Race Neutrality

Race Neutrality

Rationalizing Remedies to Racial Inequality

Samuel L. Myers, Jr. and Inhyuck "Steve" Ha

LEXINGTON BOOKS
Lanham • Boulder • New York • London

Published by Lexington Books
An imprint of The Rowman & Littlefield Publishing Group, Inc.
4501 Forbes Boulevard, Suite 200, Lanham, Maryland 20706
www.rowman.com

6 Tinworth Street, London SE11 5AL, United Kingdom

British Library Cataloguing in Publication Information Available

Library of Congress Cataloging-in-Publication Data

ISBN 978-0-7391-8561-2 (cloth : alk. paper)
ISBN 978-0-7391-8562-9 (electronic)

♾™ The paper used in this publication meets the minimum requirements of American National Standard for Information Sciences—Permanence of Paper for Printed Library Materials, ANSI/NISO Z39.48-1992.

Printed in the United States of America

Contents

Contents

Acknowledgments

Many graduate research assistants and former staff members of the Roy Wilkins Center for Human Relations and Social Justice, Humphrey School of Public Affairs, University of Minnesota have contributed to the work of this book.

We wish to thank Andriana Abariotes, Giovann Alarcon, Irma Arteaga, Akua Asare, Karimatou Bah, Del Brown, Jennifer Bynes, Juan Cardena, Xinzhi Chen, Britt Cecconi Cruz, Ana Cuesta, Shuyi Deng, Alejandra Diaz, Patryk Drescher, Thomas Durfee, Patrick Gao, Nathaniel Gibbs, Brian Hagerty, Jason Hicks, Aaliyah Hodge, Molly Illes, Cheryl Jeffries, Cheniqua Johnson, Lawrence Karongo, Hyeoneui Kim, Illenin Kondo, Yufeng Lai, Eryn Lee, Pa Houa Lee, Soomin Lee, Summe Lee, Tou Lee, Won Fy Lee, Rodrigo Lovaton Davila, Allan Malkis, Cheryl Mandala, Jose L. Mazas, Merone Meleken, Jessica Y Molina, Kevin Monroe, Jose Pacas, Jonathan Palmer, Lan Pham, Patricia Torres Ray, Michelle Revels, Julieth Santamaria, Bosu Seo, Jin Song, Terri Thao, Nathan Tiller, Diana Vega Vega, Gaozoupa Vue, David Waithaka, Quin Williams, and Man Xu.

Valuable editorial assistance was provided by Julia Blount, Jacqueline Higgins, Mary Lou Garza Iroegbu, and Shawn Monahan. Expert administrative and executive assistance over the years has been provided by Judy Leahy Grimes, Blanca Monter Monroy, Lawrencina Mason Oramalu, and Roseann Zimbro.

We would like to thank Dr. Sheila Diann Ards, former Associate Vice President of the University of Minnesota, for her support of our collaborative research and our use of parts of previously coauthored papers.

Many thanks as well to Bruce Corrie, Judge Lajune Lange, and Yuan Gao for use of parts of our previously circulated coauthored papers.

Generous support to the Wilkins Center permitting the research and writing was provided by the US Fulbright Foundation, the Roy Wilkins Endowment, the Minneapolis Foundation, the Bremer Foundation, the General Mills Foundation, the US Department of Housing and Urban Development, the National Institutes of Health, Minnesota Department of Transportation, and New Jersey Transit Corporation.

List of Figures

List of Tables

Introduction

This book has its origins in Samuel Myers and Inhyuck "Steve" Ha's collaborative research, examining the biggest affirmative action program of all time: public procurement and contracting. We, the authors, were contracted in 1999 by New Jersey Transit Corporation (NJT) to conduct a study to determine whether there were statistically significant disparities between the availability and utilization of women- and minority-owned business contractors in the market place in which NJT conducted business. We also were asked to determine whether any observed disparities could be attributed to discrimination. Based on the results of the study, conducted when Steve Ha was a graduate student and research assistant at the University of Minnesota, NJT embarked on a vigorous and sustained program of affirmative action in public procurement and contracting. Consistent with applicable rules and legislative mandates, the research team from the Roy Wilkins Center for Human Relations and Social Justice, Hubert H. Humphrey School of Public Affairs, University of Minnesota has applied novel econometric methodologies to establish the NJT participation goals for minorities and women and to partition these goals between race-conscious and race-neutral components for more than fifteen years. The methodology has withstood legal challenges in the federal courts in New Jersey and in Minnesota. Our methodology for measuring and applying the concept of race-neutrality in the case of public procurement and contracting is rooted in our collaborative work over the decades.

This book, however, is not about our econometric methodology, nor is it a defense of race-neutrality. As we will show, there are clear empirical instances where race-neutrality is economically inefficient and fails to remedy the underlying problem of persistent racial and ethnic economic disparities. There are other instances, we demonstrate, where race-neutral remedies work well or work well enough.

This book is about understanding how policy makers should care less about embracing race-neutrality as a remedy to racial inequality and care more about identifying and seeking targeted remedies that actually work. To achieve this objective, the authors draw liberally on the results of previously published research and detail some surprising findings about racial disparities in child maltreatment, racial disparities in mortgage lending, and even racial disparities in competitive swimming and in drowning. These illustrations, along with our extended discussion of the problem of racial disparities in public procurement and contracting, are designed to challenge the reader to think about why race-neutral remedies—while desireable on their face— might fail to resolve protracted and persistent patterns of racial inequality in market and nonmarket contexts.

The book is organized in the following way. We begin with an overview of the problem that race-neutral remedies are designed to solve. This chapter introduces the concept of "The Minnesota Paradox." Minnesota is a state long known for its egalitarian policies and its promise of racial equality and social justice. It is a state with some of the highest measures of social and economic well-being in the nation. But, it is also a state with some of the largest racial disparities in virtually every measure of social and economic well-being. How can that be? And, what does it mean for the willingness of the public to embrace a solution or a remedy when not everyone agrees that there is a problem to be solved or an inequality that needs to be remedied?

Chapter 2 provides the methodological foundations for understanding problem structuring and race. This chapter provides some hard evidence that there is a profound disconnect between the public perceptions about the problem that needs to be remedied and the views about specific remedies like affirmative action. One of the key take-away points from this chapter is that we cannot agree on the appropriate remedy to racial or ethnic economic inequality if we cannot agree on the nature of the problem that is to be remedied.

Chapter 3 introduces the curious case of racial disparities in drowning rates and illustrates how the failure to acknowledge that there is a racial problem can thwart efforts to solve the problem. It presents a useful metaphor for understanding why there is so much hostility and opposition to race-conscious remedies. When there is a lack of awareness of or appreciation for the underlying problem worthy of remediation, there emerges staunch opposition to remedying the problem using race-conscious mechanisms.

Chapter 4 explores measurement issues related to whether a race-conscious remedy is appropriate. The case study is child maltreatment, which poses some novel issues in its own right. This chapter relies heavily on collaborative research with Dr. Sheila Ards, former Associate Vice President for Research and Community Engagement at the University of Minnesota, and challenges the view that all racial disparities are the result of racism or racial discrimination.

Chapter 5 highlights a more detailed and nuanced analysis of the problem of public procurement and contracting disparities, using evidence from New Jersey Transit and the Minnesota Department of Transportation to highlight the fact that affirmative action programs—however, well-intentioned and legally justified—sometimes simply do not do what they were intended to do. The evidence from this chapter will point to the problem of "diversity and inclusion," where not all groups benefit from public interventions originally designed to redress prior discrimination.

The remaining chapters explore key alternatives to race-conscious programs. The alternatives to race-conscious programs are viewed through the lens of markets and market failures. Diversity initiatives and other efforts to "level the playing field" can be viewed as interventions in the marketplace to achieve efficiency. The rationale for government intervention in these instances is that the unfettered market might not produce desired efficiency outcomes. The case against targeted interventions to remedy racial disparities was proffered during the Obama administration and is known as "A Rising Tide Lifts All Ships" strategy. This approach focuses on overall economic stabilization rather than targeted entitlements to racial or ethnic minority groups. Chapter 6 presents evidence suggesting that there is no consistent pattern of narrowing racial gaps in earnings during periods of economic expansion and widening gaps during periods of contraction, as conventional wisdom would suggest. Chapter 6 offers evidence against the race-neutral method of solving problems of racial inequality via "a rising tide lifts all ships," and shows that the evidence does not support the claim that race-neutrality through overall economic stabilization policies will remedy racial income inequality.

A second set of race-neutral strategies for remedying racial inequality can be labeled "deterrence and compliance strategies." The logic of deterrence strategies is that racial discrimination in many markets is illegal. If we only enforced the existing laws, discrimination would decline and racial disparities would diminish. An excellent illustration is the case of lending disparities and the deterrent effect of U.S. Department of Housing and Urban Development (HUD) enforcement and media exposure on threats of litigation. Chapter 7 reveals that there is no strong relationship between enforcement of the anti-discrimination laws related to home mortgage lending and the resulting racial disparities in loan denial rates.

Similarly, there are already rules on the books requiring compliance with anti-discrimination in public procurement and contracting. These rules are designed to assure that preferential goals are set to maximize race-neutrality and that the goals should not discriminate against white men. Using a unique data set on the setting of federal procurement and contracting goals for women- and minority-owned business enterprises, chapter 8 examines whether threats of reverse discrimination litigation result in noncompliance or the setting of lower targeted goals. Chapter 8 offers evidence that threats of litigation neither increase nor reduce compliance.

Chapter 9 briefly reviews other alternatives to race-neutral policies and offers an assessment of what we know and what we don't know about the effectiveness of these alternatives.

In the conclusion, we offer insights about how the dramatic changes in the political landscape simultaneously demand more careful scrutiny of race-conscious programs and invite opportunities to experiment with innovative methods of delivering race-neutral programs that actually work.

Chapter 1

The Problem*

Racial and ethnic economic inequality pervades many markets.[1] In the labor market, there are persistent disparities in earnings and labor force participation (Darity and Myers 2000). In housing markets, there are wide racial and ethnic differences in ownership and access to mortgage lending (Ladd 1998; Munnell et al. 1996; Myers and Chan 1995; Myers and Chung 1996; Yinger 1986). In consumer credit markets, there are substantial differences in the terms of loans and approval rates between blacks and whites (Ards and Myers 2001; Hawley and Fujii 1991; Yinger 1998). In public procurement and contracting, where firms compete for federal, state, and local contracts worth billions of dollars for projects such as highway construction, there are huge disparities between white male-owned firms and women- and minority-owned business enterprises (Echaustegui et al. 1997; Myers and Chan 1996; Myers and Ha 2009). These racial and ethnic differences in market outcomes cannot be fully explained by differences in qualifications or human capital endowments alone.

There are also wide racial and ethnic differences in nonmarket and premarket outcomes. African Americans are three times more likely to be found in the criminal justice system than they are to be found in the overall population.[2] African American children are 1.6 times more likely to be found in child protective services[3] and two times more likely to be found in out-of-home placement than they are to be found in the overall population.[4] Moreover, in the education system there are wide disparities in important outcomes. African Americans are three times more likely to be suspended;[5]

* Portions republished with permission of Taylor & Francis, from "The Economics of Diversity" published in *Justice for All: Promoting Social Equity in Public Administration*, Norman J. Johnson; James H. Svara (eds), M.E. Sharpe, April 2011; permission conveyed through Copyright Clearance Center, Inc.

they are 1.8 more times likely to drop out,[6] and are less likely to graduate than are whites (48 vs. 65 percent).[7] Moreover, the average math SAT score for whites is 536 while the average for African Americans is 429.[8] In short, on a broad array of metrics, African Americans fare less well in markets and nonmarkets (see Figure 1.1).

Public policy *remedies* to these and other instances of racial and ethnic inequality in American society have followed six distinct phases. One phase might be called the desegregation phase; another might be called the equal opportunity phase. A next phase might be called the affirmative action phase, which was followed by an affirmative action retrenchment, post-civil rights phase. The most recent phase—prior to the unprecedented election of Donald Trump and coinciding with eight years of leadership by the first African American president of the United States—might be called the "diversity phase" where "the case for diversity" is often understood to be a case for race and ethnic inclusiveness based on efficiency grounds. Another name for the most recent phase is "post-racialism," where inclusiveness beyond racial classifications becomes the foundation for the concept of race-neutrality or color-blindness. Although the policy of race-neutrality has origins in the Clinton administration that advocated "mending affirmative action, but not ending it," it clearly remains in the forefront of efforts to dismantle affirmative action or race-based remedies in the years leading up to the election of Donald Trump. With the evolution of terminology like "disadvantaged business enterprises" as a substitute or replacement for racial classifications and aggressive litigation designed to dismantle all vestiges of race-conscious programs, one might call the emerging era the post-Obama era.

The Six Phases of Post -WWII Remedies to Racial Inequality	
1. Desegregation	1940s –1950s
2. Equal Opportunity	1960s
3. Affirmative Action	1970s – 1980s
4. Affirmative Action Retrenchment	1990s – 2000s
5. Diversity & Inclusion	2000s – 2016
6. Post-Obama Race-Neutrality	2016 – present

Figure 1.1   The six phases of post–World War II remedies to racial inequality. Author's analysis.

Efficiency is understood broadly to mean that a policy option produces net social benefits that exceed the net social benefits of all other alternatives. A looser and less precise notion of efficiency would require that a policy option produces social benefits that exceed its social costs.[9] While it is often difficult to measure social benefits and social costs, one rule of thumb for determining whether there are efficiency gains from a policy is to determine whether it is possible to make one group better off without making another group worse off. The "economic case for diversity" claims that diversity improves overall social welfare by making everyone better off.[10]

This chapter reviews the historical roots of the post-civil rights phase that has prevailed since the beginning of the twenty-first century and details the arguments for and against the diversity case. In particular, the literature exploring the relationship between ethnic diversity and economic development is juxtaposed to the literature on the putative impacts on increasing the performance of majority group members from exposure to minorities. Regardless of how attractive the case for diversity may be to supporters of affirmative action and equal opportunity, the economic arguments against it must at least be understood.

The central argument of this chapter is that one must be extremely cautious in embracing the "economic case for diversity," in the sense that the economics of diversity reveals contradictory indicators and outcomes. The putative efficiency impacts of diversity at the market level have rarely been formalized or operationalized. Even when evidence of majority group gains from diversity exists, the measured gains to the intended beneficiaries may be minimal. The case for diversity or population heterogeneity at the macro-level is also suspect. Analysts point to an inverse relationship between national wealth and racial or ethnic diversity that stems from conflict and intergroup tensions. These economic arguments point to potentially harmful impacts of factors at the macro-level that produce highly diverse populations. In short, the economic case for diversity hinges on demonstrating that there are net gains to nonminorities, or that there are no net losses to society from diversity. Ironically, to date, not much empirical evidence has been fully marshaled to sustain the economic case for diversity.

HISTORICAL UNDERPINNINGS

The context of current policies intended to increase racial and ethnic diversity in markets is rooted historically in the legal status of African American slaves, indentured servants, and others deprived of basic protections under the law. Until the abolition of slavery, the ratification of the Fourteenth

Amendment, and the guarantee of equal protection regardless of race, blacks were considered chattel property and were denied rights that were constitutionally afforded to citizens.

> For many white Southerners, however, violence was still the surest means of keeping blacks politically impotent, and in countless communities blacks were not allowed, under penalties of severe reprisals, to show their faces in town on election day. (Franklin and Moss 2000, 282)

Gunnar Myrdal (1996) encapsulated the paradox of the American constitutional framework. The legal architecture and the constitutional guarantees of freedoms given to the American people set the United States apart from many other nations of the world. Yet, its denial of basic freedoms to a sizeable portion of the population posed an ongoing dilemma long after slavery was abolished.

This historical legacy of slavery and the denial of equality under the law, even after Emancipation, is the backdrop for the post–World War II period that marshaled a sustained legal effort, undertaken in part by the NAACP Legal and Education Defense Fund and led by Charles Hamilton Houston and Thurgood Marshall (Higginbotham 2005; Myrdal 1996). The period, often called the Civil Rights Era, came at a pivotal economic period of low unemployment accompanied by a surge of migration from southern rural cities to northern industrial centers. The period also overlapped a transformation in technology and a change in labor demand (Noble 1986). The rapid migration of blacks to northern, urban inner cities following World War II, combined with the rise of policy-induced suburban housing ownership by the white middle class, reproduced in the North the very segregation that existed in the Jim Crow South (Lamb 2005). Efforts designed to eliminate the most blatant vestiges of slavery and segregation included both attempts to provide equality before the law and initiatives to dismantle racial discrimination and state-sponsored segregation. If the era from 1948 to 1989 is called the Civil Rights Era, then the era marked by major Supreme Court reversals beginning in 1989 might be termed the post-Civil Rights Era (Myers 1997).

Phases of the Post–World War II Civil Rights Policies

The entire post–World War II era of Civil Rights might be divided into five distinct phases. The first phase might be termed "the desegregation phase." It is during this period that the most vicious forms of _legal_ separation of the races, codified and legitimized after the Civil War, were dismantled (Klarman 2007, Chapters 3, 4, and 5). The beginning of this phase rests largely with the _Brown v. Board of Education_ (1954) decision by the US Supreme Court that struck down the "separate but equal" doctrine of _Plessey v. Ferguson_ (1896).

Although the decision focused largely on schooling, its impacts were far reaching due to the connection between quality schooling and labor markets (Donohue and Heckman 1991; Heckman 1990). The failure of this phase is evidenced by the fact that a half century after the ruling, public schools while no longer segregated by law nonetheless were segregated by housing patterns (Crowley 2006; Hartman and Squires 2006). Conspicuously, the policy of desegregation rested on equity grounds, with little or no attempt to make the case that racial segregation was inefficient.[11]

The passage of the Civil Rights Act of 1964 heralded the equal opportunity and anti-discrimination era. The Act banned segregation in public accommodations and discrimination in employment. The substance of the Act was to make discrimination illegal in housing and labor markets in the quest for equal opportunity. The premise was that equal treatment would lead to equal results (Graham 1990). That there were wide racial gaps in earnings and incomes that could not be attributed solely to human capital differences suggested to many analysts that market discrimination existed and was inefficient (Thurow 1969).

The next phase was officially marshaled in by Executive Order 11246, which was issued by Lyndon Johnson in 1965 and establishes the foundation for affirmative action in employment in the public and private sectors (Andorra 1998). A careful reading of the original executive order suggests that it was merely an advancement of anti-discrimination objectives (Anderson 1997). In practice, however, employers, colleges and universities, and government contracting and procurement offices rushed to implement affirmative action in ways that might at first glance be regarded as simplistic or mechanistic numerical repositioning. For example, following rules established by the Federal Transit Authority (FTA), state and local agencies receiving federal funds for highway and transportation projects established percentage goals for the allocation of funds to women- and minority-owned business enterprises. These numerical goals, often set with no penalty for noncompliance, were characterized by critics as "quotas."[12] Arguably, many affirmative action plans and timetables involved an expansion of opportunities for underrepresented groups to hear about and apply for openings, which widened recruitment efforts to attract larger pools of qualified candidates, as well as numerical goals and timetables. Some of these affirmative action efforts were, in fact, court ordered as remedies to specific instances of illegal discrimination. The rationale for these court orders was clearly based on equity considerations. The affirmative action in these cases was a redress or remedy for a prior wrong. Other efforts, however, were broad sweeping attempts to change the racial and ethnic composition of the workforce, higher education, and firms conducting business with public entities.[13] These efforts were only vaguely defined on efficiency grounds. Rather, they, too, were predicated upon equity considerations. These highly visible affirmative action efforts prompted a broad challenge from alleged victims of affirmative action: whites generally, but white males in particular. The legal challenges were founded on the premise that the Fourteenth Amendment to the US Constitution prohibited state actions that deprived any group—not just former slaves—of equal protection. The ideological framework upon which these cases arose was one of market efficiency. Why reduce employment of (better) qualified white males merely to redistribute employment outcomes? Plaintiffs in cases that reached the US Supreme Court in one single transformative year, 1989, set in place an unraveling of the entire affirmative action apparatus built up during the previous twenty-five years.

Illustrative of the reversal is the *City of Richmond v. Croson* (1989) case. In this instance, a white-owned plumbing supply company argued that the minority- and women-owned business set aside program, designed to rectify the underrepresentation of nonwhite firms among contractors in Richmond, harmed nonminority-owned firms. Croson argued that its efforts to comply with the affirmative action mandates of the City of Richmond were unsuccessful, principally because of its inability to find "qualified" minority firms with which to subcontract. Pointedly, this is an efficiency argument against the city's affirmative action program. Associate Justice Sandra Day O'Conner, writing for the majority, pointed out that the City of Richmond had failed to prove the compelling state interest (remedying ongoing discrimination), while not denying that such race-conscious set-asides were sometimes needed:

1. The city has failed to demonstrate a compelling governmental interest justifying the Plan, since the factual predicate supporting the Plan does not establish the type of identified past discrimination in the city's construction industry that would authorize race-based relief under the Fourteenth Amendment's Equal Protection Clause (498–506).
2. The Plan is not narrowly tailored to remedy the effects of prior discrimination, since it entitles a black, Hispanic, or Oriental entrepreneur from anywhere in the country to an absolute preference over other citizens based solely on their race. Although many of the barriers to minority participation in the construction industry relied upon by the city to justify the Plan appear to be race neutral, there is no evidence that the city considered using alternative, race-neutral means to increase minority participation in city contracting (*City of Richmond v. Croson*).

It is clear from the wording of the *Croson* decision that a compelling state interest is required to justify a potentially inefficient market intervention. The implicit inefficiency is the award of contracts to minority firms when nonminority firms would have prevailed in the absence of the affirmative action policy. The phase following the 1989 Supreme Court decisions that severely challenged the constitutionality of affirmative action in many markets might be regarded as the Affirmative Action Retrenchment/Post-Civil Rights Phase.

A major transformation was apparent in the 1995 California ballot initiative 209, which passed with 54 percent of the vote, which sought to eliminate affirmative action programs in all public contracts, at public state colleges and universities, and in hiring decisions within public state agencies. Constituents felt that the current affirmative action programs had become reverse discrimination. They argued that white men are harmed because less-qualified minorities are given an unfair advantage in the marketplace. Although constitutional challenges to ballot initiative 209 immediately emerged, the public outcry against affirmative action set in place other state initiatives and added credibility to efforts across the nation to eliminate affirmative action programs altogether.

Between 1992 and 1996, sixteen states faced similar ballot initiatives. From 1992 to 2000, twenty-nine states faced legislation banning affirmative action. Ards and Myers (1997, 2001) collected data on state ballot initiatives and legislative attempts to dismantle affirmative action from 1992 to 2000. The bills introduced ranged from those that would eliminate all programs giving preferential treatment to individuals on the basis of race, sex, color, or ethnicity, to bills that would curb race or other preferences in limited spheres of government activities, such as government contracting and procurement, admissions and scholarships to state institutions, and government employment. Altogether 108 anti-affirmative action in public employment bills were introduced; 113 anti-affirmative action in public contracting and procurement bills were introduced; and 107 anti-affirmative action in higher education bills were introduced. Most of the bills were introduced in California, South Carolina, Michigan, and Alabama. Only 8.5 percent of the bills made their way out of committee; only two bills actually passed (in Alaska banning affirmative action in fishery management). Although few of the anti-affirmative action bills introduced in the 1990s resulted in the formal dismantling of state affirmative action, the failed efforts served two related purposes: these efforts highlighted the resolve to attack affirmative action programs even when there may be limited support from the executive branch or from other legislators, and the efforts provided widespread media attention that gave legitimacy to contemporaneous ballot initiatives.

What were the reasons for affirmative action retrenchment as measured by ballot initiatives and legislative attempts to dismantle affirmative action? Ards and Myers (1997, 2001) estimated logistic models to predict the probability that an anti-affirmative action ballot initiative appeared in a state between 1992 and 1996 and whether anti-affirmative action legislation was introduced, voted out of committee, or passed between 1992 and 2000. They controlled for measures of unemployment, decline in manufacturing, black-white income gaps, state employment, black elected officials, minority educational attainment, Democratic voting, percent of the voting age population registered, immigration, racial diversity, crime, and welfare.[14]

Factors that emerge as significant predictors of the probability of anti-affirmative action legislation are black-white income inequality, black homeownership, percent retail and service firms, percent of the population that is black, percent receiving welfare, urbanization, and education. Affirmative action retrenchment appears to rise when black income is lower relative than white income; when black home ownership is high; when retail and service firms are a smaller fraction of all businesses; when there are larger fractions of blacks and those on welfare in the population; and when the population is urbanized and with larger shares of high school graduates. In addition, ballot initiatives are more likely to be introduced in states with high nonwhite populations combined with high white male unemployment rates. These factors suggest that economic factors matter in affirmative action retrenchment efforts and that those factors that pose the greatest threat to white males translate more readily into ballot initiatives or legislative efforts to dismantle affirmative action.

Post-Affirmative Action

Many of the efforts of traditional civil rights organizations during the Affirmative Action Retrenchment phase were geared toward preventing the passage of ballot initiatives and thwarting legislative attempts to dismantle affirmative action. These efforts recognized the equity concerns of both (a) whether race-neutral policies were capable of redressing the legacy of inequality rooted in slavery, segregation, and historic discrimination and (b) whether the privilege afforded to white males should be balanced by preferential advantages to women and minorities in order to level playing fields.

A dramatic shift in the thinking about affirmative action came about in the ensuing years. President Bill Clinton's argument that affirmative action should be mended but not ended, and the rush within the federal government to enact policies and plans that produced greater diversity without creating harm to nonminority market participants signaled concerns about efficiency. In the face of cutbacks to and elimination of many affirmative action programs, even without court orders or legal challenges, the tone of policy discourse among advocates of minority and women's equal rights seemed to embrace the efficiency criteria that were the cornerstone of the dismantlement of affirmative action programs in the first place. The tone was that "diversity is good for business" or that diversity has broad social benefits that outweigh any individual costs incurred. Indeed, the argument was that nonminorities as a group benefited from diversity. This net-social gain argument is the efficiency argument, or the "economic case for diversity." The diversity case is both a case for inclusiveness beyond just race and ethnicity and also an argument against traditional affirmative action (Slack 1997).

THE ECONOMIC CASE FOR DIVERSITY

The most compelling and articulate statement of the case for diversity, in particular the case for diversity in higher education and employment, comes from the October 16, 2000, "Fortune 500" amicus brief filed on behalf of the defendants in *Gratz v. Bollinger. Grutter v. Bollinger* challenges the University of Michigan's race-conscious admission policies in the undergraduate school and in the law school. The joint amicus brief brought together such multinational giants as Microsoft, the Dow Chemical Company, General Mills, Kellogg, KPMG, and 3M to produce a stunning statement in defense of workplace diversity:

> In the opinion of *amici*, individuals who have been educated in a diverse setting are more likely to succeed, because they can make valuable contributions to the workforce in several important ways. *First*, a diverse group of individuals educated in a cross-cultural environment has the ability to facilitate unique and creative approaches to problem-solving arising from the integration of different perspectives. *Second,* such individuals are better able to develop products and services that appeal to a variety of consumers and to market offerings in ways that appeal to these consumers. *Third*, a racially diverse group of managers with cross-cultural experience is better able to work with business partners, employees, and clientele in the United States and around the world. *Fourth*, individuals that have been educated in a diverse setting are likely to contribute to a positive work environment, by decreasing incidents of discrimination and stereotyping. *Finally*, an educational environment created by consideration of the potential promise of each applicant in light of his or her experiences and background is likely to produce the most talented possible workforce. (Brief of Amici Curiae by Fortune 500 Companies in *Gratz v. Bollinger* No. 97–75928, No. 97–75231, October 16, 2000)

The central issue addressed, that a diverse workforce is good for business, is sometimes called the business case for diversity. The business case for diversity asserts that a diverse workforce permits employers to hire and retain better qualified employees, who in turn are more productive and innovative. The business case for diversity points to the need for a workforce that mirrors the diverse consumer base to which firms market. Minnesota-based

3M detailed these issues specifically in an appended statement in the amicus brief:

> Because it serves and works with an increasingly diverse group of communities in both the United States and around the world, 3M's future hinges upon its ability to attract, deploy, and maintain a diverse workforce capable of understanding, relating to, and satisfying the needs of its broad customer base. 3M invests heavily in research and development and is known widely as one of America's most innovative companies. As such, 3M has found that bringing together the collective talents and experiences of a diverse group of employees is necessary to develop creative approaches to problem solving, and to successfully market and sell its products to a wide range of communities. Time after time, 3M has found that input from employees who are members of the communities to which 3M markets and sells its products is crucial to ensuring that it can reach those communities in the most effective way. (Brief of Amici Curiae by Fortune 500 Companies in *Gratz v. Bollinger* No. 97–75928, No. 97–75231, October 16, 2000)

A careful reading of the "Fortune 500" submission reveals that the case made is one of a compelling state interest in promoting diversity and not necessarily a specific appeal to any particular method to achieve diversity. Moreover, little or no mention is made as to whether particular subgroups within a diverse population require or need greater intervention in order to attain the desired end of workplace diversity.

The actual details of the claims that a diverse workforce is necessary, if not sufficient, for achieving profitability in the global market place reside within a burgeoning literature in industrial relations and labor relations. Jonathan Leonard and David Levine (2006) review this literature and focus their empirical analysis on the effects of workplace diversity on labor turnover and productivity. Using longitudinal data from over 800 similar workplaces, they show that low workplace diversity and employee isolation increase worker turnover. The specific impacts differ among race, gender, and age groups. They refute the hypothesis that workforce diversity undermines stability.

The efficiency case for diversity in higher education is documented principally in an expert report by Professor Patricia Gurin in the *Grutter* and *Gratz* cases. After examining national institutional data, survey data, and classroom information, she found that

> students who experienced the most racial and ethnic diversity in classroom settings and in informal interactions with peers showed the greatest engagement in active thinking processes, growth in intellectual engagement and motivation, and growth in intellectual and academic skills. (Gurin 1999)

The Harvard Civil Rights Project in its amicus brief in *Gratz v. Bollinger* provides a summary of the social science literature that documents the positive impacts of diversity on student outcomes. They review the literature that shows that (a) student body diversity improves classroom learning environments, (b) diverse learning environments promote critical thinking skills, and (c) cross-racial interaction has positive effects on retention, college satisfaction, self-confidence, interpersonal skills, and leadership (Brief of Amici Curiae for The Civil Rights Project at Harvard University in *Gratz et al. v. Bollinger et al., Patterson et al.* [Nos. 01–1333, 01–1416, 01–1418] May, 2001). These findings support the idea that diversity in educational and training environments improves educational and training outcomes.

Chang, Astin, and Kim (2004), using a national longitudinal data set on college students, note that diversity in student bodies produces cross-racial interactions for different groups and at different levels of student body diversity. Whereas cross-racial interaction is shown to produce improvements in cognitive outcomes, the primary beneficiaries of cross-racial interactions across all levels of diversity are white students.

Other areas that make the case for diversity include real estate markets and corporate boards. Real estate firms with greater diversity in their workforces capture larger shares of the diverse customer base (Bond, Seiler, and Seiler 2003). Firms with more diverse corporate boards have higher firm value (Carter, Simkins, and Simpson 2003).

THE ECONOMIC CASE AGAINST DIVERSITY

The economic case against diversity recognizes a trade-off between benefits and costs associated with diverse societies or workforces. This literature argues essentially that heterogeneity in populations has the potential for exacerbating existing ethnic hostilities and hatreds, thus retarding economic growth. In their review of this literature, Alesina and La Ferrara (2005) note:

> The potential costs of diversity are fairly evident. Conflict of preferences, racism, and prejudices often lead to policies that are at the same time odious and counterproductive for society as a whole. The oppression of minorities may lead to political unrest or even civil wars. But a diverse ethnic mix also brings about variety in abilities, experiences, and cultures that may be productive and may lead to innovation and creativity. (Alesina and La Ferrara 2005)

In this view, the cost of diversity is conflict and interethnic conflict, which must be balanced against the benefit associated with possible gains to productivity from a more heterogeneous population. The literature points to extensive examples, particularly from Africa, where these costs tend to outweigh the benefits (Easterly and Levine 1997). There is an important distinction in this literature between how advanced economies are able to resolve these

conflicts and how ethnic fractionalization in emerging economies may dominate the trade-off between the costs and benefits of diversity.

On balance, the economic case against diversity hinges on showing that
these costs outweigh the benefits. Note the qualifier that Alesina and La Fer-
rarar use in denoting the possible benefits of diversity: they say that a diverse
mix *may* produce higher productivity and *may* generate innovation and
creativity.

Part of the economic case against diversity derives from the organizational
behavior literature on teams. When examining new product development,
Ancona and Caldwell (1992) point out that engineers working alone may not
be as successful as teams working with specialists from many disciplines.
They write:

> As teams increasingly get called upon to do more complex tasks and to cross-
> functional boundaries within the organization, conventional wisdom has
> suggested that teams be composed of more diverse members. (Ancona and
> Caldwell 1992)

But, Ancona and Caldwell (1992) also caution that there can be offsetting
impacts of diverse product development teams:

> While it [diversity] does produce internal processes and external communica-
> tions that facilitate performance, it also directly impedes performance. That is,
> overall the effect of diversity on performance is negative, even though some
> aspects of group work are enhanced. It may be that for these teams' diversity
> brings more creativity to problem solving and product development, but it
> impedes implementation because there is less capability for teamwork than
> there is for homogeneous teams.

What specifically about group or team diversity might be inefficient, in
the sense that it reduces productivity? One hypothesis is that it increases
emotional conflict and that conflict impedes performance. Race and ethnic
diversity in particular are believed to be sources of emotional conflict (Pelled,
Xin, and Eisenhardt 1999).

At the macro-level, the argument is that ethnic divisions, particularly in
African countries, are associated with low rates of income growth and high
rates of poverty. Of course, many of the most careful analysts of these patterns are quick to point out that it is not ethnic diversity itself that produces
the tragic poverty in Africa, but rather the policies that arise from conflict-
ridden, ethnically diverse populations that are responsible (Easterly and
Levine 1997). It is polarization and civil conflict that produce the observed
outcomes of retarded growth and poverty, not necessarily population heterogeneity alone (Montalvo and Reynal-Querol 2005).

Alesina and La Ferrara (2000) construct indices of social capital that capture measures of trust, group membership, and civic participation. They show that there is a strong, inverse relationship between their social capital measures and community heterogeneity. In states like Minnesota, North Dakota, Montana, Utah, and Wyoming where there is little racial diversity and low-income inequality, there are high levels of social capital. In states like Florida and Texas, which have higher levels of racial and ethnic diversity as well as greater income inequality, there are lower measures of social capital. Of the different types of heterogeneity (i.e., diversity), racial heterogeneity has the greatest impact on inhibiting the formation and transmission of social capital.

Bates (2000) reviews the literature on the adverse impacts of ethnic diversity on instability and poverty in Africa. He summarizes the conventional wisdom:

> Those who study modem Africa commonly highlight three features: its poverty, its instability, and its ethnic diversity. Whether in lurid popularizations or in social scientific research scholars reason that Africa is poor because it is unstable and that its instability derives from its ethnic complexity. Ethnicity thus lies, it is asserted, at the root of Africa's development crisis.

Although Bates's critique challenges this view, the data he uses is limited and does not permit a full rejection of the underlying conventional wisdom. Paul Collier's World Bank study provides a more nuanced interpretation of the Easterly-Levine hypothesis concerning the adverse impacts of ethnic diversity on economic growth. He correlates the measure of ethnic fragmentation with measures of political dominance. He finds that in democratic societies ethnic diversity promotes economic growth, but in dictatorships fragmentation contributes to diminished growth (Collier 2000).

Another way of conceptualizing racial/ethnic diversity is to consider the blurring of traditional black-white boundaries. Bean and Leach (2005) report that states with the largest immigrant populations have the highest blurring of these traditional boundaries and represent greater racial and ethnic diversity. Patterns of multiracial identification occur more frequently in California, Florida, Hawaii, Illinois, Michigan, New Jersey, New York, Ohio, Texas, and Washington than in other parts of the United States. These states also have high immigrant populations. In states in the South with large black populations, or in the North with large white populations, multiracial categorization (i.e., greater racial or ethnic diversity) is lower.

The specific mechanism by which diversity produces adverse outcomes can come from other sources. Alesina, Baqir, and Easterly (1999) show that there are lower public expenditures in more diverse communities, perhaps, as Ferraro and Cummings (2007) argue, as a direct result of racial discrimination. Others have shown lower public goods provision in ethnically diverse communities arises from the problem of enforcing sanctions through common norms (Habyarimana et al. 2007). Lazear (1999) posits that the adverse outcomes derive from culture and language that inhibit communications within the firm. Using information on teams and within organizations, researchers have found that the gains to group performance from diversity can be offset by difficulties within groups to agree on strategies or difficulties in communicating with one another. On balance, the net effect of diversity on organizations depends in part on how and whether benefits outweigh costs.[15]

Few researchers have identified the time element in their analysis. A notable exception is Putnam who argues that—at least for modern industrialized societies—the initial negative impacts of diversity ultimately are reversed once a society embraces the intrinsic value of the benefits from ethnic diversity. Importantly, Putnam (2007) argues that the ethnic diversity is prompted in industrial societies largely through immigration. Using the example of the United States, he argues that the infusion of diverse languages and cultures enriches society and even if there are short-term losses, in the long-run net gains are likely to be sustained. This distinction, however, does not comment on whether populations *initially disadvantaged*, such as indigenous populations or former slaves, necessarily benefit or lose from immigration and thus diversity.

There are other cases to be made for diversity besides the economic one. For example, Mitchell Rice (2005) details and clarifies the substantive case for diversity in public sector employment as paramount for achieving democracy and a representative bureaucracy. These foundations for diversity clearly deserve as much merit as do the factors related to economic efficiency. In the Michigan case, the more uncontroverted evidence offered about diversity benefits referred to civic engagement and democratic participation rather than improved test score performance or heightened cognitive or problem-solving skills. Thus, the putative efficiency benefits associated with diversity might be less important than the general societal benefits from improved civic participation.

Nevertheless, the economic case for diversity hinges on a balancing of benefits and costs that are rarely assessed directly. Moreover, programs that purport to enhance and promote diversity are rarely evaluated or assessed based on these trade-offs of benefits and costs. When such assessments are made, more often than not they are done without the rigor of experimental or quasi-experimental designs that NSF's Committee on Equal Opportunity in Science and Engineering (CEOSE) (2003, 2004) has recommended in its reports.

The contradictory evidence for and against the impacts of workforce diversity and classroom diversity on productivity may be explained in part by nonlinearities between diversity and performance outcomes. For example, in their study of problem-solving skills and group performance indicators, Terenzini et al. (2001) show that there are moderate levels of performance at low diversity levels that initially decline as diversity goes from the lowest levels to not-so-low levels. Then, as diversity increases beyond the low points, performance indicators increase. This positive relationship continues up and until the very highest levels of diversity wherein diversity and performance move in opposite directions. The nonlinear relationship between diversity and performance may reflect the fact that in economic terms there exists some optimum level of diversity between the extremes of completely homogenous groups to the other extreme wherein there is no critical mass of any group. Some researchers have attempted to compute what this optimum level of diversity would look like. Generally speaking, the optimum proportions, in democratic societies, are likely to be such that no one group dominates.[16]

Using the metaphor of biological diversity and the preservation of species, Weitzman (1992) postulates that there must exist a "diversity function" and that any good economic theory of diversity ought to consider the optimization role that diversity might play. If as in ecological systems, diversity matters, so too should diversity matter in economic systems. This manner of thinking, however, which focuses almost exclusively on the efficiency of species within a larger ecosystem, may inadvertently lead analysts to rank groups according to their overall productivity and they might ultimately conclude that at the optimal level of diversity, the representation of certain less productive groups might be lower than it might be under other organizational schemes. Moreover, if the current productivity of specific groups is intricately linked to historic barriers and inequalities, it is difficult to know whether a model of "optimal diversity" would impede the ability of these groups to move into the mainstream of the economy and become productive contributors to society in the manner that the Fortune 500 amicus brief postulates. It is entirely possible that the "optimal" amount of diversity will vary across time as groups assimilate and the negative aspects of diversity become less apparent. Assimilation may also erode the creativity and innovation that is the cornerstone of the benefits to diversity, suggesting that at some point diversity no longer will produce huge net social benefits.

It is ironic that the key explanations provided by those who present evidence that the costs of diversity might exceed the potential benefits point to the strife, the conflict, the tensions, and the hostilities that arise from heterogeneous populations that face historic animosities. If, in fact, the purpose of race-conscious efforts is the equity goal to remedy and redress historic wrongs, then the fact that there are possibly efficiency reducing, redistributive impacts should not be surprising. Ideally, of course, one would want to design remedies that are both efficient and equitable. But, if the cost of diversity is rooted in the ills that create bias, discrimination, and racism, perhaps the short-term costs that are attendant to creating more diverse communities can be justified based on longer-term transformations that ultimately reduce racism and discrimination. Furthermore, can we permit the opponents of inclusion to veto it by their hostility? If we must choose between efficiency and equity, do we not have to choose equity (narrowly tailored) based on Constitutional grounds or principles of fairness and justice? Putnam argues that we can expect that efficiency (or at least democracy) will rebound over time.

In summary, the economic case for diversity hinges on being able to show that benefits of heterogeneous groups in the workforce or in the classroom exceed the costs associated with studying, living, and working outside of the comfortable, reassuring, and customary confines of homogeneous settings. While the evidence is mixed about the net social benefits of diversity, it is clear that the logic of diversity takes a significant turn away from the original purpose of affirmative action: to redress historic inequalities against specific groups, including African Americans harmed by the institution of slavery and state supported segregation. Advocates for advancing the social and economic status of this group who shift attention and adopt the language of diversity run the risk of accepting policy proscriptions (e.g., about optimum levels of diversity) that enhance the well-being of majority group members without necessarily improving the relative economic well-being of the intended beneficiaries of the affirmative action policies that diversity programs replace. The calculus of net social benefits does not require that all groups benefit. Importantly, the logic of the efficiency claims of diversity does not require that disadvantaged racial or ethnic minority group members gain or gain as much as majority group members. Efficiency, as it is commonly defined by economists, will prevail even if all of the net-benefits accrue to the majority and none to the minority. It is precisely for this reason that advocates for reducing racial and ethnic economic inequality should be cautious about embracing "the efficiency case for diversity" without being attentive to the resulting distribution of outcomes that such a policy might produce.

THE POST-OBAMA/RACE-NEUTRALITY PHASE

Ambivalence about the effectiveness of the diversity and inclusion remedies to racial inequality combined with outright hostility lingering from the anti-affirmative action phase produce the foundations for the post-Obama/race-neutrality phase. The most sophisticated and well-developed scheme for advancing race-neutrality is found in US Department of Transportation regulations mandating that public procurement and contracting goals for women- and minority-owned business enterprises *maximize race-neutral alternatives* over race-conscious goals. In other words, recipients of federal funding must find color-blind alternatives to race-conscious affirmative action efforts to remedy underlying problems of racial inequalities in the marketplace. Other areas where race-neutrality is in the spotlight include admissions to state colleges and universities and financial aid for graduate students in the sciences. Increasingly, though, many Americans, particularly white working class, do not believe that there is a rational basis for race-conscious remedial policies because they do not believe that there is a racial problem that requires public policy remedies. This belief arises partly from the wide separation of the experiences of many whites and blacks in America. It also arises because of the rapid growth of other racial and ethnic groups in the diverse fabric of American life who appear to be succeeding against the same odds that African Americans face. Many "good people" are not racist opponents to the achievements and integration of those left behind. Rather, they simply disagree about the nature of the problem we are trying to solve.

There is no better illustration of this tension between wanting to support equality while being unwilling to support race-conscious programs that would directly address racial inequality than the problem of racial inequality in Minnesota. Minnesota is one of the best performing states in the nation on many social and economic indicators but has one of the worst racial gaps in almost all major indicators of social and economic well-being. This situation is the "Minnesota Paradox."

THE MINNESOTA PARADOX[17]

For the last seventy years, a racial gap in unemployment has existed in the United States. From near parity in the 1940s, the black-white ratio in unemployment has grown today to over 2 to 1. Minnesota, which consistently has much lower unemployment rates than elsewhere in the country, also has one of the largest racial disparities in unemployment in the nation. In 2008, the Minnesota black-white unemployment gap was 4.2 to 1 and 3.7 to 1 for males and females in 2008, more than twice the disparity than in the rest of the country.

The simple explanation for the very high racial gap in unemployment rates in Minnesota while the overall unemployment rates are low is that *whites in Minnesota* are much better off than whites elsewhere in the nation; but blacks in Minnesota face about the same outcomes as blacks elsewhere. Table 1.1 gives some background on the growth of Minnesota's black and white labor force in the years prior to the recession.

Chapter 1

Table 1.1 Growth Rates in the Number of Persons in the Civilian Non-Institutionalized Labor Force vs. Employment (Minnesota)

	2000–2005 (%)	2005–2010 (%)
Civilian Noninstitutionalized Labor Force		
White	3.7	0.9
African American	25.3	5.8
Employment		
White	3.2	–2.1
African American	19.5	–6.5

Source: Authors' computations from BLS-LAUS, 2000–2010.

From 2000 to 2005, growth in the African American civilian noninstitutionalized labor force was rapid, at 25.3 percent, almost seven times greater than growth in the white civilian noninstitutionalized labor force, which grew at 3.7 percent (Table 1.1). Growth in employment for African Americans was also robust, at 19.5 percent, while white employment was growing more slowly at 3.2 percent (Table 1.1), meaning African American employment was growing at six times the speed of white employment during the period between 2000 and 2005. But, black employment during this period was growing more slowly than the civilian noninstitutionalized labor force.

From 2005 to 2010, there was slower growth in the civilian noninstitutionalized labor force for both blacks and whites. Whereas the African American labor force grew at a rate of 5.8 percent, the white civilian noninstitutionalized labor force only grew at 0.9 percent (Table 1.1). Again, black labor force growth outpaced white growth by some six times. During this period, both populations faced employment retrenchment. Growth in white employment declined by 2.1 percent, while black employment declined by 6.5 percent (Table 1.1). Black employment therefore fell three times as quickly as it did for whites. Once again, the black labor force growth outstripped changes in black employment. This background explains the widening racial gap in unemployment rates.

Table 1.2 gives a more thorough account of why the gap narrowed during the recession.[18]

Using merged American Community Survey (ACS) data from 2007 to 2009, we computed unemployment rates for the seven-county Twin Cities Metropolitan area as well for the two most populous counties in Minnesota: Hennepin and Ramsey. In the period from 2007 to 2009, white male unemployment nearly doubled, from 5.14 percent to 8.99 percent (Table 1.2), not an unexpected effect, given the recession.[19] The national recession began in the fourth quarter of 2007 and ended in the second quarter of 2009. Black male unemployment increased as well, but not as substantially as it did in the white male population. The black male population saw rates rise from 17.2 percent to

Table 1.2   Rates of Unemployment during the Recession (Minneapolis-St. Paul)

	Men						Ratio		
	White			Black			Black/White		
	2007	*2008*	*2009*	*2007*	*2008*	*2009*	*2007*	*2008*	*2009*
Minneapolis-St. Paul Metro Area	5.14	4.6	8.99	17.2	19.2	21.4	**3.34**	**4.16**	**2.37**
Hennepin County	5.17	4.65	8.48	15.9	21.4	26.2	**3.07**	**4.6**	**3.09**
Ramsey County	5.84	5.71	9.72	24.9	26.2	19.9	**4.26**	**4.6**	**2.05**
	Women						Ratio		
Minneapolis-St. Paul Metro Area	4.59	3.67	5.7	16.9	13.6	14.9	**3.69**	**3.72**	**2.62**
Hennepin County	5.15	3.99	5.09	19.7	16.2	16.1	**3.83**	**4.05**	**3.17**
Ramsey County	4.47	6.52	4.8	7.34	7.45	8.55	**1.64**	**1.14**	**1.78**

Bold are the ratios of the numbers in the columns to the left of those numbers.
Source: American Community Survey (2007–2009).

21.4 percent (Table 1.2). While both white and black male unemployment increased during the recession, white male unemployment outpaced that of black males and thus, the ratio of black male unemployment to white male unemployment actually decreased during the recession from 3.34 to 2.37 (Table 1.2).

In short, the racial gap in unemployment rates widened at the start of the recession and then narrowed toward the end of the recession. However, labor force participation rates dropped significantly for black males and black females from 2007 to 2009, and the decline was much greater for blacks than it was for whites. Another reason for the finding that the racial gap in unemployment rates narrowed during the last stages of the recession is that unemployment rates for black males during that period were already extraordinarily high, so black male unemployment simply lacked the flexibility to escalate, whereas the white male population had more jobs to lose.

The racial gap in unemployment rates widened only slightly between 2007 and 2008 between black women and white women, but then narrowed significantly from 2008 to 2009. Whereas white women experienced an increase in unemployment from 4.59 percent in 2007 to 5.7 percent in 2009 (Table 1.2), black females saw their unemployment levels decrease from 16.9 percent to 14.9 percent (Table 1.2) in the same period. Much of this decrease can be attributed to withdrawals from the labor market.

There was a substantial drop in black labor force participation from 2007 to 2009 in the Twin Cities Metropolitan area. The evidence shows that black women were abandoning the job search, thereby dropping out of the unemployment figures. This explanation is supported by a decrease in the labor force participation rate for black women. In 2008, the rate was 69.5 and by 2009, the rate had dropped to 66.11 (American Community Survey 2007–2009).

The net effect of the abovementioned fluctuations was a narrowing of the racial gap in unemployment during the recession. This is especially unnerving considering Minnesota's historically low unemployment and highly educated populace.

We know that there were fluctuations in unemployment, but how can we explain them? Charles Betsey, one of the first economists to recognize the black and white unemployment gap, published an important article in 1978 stating that differences in schooling, age, previous training, and other demographic characteristics accounted for only two-fifths of the black-white gap. Interestingly, he pointed to the duration and number of spells of unemployment as having a significantly greater negative effect on black males than white: "Among blacks," he said, "each spell of unemployment results in about two additional weeks of future joblessness; for whites, on average, each occurrence results in a day's future job loss."

Utilizing merged ACS data from 2007 to 2009, we ran a similar regression to Betsey's to determine how much Minnesota unemployment could be explained by the following characteristics: age, education, location, industry, occupation, and year. The results showed that only about 25 percent of the racial gap in unemployment rates could be explained by more than fifty independent correlates capturing demographic, location, industry, and occupational determinants.[20]

In short, conventional wisdom and conventional explanations do not seem to explain why the racial gaps in unemployment rates are much larger in Minnesota than they are elsewhere. There is a statistical term that is often used to characterize these large "unexplained gaps." The common term used is *discrimination.*

But, how could "discrimination" explain these gaps when Minnesota is nationally known for its egalitarianism and its model of racial fairness. Minneapolis was one of the first predominantly white cities to elect an African American woman as its Mayor. Hubert H. Humphrey, one of the state's most famous elected officials, was the floor manager for the 1964 Civil Rights Act. Major Minnesota-based corporations like 3M, Honeywell, Pillsbury, General Mills, Best Buy, and Target have a legacy of diversity hiring and promotion of African Americans and other minorities to top executive positions.

ARE BLACKS WORSE OFF IN MINNESOTA THAN IN MISSISSIPPI?[21]

Recent news reports cite findings from the 2014 ACS that show that blacks are worse off in Minnesota than in Mississippi. The *Star Tribune* reported:

From 2013 to 2014, the median income for black households in the state fell 14 percent. In constant dollars, that was a decline from about $31,500 to $27,000—or $4,500 in a single year. . . . The median black household in Minnesota is now worse off than its counterpart in Mississippi. Among the 50 states, along with Puerto Rico and Washington, D.C., Minnesota ranked 45th in median black household income. Mississippi ranked 44th.[22]

This conclusion prompted many local leaders to conclude the worst. In a subsequent *Star Tribune* article, State Senator Jeff Hayden (DFL-Minneapolis), referencing Governor Dayton's request for a special legislative session regarding the walleye shortage, is quoted as saying: the black community is hearing the message that "Fish are more important than black people."[23] Or, as Louis King, president of the Minneapolis-based Summit Academy, is reported to have said: "If you're black in Minnesota, you're better off in Mississippi."[24]

The problem with these claims, and conclusions drawn from them, is that the statistics reference one-year changes that do not tell the full story about underlying shifts in the distribution of income among blacks in Minnesota. Elsewhere, we have documented that there are year-to-year fluctuations in various measures of income for blacks in Minnesota and in Mississippi.[25] We argue in our policy brief that, over the past thirteen years, there have been both increases and decreases in black incomes in Minnesota, justifying an examination of longer-term trends rather than year-to-year fluctuations.

Are Blacks Worse Off?

We looked at two different measures of economic well-being of blacks: wage and salary incomes and household incomes using the Current Population Survey (CPS). We found that wage and salary incomes and the household incomes for blacks in the 2014 survey were higher than the wage and salary incomes and the household incomes in the 2013 survey. The median household income for blacks rose from $29,780.00 to $30,020.00 in 2013 to 2014. This increase is not statistically significant (Pearson chi-squared $(1) = 0.0951$, $P = 0.758$). Mean wage and salary income for blacks rose from $28,980.91 to $30,198.60; median wage and salary income rose from $21,000 to $24,000. Mean household income rose from $41,142.64 to $44,639.72. None of these changes are statistically significant. We conclude that the claim that black income declined in Minnesota from 2013 to 2014 is not robust across alternative data sets or alternative measures of income.

We also examined the past thirteen years of annual ACS Public Use Microdata Sample (PUMS) data and found that in six of the past thirteen years, there were declines in median black incomes in Minnesota. In seven of the past thirteen years, there were increases. None of these year-to-year changes are statistically significant. These findings suggest that there are wide fluctuations from year to year in the black median incomes, and thus, one should be very careful in drawing policy implications from these abrupt changes.

Are Blacks Worse Off in Minnesota Than in Mississippi?

Using the five-year, five percent sample of the population from the American Community Survey-PUMS (2009–2013), we computed the mean and median wage and salary incomes and mean and median household incomes for blacks and whites in Minnesota versus Mississippi. On each of these measures, the black income in Minnesota exceeds the black income in Mississippi. These differences are all statistically significant. Since white income in Mississippi is also uniformly lower than white income in Minnesota, the black-white ratio is higher in Mississippi than in Minnesota (.57 vs. .51) on the measure of median household income. On other measures the black-white ratio is higher in Minnesota than in Mississippi: the ratios of black-to-white mean and median wage and salary incomes are higher in Minnesota than in Mississippi (.65 vs. .63) and the ratio of black-to-white mean household income is higher in Minnesota than in Mississippi (.62 vs. 57). The conclusion is that it is premature to claim that blacks are worse off in Minnesota than in Mississippi.

Are Blacks Worse Off Relative to Whites in Minnesota?

At the Summit on Black Income, hosted by Congressman Keith Ellison on November 10, 2015, at the Franklin Middle School, we reported findings comparing the incomes of blacks and whites in Minnesota in 2005–2009 versus 2009–2013 using the ACS-PUMS. This comparison is useful because it shows two distinct time periods: the pre-recession and recession compared with the post-recession. Unmistakably, the ratio of black-to-white household incomes declined between the two time periods. Whether measured by means or medians, the declines are statistically significant. The black-white ratio of mean household incomes in Minnesota dropped from .54 in 2005–2009 to .50 in 2009–2013. Or put differently, for every dollar that a white household earned in total income, black households received 54 cents in 2005–2009; this dropped to 50 cents in 2009–2013. These drops are statistically significant and are largely attributable to white household incomes recovering after the recession but black household incomes remaining stagnant.

We also computed the black-white ratios of wage and salary incomes for the two periods. This ratio dropped from .67 to .65, barely statistically significant on conventional grounds. The black-white ratio among native-born residents dipped insignificantly from .66 to .65 while the black-white ratio among foreign-born residents dropped from .67 to .65. Thus, the relative size and statistical significance of the drop in household incomes is of a greater magnitude than the drop in wage and salary incomes. To be sure, the comparison of wage and salary incomes is for persons who worked and persistent unemployment differentials may help explain the difference.

Explaining the Deterioration in Relative Household Incomes

There is no dispute that in Minnesota the ratio of black-to-white household incomes declined from 2005–2009 to 2009–2013. But little of the gap can be explained by changes in black-white wage and salary incomes. If labor market processes are behind these household gaps, then the problem of widening income disparities is more likely to be rooted in differential hiring than in differential wages and salaries. We do not discount the fact that blacks earn less than whites in Minnesota. Rather it is to say that the cause of the widening gap in household incomes might rest in the entry points of labor markets rather than in the wage setting.

Another important component of household incomes is transfer payments. One unintended impact of welfare reforms in Minnesota and elsewhere is the drop in the portion of total income coming from public assistance payments. Coming out of the recession, many black households face a double whammy: higher unemployment and lower transfers.

Not to be discounted is the role of self-employment in explaining the widening gap in black and white household incomes. There has been a nontrivial growth in the share of black households with foreign-born heads. Foreign-born blacks disproportionately rely on self-employment income. But, even native-born blacks have turned to self-employment as a cushion from unemployment. In the absence of vigorous implementation of public agency goals for minority business enterprises and in the presence of discrimination against these business enterprises in the private sector, self-employment incomes lag and contribute to lower household incomes. Coupled with documented lending discrimination, market barriers persist to make it difficult for these emerging small businesses to succeed.

Undoubtedly, low wages for black immigrant workers and heavy concentrations of black workers in industries paying low minimum wages contribute to the low ratio of black-to-white incomes in Minnesota. But, the widening gap in household incomes belies the smaller disparity in wage and salary incomes, pointing to factors other than labor market disparities as the culprit. In short, there is a real and persistent black-white disparity in household incomes in Minnesota and this gap is widening.

Unemployment gaps and income gaps are not the only aspects of the Minnesota Paradox. Minnesota also leads the nation in racial disparities in incarceration rates, racial disparities in child maltreatment report rates, racial disparities in loan denial rates, racial disparities in educational outcomes, and even racial disparities in drowning rates. In a state known for its low incarceration rates, its excellent child protective services and child welfare system, its progressive lenders with strong community engagement, outstanding schools, and widespread access to aquatic programs for middle school students, how can it be that there are such wide racial disparities?

The Minnesota Paradox is helpful for understanding the difficulties in attempts to implement race-conscious programs. The overwhelming sentiment among residents of Minnesota is one of alarm and concern about these racial disparities but reluctance to attribute these disparities to systemic discrimination or racism. For some residents, there is a bit of ambivalence about whether these disparities are real or the consequence of other non-race factors, such as poverty, immigration and language barriers, or cultural differences. If one cannot get agreement about race-conscious remedies in a state with wide undisputed racial disparities, then where else would one expect to see support for such remedies?

SUMMARY

In this chapter, we have sketched a post–World War II progression from desegregation to race-neutrality. This progression is seen as encompassing distinct phases of policy remedies to the problem of racial inequality. The phases of desegregation (1940s–1950s), equal opportunity (1960s), affirmative action (1970s–1980s), affirmative action retrenchment (1990s–2000s), and diversity and inclusion (2000s–2016) bring us to the current post-Obama and race-neutrality phase. Much of the shift over the years comes with ambivalent views toward race-conscious remedies. We provide an illustration of this tension between wanting to support equality but being unwilling to support race-conscious programs that would directly address racial inequality by introducing the concept of the Minnesota Paradox. We argue that Minnesota is one of the best performing states in the nation but one of the worst performing states relating to racial equality. The problem is not that Minnesotans consciously harbor ill will toward racial minority group members. Rather, the problem is that not everyone agrees on the nature of the problem that needs to be remedied, and therefore, there are strong opinions about why race-conscious remedies are not necessary. Although our illustration comes from one state, one can argue that the difficulty in embracing a race-conscious remedy prevails more generally in the United States and stems from widespread disagreement that there is a racial problem that needs to be solved.

NOTES

1. This chapter draws on Myers, Samuel L., Jr., "The Economics of Diversity," in *Justice for All: Promoting Social Equity in Public Administration*, Norman J. Johnson and James H. Svara (eds.). M.E. Sharpe, April 2011.

2. Estimation based on Sabol and Couture (2008).

3. Estimation based on US Department of Health and Human Services, Administration on Children, Youth and Families (2008b).

4. Estimation based on US Department of Health and Human Services, Administration for Children and Families (2008a).

5. See Table 153. Number and percentage of students suspended from public elementary and secondary schools, by sex, race/ethnicity, and state: 2004 in Snyder, Dillow, and Hoffman (2008).

6. See Table 105. Percentage of high school dropouts among persons 16 through 24 years old (status dropout rate), by sex and race/ethnicity: Selected in Snyder, Dillow, and Hoffman (2008).

7. See Table 8. Percentage of persons age 25 and over and 25–29, by race/ethnicity, years of school completed, and sex: Selected years, 1910 through 2007 in Snyder, Dillow, and Hoffman (2008).

8. See Table 131. SAT score averages of college-bound seniors, by race/ethnicity: Selected years, 1986–87 through 2005–06 in Snyder, Dillow, and Hoffman (2008).

9. The broad definition here approximates the notion of Pareto optimality, wherein an allocation cannot be achieved that makes one person better off without making another person worse off (Friedman 2002, 45). This concept of "efficient" differs from cost effectiveness, wherein no other allocation exists with lower costs. There is no single, commonly accepted definition of equity, although we will often use in this chapter the notion of "fairness," wherein no one group prefers an allocation other than their own (Baumol 1986, 15). The competing definitions of equity include equality (in outcomes or in opportunities) and procedural fairness.

10. Or, at least by making some groups better off without making other groups worse off.

11. Gary Becker (1971) says: Let us first examine discrimination by a factor W, which is a perfect substitute for N. Each employer must pay a higher wage rate to a member of W if he is to work with N rather than with other W. An income-maximizing employer would never hire a mixed work force, since he would have to pay the W members of this force a larger wage rate than members of W working solely with other Ws. He hires only W if W's rate is less than N's and only N if N's is less than W's. He is indifferent between hiring them if and only if their wage rates are equal. Both N and W can be employed (in different firms) only if each employer is indifferent between them. Therefore, if a perfect substitute for N has a taste for discrimination against N, market segregation rather than market discrimination results: a firm employs either teams of N or teams of W; W and N are not employed in the same work force.

12. See the review of myths about affirmative action as discussed by Fryer and Loury (2005).

13. In one of the best reviews of the benefits and costs of affirmative action, William Darity (2005) provides a comprehensive interactional comparison of who benefits and why.

14. The full set of factors in the ballot initiative model includes percent change in median housing values, 1980–1990; percent black owner-occupied housing; black-white per capita income ratio; Hispanic-white per capita income ratio; Asian-white per capita income ratio; percent change in state employment per 10,000 population; percent change in state employment earnings, 1986–1992; state employment 1992 per 10,000 population; percent change in average annual pay, 1979–1989; percent change in state employment 1986–1992; labor force participation rate for females; white male unemployment rate; disposable personal income per person, percent change 1990–1993; labor force participation rate, males; percent retail trade of all non-farm establishments; percent services of all non-farm establishments; total black elected officials; total black statewide and federal elected officials; black federal, state, and local elected officials per 1000 blacks; percent popular vote cast for Democratic candidate for president in 1992; the percent of the voting age population that was registered in 1992; the percent of the voting age population that voted in 1992; net international migration 1990–1993; percent of the population that is 65 years old and over, 1993; percent change in crime 1981–1991; percent change in crime 1986–1991; percent of the population with greater than high school education; percent of the population with college education; the percent of the population residing in a metropolitan area, 1992; the violent crime rate in 1991; percent nonwhite; ratio of net international migration, 1990–1993 to population in 1993; percent black; percent college enrollment, among minorities 1991.

There are significant differences between the affirmative action retrenchment states and the non-retrenchment states in many of the economic factors. In states with affirmative action retrenchment efforts, black homeownership is higher, black-white income ratios are lower, state employment is lower, and unemployment is higher.

15. Alesina and Ferrara (2005, 766) write: "This trade-off also emerges from a number of recent studies on organization performance, surveyed among others by Jackson and Ruderman, Katherine Williams and Charles O'Reilly, and Orlando Richard, Kochan, and Amy McMillan-Capehart. The majority of these studies rely on laboratory experiments to test the link between diversity and performance, and generally find a positive effect of racial and gender diversity on creativity and task completion. For example, O'Reilly, Williams, and Sigal Barsade analyze thirty-two project teams and find that more diversity leads to more conflict and less communication, but controlling for the latter it also leads to higher productivity."

16. See Alessina and Ferrara (2005, 770) write: "[I]f a group is politically dominant, it may impose a type of government that restricts freedom of the minority. On the other hand, a more fractionalized society in which no group is dominant may end up with a constitution especially careful to defend the rights of minorities."

17. See Myers, S. L., Jr., "Understanding Racial Disparities in Unemployment Rates," Prepared for Minnesota Advisory Committee to the US Commission on Civil Rights. September 30, 2011.

18. Cautionary notes: This analysis is based on a small sample. Another important caveat is that unemployment is calculated based only on those actively looking for work. Therefore, if would-be laborers get discouraged and discontinue their search for work, they are effectively dropped from the unemployment count.

19. According to the National Bureau of Economics, the recession officially began in December, 2007.

20. The details of the full regression results can be found at www.hhh.umn.edu/centers/Wilkins/USCivilRightsHearings/Regression_results.xls.

21. Parts of this section come from Samuel Myers and Man Xu, "Relative Incomes of Blacks in Minnesota," *Minnesota Economic Trends*, December 2015.

22. See Reinan, John, and MaryJo Webster, "Black Household Income Plunges in One Year in Minnesota," *Star Tribune* (Minneapolis, MN), September 17, 2015.

23. See Lopez, Ricardo, "Black Leaders Say State Has Done Too Little On Racial Income Disparity," *Star Tribune* (Minneapolis, MN), September 18, 2015.

24. See Lopez, Ricardo, "Black Leaders Say State Has Done Too Little On Racial Income Disparity," *Star Tribune* (Minneapolis, MN), September 18, 2015.

25. See Myers and Xu, "Are Blacks Better off in Mississippi than in Minnesota? Research Brief, Revised and Are Blacks Better Off in Mississippi than in Minnesota?" Research Brief, Revised and Update; Roy Wilkins Center, University of Minnesota, November 10, 2015. http://www.hhh.umn.edu/news/roy-wilkins-center-research-brief-disputes-reports-income-disparity-minnesota.

Chapter 2

Problem Structuring, Race, and Policy Analysis*

One reason many policy makers disagree about how to remedy racial inequalities is that they disagree over the nature of the problem, its causes, and its consequences.[1] For example, in the area of child welfare, some policy makers dispute the claim that black children are really overrepresented among those cases reported to, and substantiated by, the child welfare system. They dispute that there is racial bias in the child protective system. They contend that much or all of the disproportionality occurs before children even enter the child welfare system. Or, stated differently, they claim that blacks are overrepresented in the child welfare system because they are overrepresented among those who are abused and neglected.

The technique of problem structuring is helpful in deconstructing the various debates about racial inequality and is helpful in answering the question: "What is the underlying problem we are attempting to solve?" before one proceeds to discuss race-conscious versus race-neutral remedies.

Problem structuring is a tool for defining problems, identifying the causal relationships underlying the problems, and distilling the value implications. A core ingredient in the task of problem structuring is asking: what groups are affected by the problem and why do we care about these groups? Understanding the stakeholders involved and those who wield or do not wield power helps to deconstruct elements of the problem. Problem structuring is like putting together a complex puzzle with perhaps many missing pieces. As we puzzle through the process of understanding the problem, we learn something about why there may be disputes about the remedy to the problem. This process is particularly helpful in the case of racial problems.

* Portions republished with permission of John Wiley and Sons, from *Journal of Policy Analysis and Management* 21(2)(Spring 2002): 169–190; permission conveyed through Copyright Clearance Center, Inc.

Policy analysts often place a self-conscious emphasis on quantitative and economic approaches to public policy problems. While there are many quantitative tools used to undertake policy analysis—ranging from simple descriptive methods of comparison of inputs and outputs to more complex methods of modeling queuing and dynamic processes—one core ingredient is often present: a focus on efficiency.

The efficiency criterion is central to many components of policy analysis: problem structuring, forecasting, recommendation, monitoring, and evaluation. One of the most popular and widely used textbooks on policy analysis, Lee Friedman's *The Microeconomics of Policy Analysis* (2002) identifies "cost-benefit" reasoning as key to understanding the logic of public choices. Of course, the reason economics is needed at all is that sometimes markets fail to provide the guidance public decision makers need when making thorny choices. It is no wonder, then, that risk and uncertainty, discounting of the future, and many aspects of informational imperfections and asymmetries enter explicitly into texts such as Friedman's.

The more important lesson of conventional microeconomic approaches to policy analysis is that the efficiency criterion is often at odds with alternative criteria that must enter into the political decision-making process. The most obvious alternative criterion is that of fairness or justice. While we have developed broadly accepted paradigms for examining the efficiency criterion—along with well-illustrated examples of how public decision-making can achieve this criterion despite market failure or what former Humphrey School of Public Affairs Dean John Brandl calls "government failure"[2]— there are few universally agreed upon or accepted metrics for the fairness, or equity, criterion. Fairness can mean equality of outcomes, or equal treatment, or consistency in the application of the rules of the game, or where the worst off person is as well off as they can be, or distributions of outcomes where nobody envies someone else's share of the pie. In short, while there are commonly accepted metrics for measuring efficient, a common or uniform notion of fairness often eludes policy analysts.

What is evident in the policy analysis discipline, however, is there is a tension between equity—however measured—and efficiency and that there are inherent trade-offs between the two. Transportation policies that seek to impose congestion taxes on drivers inherently disadvantage those whose income is low or who must use public transportation (Myers, Chung, and Saunders 2001; Myers and Saunders 1996). Environmental policies that seek to reduce pollution often pit gainers in some industries against losers in other industries. Analysis of income-transfer policies typically confronts the tensions between efficiency and equity.[3] Indeed, one could argue that the tension between equity and efficiency is characteristic of virtually every resource allocation dilemma faced by modern policy analysis. One of the strengths of microeconomic approaches to policy analysis is the ability to make these tensions and trade-offs explicit as a tool for more effective and useful advice and policymaking.

RACE ANALYSIS

Race analysis is the systematic application of the tools of historical and cultural analysis to understand the social and economic circumstances facing blacks and other racial minority group members. W. E. B. DuBois may have been the first architect of modern race analysis. His pioneering *The Philadelphia Negro* set the standard for analysis for a century, by combining careful historical and cultural observations with quantitative measures of social and economic well-being among racial groups. It is notable that DuBois's work appeared during an era when economists and others often began with a set of ahistorical assumptions about the behavior and traits of racial minority group members. DuBois, cognizant of this dominant way of viewing the problem of race, began instead with an attempt to understand *why* divergent racial and ethnic behaviors were evident in the population. It was DuBois who asserted that the problem of the twentieth century was the problem of the color line.

While much of race analysis was developed by the Chicago School of Sociologists, which produced such African American notables as E. Franklin Frazier and Oliver Cromwell Cox, it has not necessarily been a part of the body of work of modern policy analysts. Reading the literature on racial earnings inequality, for example, one would think that history has played only a small, if any, role in explicating the pathways toward creating different family structures, different neighborhood locations, different types of schools, and different outcomes on predictors of pre-labor market success. These factors are often regarded as exogenous in the economics literature.

Race analysts—such as the late Rhonda M. Williams, William A. Darity, Jr., James B. Stewart, Patrick L. Mason, William E. Spriggs, and William M. Rodgers III—have argued individually and collectively for interpreting race within economic models, as an endogenous factor (Darity 1995; Darity, Guilkey, and Winfrey 1995; Darity, Hamilton, and Dietrich 2001; Darity and Myers 1995; Darity, Stewart, and Mason 2000; Darity and Williams 1985; Mason 2001, 1999, 1997, 1996, 1995; Myers 1993, 1985; Myers and Chung 1996; Myers and Sabol 1988; Rodgers and Armentrout 1996; Rodgers and Spriggs 2002, 1996; Shulman and Darity 1989; Spriggs and Williams 1996; Williams and Kenison 1996). The endogeneity can take the form of making test scores endogenous in an earnings equation, rethinking the direction of causation between competition in markets and unequal market outcomes, and, indeed, by making the selection of an individual's race on a census form subject to complex decision-making based on culture, skin color, and self-identification. Modern race analysis draws on history, psychology, economics, and even biology for its inspiration. The subjects explored range from African Americans in sports to issues of voting and participation in policy arenas. Race analysis is practiced by legal scholars, political scientists, sociologists, and, more generally, those specializing in ethnic studies. Race analysis, however, is largely absent in the discipline of policy analysis.

Illustrations Drawn from Race Analysis

Many of the core problems that occupy the study of race relations can be characterized as problems that pit efficiency against equity. The Pareto criterion—can we make one group better off without making another worse off—seems to loom in the background when remedies to various forms of racial and ethnic economic inequality are discussed. This equity concern is at the root of many discussions about racial inequality. Yet surprisingly, the centrality of policy analysis tools to the body of race-relations research literature is seldom used in the illustration of policy analysis concepts. A few examples will suffice.

Racial Disparities in Credit Markets and the Use of Credit Scores to Screen for Credit Risk

Helen F. Ladd (1998) and John Yinger (1995) have long contended that racial disparities in loan rejection rates cannot be explained by racial differences in qualifications of loan applicants alone. They trace the history of the use of the Home Mortgage Disclosure Act (HMDA) data from the days when the data were collected at the census-tract level—and thus were virtually useless in testing hypotheses about racial discrimination based on individual characteristics—to the post-1990s era when individual-level data were routinely used by such advocacy groups as ACORN to contest lender policies and to challenge regulatory approval for bank mergers and acquisitions. The now-famous analysis by the Boston Federal Reserve of racial gaps in lending Bank (Munnell et al. 1992), which combined information on borrower credit worthiness with characteristics of loans, lenders, and census tracts, stands out as one of the historic policy research documents of the decade that influenced policymakers' understanding and views on a major race-related issue.

Before the publication of the Boston Fed's report, the overwhelming policy view about *why* blacks and Hispanics were much less likely to obtain mortgage credit and thereby less likely to own homes was that they are far worse credit risks than whites. When the Boston Fed examined the credit and employment history of blacks, Hispanics, and whites, they found that nonwhites were greater credit risks, but they also found that controlling for risk did not eliminate the racial gap in loan outcomes. There remained a substantial racial gap in mortgage loan rejection rates.

Although a debate as to whether the Boston Fed's work was sufficient to establish racial discrimination ensued within the narrow confines of the applied econometrics literature, the policy response at the federal level seemed to embrace the view that racial discrimination was partly responsible for lending disparities. A host of successfully argued lawsuits filed on behalf of minority plaintiffs further underscored the legitimacy of the policy research showing large "unexplained" racial gaps in loan outcomes.

In part, as a result of the findings of lender discrimination, many commentators began to ask: "If lenders do discriminate, then why?" One prominent explanation was that lenders were merely responding to underwriting criteria imposed on them by government-sponsored enterprises (GSEs). Since these federally chartered, private organizations generate billions of dollars of profit in exchange for the fulfillment of various social equity objectives, it is appropriate to ask whether the efficiency criterion of improving the performance of loans sold on the secondary market comes at the expense of reducing racial minority group members' access to loans. Much is at stake in this policy analysis, and understanding the effects of race is a crucial aspect of doing the policy analysis correctly.[4]

In the fall of 1999, Freddie Mac, one of the two leading GSE secondary market participants (the other is Fannie Mae), released a report summarizing an analysis of data collected on its behalf by Market Facts. The report showed that blacks had worse credit than whites (Ards and Myers 2001a). While not the most important or statistically compelling finding of the report, it quickly became the most controversial finding. Almost immediately, members of the US Congressional Black Caucus denounced the report and questioned the GSE's motives. Congresswoman Maxine Waters held a press conference to denounce the derogatory language used and demand a further examination of the issue. The underlying theme seemed to be that focus on credit scores inherently causes a form of discrimination. While credit scores may not necessarily reflect disparate treatment, the hint was that it resulted in a disparate impact. This episode is an example of a policy situation where race is the subject of analysis and a critical component of the policy process.

In all fairness, Freddie Mac had commissioned five historically black colleges and universities (HBCUs) to hold focus groups, design the questionnaire, and pretest some of the questions before Market Facts collected its data. Benedict College was contracted to perform the statistical analysis. Interestingly, that analysis discovered that much of the racial gap in loan outcomes could be explained by racial differences in credit scores and that there was indeed a major justification for focusing on borrower education and credit improvement as a way of reducing the racial gap in loan outcomes (Ards and Myers 2001b; Betsey, Lindsey-Taliaferro, and Amdet 2001). Another important outcome of the HBCU research was that in addition to the problem of minority borrowers who were high credit risks, was the problem of minority non-applicants who were of low credit risk. The analysis showed that a nontrivial number of persons who otherwise might obtain loans do not apply for loans because they believe they will be turned down. The resulting pools of applicants who do apply, therefore, are actually of higher risk than the (unobserved) total population of potential applicants. The lender, unfortunately, only observes those who apply and then correctly predicts that minorities on average have a higher risk. This outcome clearly is undesirable from an efficiency point of view and also thwarts efforts to obtain a fairer or more equitable distribution of loans to racial minority group members (Ards and Myers 2001a).

The policy response was to contest or restrict the use of credit scores or to use automated underwriting criteria as a way of forcing lenders and secondary market buyers to make more loans to minority members. This approach was apparently flawed. Advocates for minority homeownership were committing what Howard Raiffa coined the "error of the third type (E_{III})."[5] This process of getting the right answer to an incorrectly formulated policy question is characteristic of many race-related policy questions. Industry proponents were no less guilty of this error, for while their own data showed possible efficiency improvements in making loans to minority borrowers, the debate somehow ended as if they were arguing *for* efficiency and *against* equity, hardly something that businesses under federal and state regulatory control and oversight should do.

Neither the advocates of fair lending in minority communities nor industry proponents of efficiency-first seemed to be aware of the historical backdrop of minority involvement in credit markets. Both appeared to believe the "bad-credit" myth as if it has always been true that blacks have worse credit than whites. As Ards and Myers demonstrate, however, blacks have historically had higher-than-average savings rates, and until World War II actually had fewer opportunities than whites to display high risk in credit markets (Ards and Myers 2001a). Many saved merely to purchase consumer items and never sought loans at all. The failure to explore the historical and cultural antecedents to the existing racial disparities in credit markets can easily lead to faulty policy prescriptions.

Historical analysis and examination of the policy process for improving minority access to home mortgage loans illustrate both the inherent tensions between equity and efficiency *and* an important aspect of race analysis. The analysis of race provides the historical and cultural context needed to enhance the analysis of mortgage lending disparities.

Minority Admissions and Scholarships

One can easily see the tensions between equity and efficiency in the analysis of minority admissions and scholarships to college. But one can also see how important it is to understand the historical background and contemporary political climate regarding race relations when analyzing the many issues related to minority representation in higher education. The case of *Podberesky v. Kirwan* is a classic illustration.[6]

Daniel Podberesky, a student of Hispanic heritage, graduated from high school with a 4.0 average and scored 1,340 on the SAT examination. He applied to the University of Maryland, College Park for admission in the fall of 1989. He requested that he be considered for a scholarship.

One scholarship for which he applied was the Benjamin Banneker scholarship, named after the black mathematician and native Marylander. The scholarship was created in part to respond to complaints over the years from the Office of Civil Rights (OCR) of the US Department of Health, Education and Welfare (HEW) alleging that the state of Maryland operated a segregated system of higher education. To increase African American student enrollments, the University of Maryland initiated a merit-based scholarship program ostensibly to attract middle-class black students who might play a formal leadership role in the college and thereby attract more and better qualified African American students. By 1988, the scholarship was worth more than $33,500 over four years. The minimum requirements for consideration were a 900 SAT score and a 3.0 high school grade-point average.

Podberesky was denied a Banneker Scholarship because he was not black. He was also denied another merit scholarship open to all students (the Francis Scott Key scholarship) because he did not meet the academic qualifications for that scholarship. He filed suit in federal court alleging that he had been discriminated against in violation of Fourteenth Amendment to the United States Constitution, guaranteeing equal protection under the law. The US District Court for the District of Maryland at Baltimore granted summary judgment for the university. The plaintiff appealed, and the decision was reversed and remanded for a showing that the race-conscious policy was narrowly tailored and served a compelling governmental interest. The appeals court required that there be a showing of sufficient present effects of past discrimination to justify the race-conscious program.

The University of Maryland made four claims to support its contention that there were lingering effects of prior discrimination, justifying the continued use of a race-based remedy. First, it cited the poor reputation that the University has within the black community, stemming from a long history of segregation. Second, the University pointed to the significant underrepresentation of African American students on campus. Third, the University identified the problem of low retention rates and graduation rates among African

American students. And, finally, the University stated that African Americans faced a hostile campus climate. The district court agreed. Plaintiff appealed. The appellate court ruled that the evidence was insufficient to conclude lingering effects of prior discrimination.

This case is a tailor-made example of the tension between equity and efficiency. The University, attempting to craft a remedy for prior discrimination, is faced with the challenge of finding a means to improve minority student representation, retention rates, and graduation rates *without* taking race into account to achieve an equity goal, but also taking race into account to achieve the goal most effectively. The University believed, perhaps correctly, that without taking race into account, it would not be able to improve black representation, retention, and graduation rates. The University, without fully documenting or appreciating the paths by which prior discrimination is transmuted into current inequality was unable to persuade the appeals court.[7]

In addition to the obvious equity versus efficiency trade-off is the more intimate understanding of race that is required to appreciate this case fully. The previous president of the University of Maryland was John Slaughter. Slaughter, an electrical engineer by training and a member of the National Academy of Engineering, had been the executive director of the National Science Foundation before being selected to be the University's first (and only) African American chief administrator. Slaughter was charismatic, highly respected both within the black community and the broader academic community, and, in the words of many, "worked miracles" at the University. He helped to establish credible programs in science, technology, and minority communities and oversaw a significant increase in minority enrollment. The University's national standings rose and its prestige increased.

During Slaughter's tenure, William Kirwan, a mathematician who had spent nearly his entire career at the University of Maryland, was provost and vice president. Kirwan succeeded Slaughter as president and was a popular and well-respected administrator in his own right. One of his former graduate students, Howard P. Rawlings (who never completed his dissertation), had become one of the most important black power-brokers in the state of Maryland. Delegate Rawlings chaired the appropriations committee of the Maryland House of Delegates. It was no secret within the black community that the selection of Kirwan as Slaughter's successor came with the expectation that Kirwan would at minimum continue the progress begun under Slaughter's leadership to increase black representation, black retention, and graduation and improve the campus climate for people of color.

Rational policy analysis may argue for finding ways to improve the representation of African Americans without diminishing the opportunities for other students, particularly other students of color. But, as Richard Nelson (1977, 13–17) notes in *The Moon and the Ghetto*:

What is a problem, and what is a solution, are not questions that rational analysis alone can decide. The questions of what values, and whose values, ultimately are to count inherently must be answered through political process, not rational analysis alone. Some groups may be unhappy with their lot. However, all demands and all groups can never be satisfied. Some "problems" simply reflect the realities of political power that cannot be influenced by rational analysis.

Understanding how certain choices are made in race cases, such as the Banneker case, requires knowledge about the political, personal, and historical aspects of policy evolution as much as it does about the analysis of efficiency. While these aspects of race analysis make the case more complex, more unwieldy and more difficult to resolve, they offer a glimpse into a reality that might improve policy analysis and policymaking.

Racial Disproportionality in Child Protection Services

Another classic example of the interface between equity and efficiency as well as the role of race analysis is the problem of the overrepresentation of African American children in the child protective services and out-of-home placements. African American children make up about 15 percent of the overall population, but they comprise more than 25 percent of reported and substantiated cases of abuse and neglect. In part, because of the higher-than-average representation among substantiated cases, African American children are disproportionately found in foster care and out-of-home placements (Ards, Chung, and Myers 1998).

No social workers or caseworkers want to find their name or case on the front pages of the *New York Times*. Difficult decisions at a minute level are made several times a day about whether to remove a child from an abusive home, what type of services to provide and when and whether to return the child to its biological parents. But, no matter how well-intended, decisions sometimes are accompanied by unexpected and often gruesome outcomes. One example is that of a child in New York who died from being scrubbed with Brillo pads (Bernstein and Newman 2001). The parents had been accused of child maltreatment on numerous, previous occasions. Literally hundreds of thousands of dollars in services had been spent over the years to support the family through social services. But no matter how well-intentioned, the decision to keep the children in the abusive family environment backfired.

In part, to shield caseworkers from individual recrimination from their administrative decisions, such as in the Brillo pad case, many states have begun to initiate risk assessment protocols. The logic is that if we are able to determine statistically whether a child is likely to be subjected to additional abuse or neglect by returning to the biological family, we can reduce the human error associated with these deeply emotional decisions.

Factors that often enter into the risk assessment criteria include whether the parent is a drug user; whether there has ever been a criminal complaint or arrest; the social and demographic characteristics of the family; and whether the household is headed by a woman. The head of the Child Welfare League, Thomas Morton (1999) has argued that such risk assessment protocols have a disparate impact on African American children. He contends that the over-representation of African American children is due principally to reporting bias and other forms of racial bias within the child protective services that, in turn, render statistical analyses using data on reported and substantiated cases suspect.

This area of policy analysis is controversial because of unresolved issues of race. Are African American children really discriminated against in the child protective services, and what is the nature of the discrimination? If they are overrepresented in the system are they more likely to receive needed services? Or, as many black social workers contend, while they may be overrepresented among reported and substantiated cases, their families are not getting the expensive services they need in order to reunite. As a result, black children are disproportionately found among those languishing in foster care, and are neither in a permanent adoptive home nor reunited with their biological parents.

The controversy hinges partly over whether services provided are "cultur-ally appropriate" and whether service providers have the necessary training or experience to deal with clients of diverse backgrounds. But the controversy is also partly about *analysis*. How is racial disproportionality in reported abuse cases measured? Does one compare the child population to the population of reported cases? Does one estimate the "at risk" population and compare that to the reported population? One series of national surveys, the National Inci-dence Studies (NIS), provides underlying data needed to compute racial gaps in report rates. Surprisingly, blacks are not more likely to be reported than are whites, even when one accounts for differences in characteristics of report-ers, type of maltreatment and characteristics of the child and family, as well as possible sample selection bias (Ards, Chung, and Myers 1998). If racial disparities in reporting are to explain the overrepresentation of black children among reported abuse and neglect cases, then black children will need to have higher report rates than whites. This finding does not seem to emerge when the NIS data is examined.

Of course, bias might exist elsewhere, as Thomas Morton (1999) and oth-ers (Ards, Chung, and Myers 1999, 2001; Sedlak, Bruce, and Schultz 2001) contend. The bias might occur in the opening of a case for investigation; it might occur at the stage of substantiation; it might occur at the stage of ser-vice provision; it might occur at the stage of placement in foster care. Still, without any substantial data supporting these possibilities, there is a generic belief among many black professionals working in child protective services that racial bias is the explanation for the overrepresentation of black children in the child protective services.

How does one undertake good policy analysis in an area where a huge segment of the stakeholder population believes that there is bias? How does one undertake efficiency improvements, such as the risk assessment protocols being initiated around the nation, when many believe that the data used to calibrate these efficiency tools is tainted by prior racial disparities? Unresolved issues of racial bias and the limited availability of careful race analysis in the area of child abuse and neglect could hinder the implementation of effective new tools to improve the administration of public services.

Racial Profiling

A quick search of Lexus/Nexus database reveals literally hundreds of law review articles on racial profiling. The entire subject has emerged under an umbrella called "driving while black." This literature has produced not only technical articles examining various aspects of Fourth Amendment protections that are forfeited when suspects are in their automobiles rather than in their homes, but also a broad array of popular articles and journalistic reports (e.g., Bustillo 2000; Doxsey 2001; Eddings 2001; FindLaw Legal News 2000; Higgin and Mihalopoulos 2000; Jones 2001; Kennedy 1999; Nando Times 2000; Poughkeepsie Journal 2001; Still 1999; Times Union 2001; Wilson 2000).

Racial profiling, or the use of race as a marker for possible illegal behavior, has all the characteristics of screening and information imperfections that have occupied the economics literature over the past quarter century. Nobel laureate Joseph Stiglitz, for example, has examined the problem of credit market signaling that anticipates much of the current debate surrounding the use of credit scores that have been calibrated on a possibly biased sample of loan applicants (Stiglitz and Weiss 1981). In the case of US Customs screening for drug dealers, for example, black women are believed to be more likely than others to serve as couriers, or "mules," in the drug trade. This belief justifies in part the higher rate of intrusive searches conducted on this group as compared to other groups. And, indeed, many black women, once stopped, do in fact turn out to be carrying drugs. In traffic stops, state highway patrols believe that Latino and African American males are more likely to transport drugs than others. And, indeed, many Latino and African American males stopped and searched are found to be carrying illegal drugs. The problem is that in both instances—in airport searches and traffic stops—carefully assembled evidence often suggests that racial minorities stopped and searched are no more likely, and are often less likely, than others to be found guilty of other crimes for which they have been stopped.

The US General Accountability Office (2000a) reviewed a database of more than 100,000 arriving international passengers for the years 1997 and 1998, who were subjected by US Custom Service officials to personal searches. The vast majority of these searches arose from the suspicion of contraband or weapons. Searches could take the form of pat-downs, strip-searches, or x-ray searches. African American women were nine times more likely to be x-rayed after being frisked or patted down than were white American women. Yet, African American women were only half as likely as white women to be found carrying drugs or weapons.

Temple University social psychology professor John Lamberth designed and conducted a data collection strategy in 1995 to determine whether there was racial profiling along the I-95 corridor from the White Marsh, Maryland exit to the Elkton, Maryland exit. The test consisted of driving along the highway at the speed limit and observing the number and race of persons who passed the tester and who did not pass the tester. The sample of persons who passed the tester (speeders) was considered to be the at-risk population. Most of the drivers on the highway were speeding. Lamberth found that of those speeding, 21.8 percent were minorities. Of all drivers, 21.1 percent were minorities. Next, Lamberth examined the distribution of those stopped by Maryland State police from data mandated by a consent order. Of all drivers stopped, 80.3 percent were minorities (Lamberth 1996). Using statewide data on the discovery of drugs in the automobiles or on motorists' persons, Lamberth shows that blacks and whites have nearly the same rates of offending.[8] The probability that the resulting disparity between the minority share of the at-risk population (those speeding) and the minority share of the stopped population could occur by chance "is less than one in one quintillion."

Although both the National Association of Police Organizations and the International Association of Chiefs of Police have condemned racial profiling, neither organization initially supported racial data collection on traffic stops (US General Accountability Office 2000b, 4). Nonetheless, by spring of 2000 legislation had been introduced or passed in thirteen states, from Arkansas to South Carolina, requiring the collection of such data. Bills were introduced in another seventeen states by November 2001. Organizations such as AELE (Americans for Effective Law Enforcement, Inc.) have set up high-profile training sessions to assist state and local law enforcement agencies in shielding themselves from liability in racial profiling litigation.[9] These actions have been initiated despite the fact that little or no policy analyses had been conducted to determine the trade-offs between the efficiency goals of improved policing through targeted stops and searches and the equity goals of equating minority shares of stops to minority representation in the at-risk population.

On one hand, the study of racial profiling can help enhance the understanding of the tools and techniques of policy analysis. There are resource allocation issues involved. There are issues of imperfect information and screening involved. There are issues of conditional probabilities and inferences drawn from potentially biased samples involved. These sorts of issues are illustrated in detail in a case note found elsewhere in this volume that deals with the attempted passage in Minnesota in 2001 of a bill mandating race data collection in traffic stops.

On the other hand, understanding the dynamics of race could better help those who conduct research on topics like racial profiling. It is no secret that Congressman James E. Clyburn (D. South Carolina) was the chair of the Congressional Black Caucus and requested the GAO to conduct an analysis of what federal and state data was available to measure racial profiling. It is no secret that Congressman John Conyers, Jr., one of the most senior members of the Congressional Black Caucus, was the lead sponsor of the House version of the "End Racial Profiling Act of 2001" (H.R. 2074).[10] These African American legislators have chosen a particular approach to racial profiling, data collection on stops, and searches, that begs for an intimate understanding of both the individual lawmakers and of the larger constituencies and stakeholders they represent.

The Racial Divide and Problem Structuring

Race analysis helps uncover some of the complexity in policy analysis. Many policy analysis questions are poorly structured because they fail to incorporate the messiness of race. Discourse about racial disparities, for example, often centers on debates about remedies to those disparities and not about the problem the remedies are attempting to resolve. There is an apparent racial divide in understanding the nature of problems of racial disparities and as a result there is a thorny divide in public opinion about what to do about these racial disparities.

An illustration is discourse about affirmative action. Affirmative action is a remedy. It is a race-conscious remedy. What problem is it that people feel that the remedy is attempting to solve? Perceptions of the problem of racial disparities, say, in incomes or housing or jobs, arguably contribute to differing opinions on remedies. Part of the reason why there is a wide difference in views about proposing a solution to the problem of racial inequality can be attributed to the fact that there are wide differences in perceptions about why there are racial disparities to begin with. This discrepancy between perceptions about causes of a problem and beliefs about remedies to a problem can be observed by looking at the population's opinions on preferential treatment in hiring, commonly referred to as affirmative action. The General

Social Survey (GSS) asked this question. The GSS is an annual survey of the nation's attitudes and behaviors on an extensive range of topics such as morality, national spending priorities, and social mobility. Since 1972, the National Opinion Research Center (NORC) at the University of Chicago has been conducting this annual survey. It is the most commonly used resource for research in the social sciences after the US Census database. In this analysis, we included 27,055 valid cases between 1988 and 2016.

Some people believe that blacks should be given preference in hiring and promotion due to past discrimination. But others believe that such preferences in hiring and promotion of blacks would discriminate against whites. In the GSS survey, respondents were asked about their opinion: "Are you for or against preferential hiring and promotion of blacks?" This question captures aptly and concretely the respondent's opinion about preferential treatment based on affirmative action programs. According to the GSS, national support for affirmative action has been about 17 percent for the past twenty years. However, if we look at the responses of white Americans and black Americans separately, we see that support for affirmative action is drastically different for the two groups, averaging at just below 12 percent for white Americans and over 45 percent for black Americans.

As shown in Figure 2.1, 56.4 percent of blacks were in favor of preferential hiring and promotion of blacks in 1994. Black support dropped to 39.4 percent by 1998. But it has stayed between the 40 and 50 percent range since then. Whites, who overwhelmingly disfavor affirmative action, have recently shown an uptick of support. The rate increased from 11.4 percent in 2006 to 18 percent in 2016. Still, the vast majority of whites are opposed to affirmative action.

If we further parse the population by level of education, as depicted in Figure 2.2, we see that among white Americans, a huge majority of those without a college degree and those with only a bachelor's degree "strongly oppose" affirmative action. Among white Americans with graduate degrees and professional degrees, there is strong opposition to affirmative action for blacks but to a lesser extent than among whites with no college education. There is about a 15-percentage point gap in the opposition to affirmative action between whites with advanced college degrees and those without college degrees. This gap has persisted over time.

This is an example of how our national population holds differing views on affirmative action, a proposed solution to racial inequality in the workforce.

Now to explore differences in perception about the underlying problem, we looked at other questions that the GSS addressed. The survey queried respondents about what could be possible causes of African Americans holding bad jobs, earning lower incomes, and living in poorer housing than white Americans. The respondents were able to choose among a wide range of

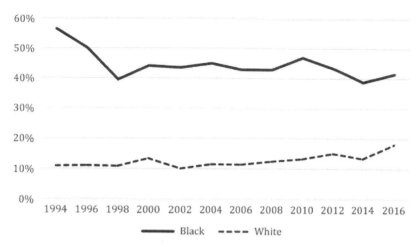

Figure 2.1 Favor preference in hiring Blacks. General Social Survey, 1994–2016.

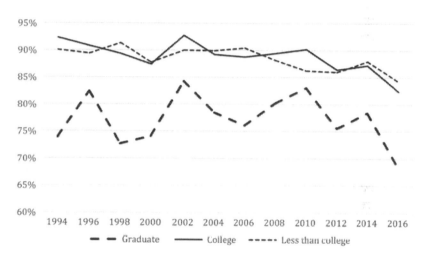

Figure 2.2 Opposed to affirmative action by education: whites only. General Social Survey, 1994–2016.

possible causes. Possible responses included "discrimination," "inborn [in] ability to learn," less "chance for education," and less "motivation." Over twenty-five years, "discrimination" as the cause for inequality has steadily declined as shown in Figure 2.3, while the share of persons checking "yes" on other factors has also declined.

Until the mid-1990s, more than 70 percent of blacks thought racial discrimination had contributed to unequal distribution of quality jobs, income, and housing, but the percentage declined in the 2000s and even lower in the 2010s. However, since 2012 it has been again increasing—from 46.4 percent

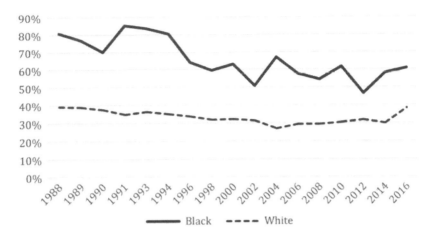

Figure 2.3   Differences due to discrimination. General Social Survey, 1988–2016.

in 2012 to 58.0 percent in 2014 and 60.7 percent in 2016. The same trend can be observed among whites—an increase from 31.6 percent in 2012 to 38.2 percent in 2016.

Among white Americans who responded that the differences in quality jobs, income, and housing were "not" due to discrimination, there is noticeable difference by level of education. According to the 2016 survey, 40 percent of white American with a graduate degree responded that the differences were not due to discrimination while the other groups show relatively higher percentages—college education (61.6 percent) and less than a college education (65.2 percent). In short, other than the most educated whites, the vast majority of whites believe that discrimination is not the cause of the problems that blacks face. It is no wonder, then, that there is so much opposition among whites to affirmative action as a remedy to inequality; most whites simply do not believe that the problem to be remedied is rooted in the past or current vestiges of racial discrimination.

In recent years, however, the majority of white Americans attribute the causes of racial inequality to black American inferiority or individual behaviors. In other words, most white Americans chose options of "inborn [in] ability to learn" or less "motivation" when queried about why blacks are less likely to have equality in incomes and housing. On the other hand, most black Americans viewed causes of black inequality to be rooted in structural factors and chose the options of "discrimination" or less "chance for education." The differing trends in the extent to which each racial group attributes inequality shows how the two cohorts view the underlying problem of inequality differently (see Figure 2.4).

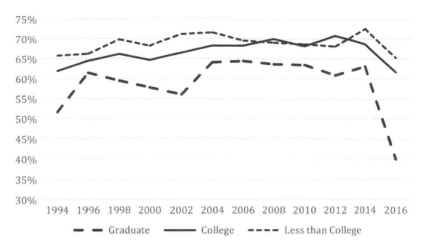

Figure 2.4   Difference "not" due to discrimination: whites only. General Social Survey, 1994–2016.

Since the respondents were allowed to choose more than one reason to account for the difference, we examined several alternative measures. Obviously, we're interested in looking at those who checked yes on discrimination only. Over the last couple of decades, "discrimination" as the cause for inequality has increased slightly as shown in Figure 2.5, although black Americans' responses have fluctuated over time. This trend was concealed, to some degree, by other factors in aggregation. Almost one out of three people who answered that discrimination contributed to inequality strongly believed that discrimination was the only cause for inequality. It is still unclear why black Americans' responses are more volatile compared with those of white Americans.

Figure 2.6 shows the share of people who checked yes on discrimination but did NOT check yes on options of inborn [in]ability to learn or less motivation, that is, discrimination without a belief in inferiority of blacks or lack of will. There is no noticeable change over time among whites, but the share of blacks was declining.

We also examined two more alternatives: (1) the share of people who only checked yes on options of inborn [in]ability to learn or less motivation and (2) the share of people who checked yes on options of inborn [in]ability to learn, less motivation, or lack of education. Both measures are increasing (racism plus paternalism).

We also looked at the white Americans who responded that they were hurt by affirmative action. The question in the survey reads, "What do you think the chances are these days that a white person won't get a job or promotion

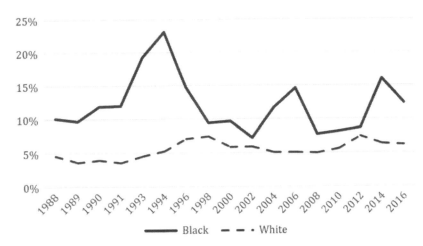

Figure 2.5   Difference due to discrimination only. General Social Survey, 1988–2016.

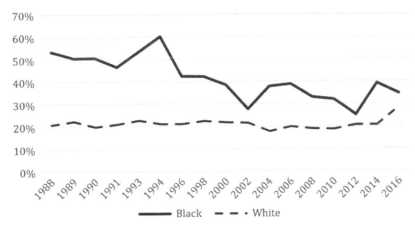

Figure 2.6   Differences due to discrimination without a belief in inferiority of blacks or lack of will. General Social Survey, 1988–2016.

while an equally or less qualified black person gets one instead?" As shown in the graph below, the overall trend has been declining in all groups broken down by level of education. According to the 2016 survey, 67.9 percent of white Americans responded that they were somewhat likely or very likely hurt by affirmative action (see Figure 2.7).

The Gallup Poll also surveys directly and explicitly people's perceptions about affirmative action. According to the Gallup Poll, in 1981, 7 percent of whites and 29 percent of nonwhites supported affirmative action or preferential treatment in hiring. These figures changed little by 1991; nationally

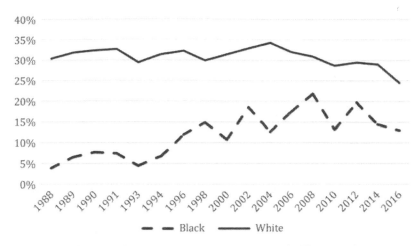

Figure 2.7 **Differences due to inborn disability or lack of will.** General Social Survey, 1988–2016.

11 percent favored affirmative action, including 8 percent of whites, and 24 percent of blacks. Furthermore, 55 percent of Americans believed the United States had enough laws aimed at reducing discrimination (see Figure 2.8).

In 2003's Gallup poll, Americans were split in their opinion toward affirmative action. In total, 45 percent of the surveyed adults favored affirmative action programs for racial minorities, while 43 percent opposed it; 70 percent of blacks and 63 percent of Hispanics favored affirmative action, compared to 44 percent of non-Hispanic whites. The Gallup poll mirrors the results of the GSS: the vast majority of whites oppose affirmative action and race-conscious remedies to racial inequality.

Perceptions about the nature of the problem that affirmative action is attempting to solve affect people's opposition to affirmative action. Recall that Figure 2.2 shows that the overwhelming majority of whites oppose affirmative action, with less well-educated whites showing greater opposition than better educated whites. How does opposition to a remedy like affirmative action relate to respondents' understanding of the problem of racial inequality? To answer this question we have estimated a logistic regression where the dependent variable is strong opposition to affirmative action among white respondents in successive waves of the GSS from 1994 to 2016. Independent variables include age, education, and gender of respondent and an indicator of whether the respondent does not believe racial disparities are due to discrimination. Figure 2.9 reports the odds ratios associated with the independent variables "does not believe racial disparities are due to discrimination" and "high school or less education." The results are reported for three different model specifications: Model 1, with controls for education, age, and

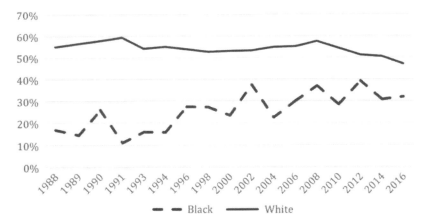

Figure 2.8   Differences due to inborn disability, lack of education, or lack of will. General Social Survey, 1988–2016.

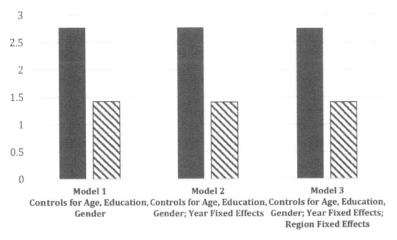

■ Does not believe discrimination is the cause of racial disparities

◪ Education: high school or less

Figure 2.9   Odds of strong opposition to affirmative action: whites only, 1994–2016. Author's Computations of General Social Survey, 1988–2016.

gender; Model 2, with controls for education, age, and gender and with year fixed effects; and Model 3, with controls for education, age, and gender and with region and year fixed effects.

For whites who don't believe discrimination is the cause of racial disparities, the odds of being strongly opposed to preferential hiring of blacks are 2.7 times higher than the odds for people who believe discrimination might be the cause for racial disparities. For those whose education is high school or less, the odds of being strongly opposed to preferential hiring of blacks are 1.4 times larger than the odds for people who have greater than high school education. These results, all statistically significant, are robust across all model specifications. The results provide compelling evidence of a strong relationship between whites' beliefs about the causes of racial disparities and their opposition to specific remedies to these disparities.

SUMMARY

People disagree about remedies to racial inequality because they disagree about the causes of racial inequality. Whether the problem is one of observed racial disparities in lending, college admissions, child maltreatment, or police stops, the debate about how (or whether) to remedy these disparities hinges upon disagreements about the underlying causes.

Two major sources of information about perceptions of remedies and the causes of inequality are the General Social Survey and the Gallup Poll. Both surveys reveal sizeable opposition to race-conscious remedies like affirmative action. The GSS reveals, moreover, that the vast majority of whites do not believe that the cause of racial disparities is discrimination, a viewpoint that is especially pronounced among less-well-educated whites. A troubling minority of whites also believes that the cause of racial inequalities is inborn inferiority or lack of will on the part of blacks. Because so few people believe that the cause of inequality is discrimination and because a nontrivial pool of whites also feels that the cause rests in inherent inferiority or lack of will, it is not surprising that there is split support at best for race-conscious programs.

Another perspective gleaned from the GSS concerns beliefs that race-conscious programs hurt whites. The vast majority of less well-educated whites believe that whites are hurt by affirmative action. Lower percentages of better educated whites share this view, but still whites as a group fear that affirmative action hurts whites. Optimistically, these perceptions have declined overtime. In 1994, about 80 percent of lower-educated whites and 65 percent of highly educated whites believed that race-conscious programs hurt whites. By 2016, about 65 percent of lower-educated whites and 50 percent of highly educated whites believed that whites were hurt by race-conscious affirmative action. While the decline in white perceptions about the harm to whites of affirmative action is notable, the vast majority of whites still remain convinced that race-conscious programs hurt whites.

Thus, on two levels one can see why there is so much opposition to race-conscious remedies. On one level, there is the view that the underlying problem is not something that ought to be remedied by state action, for example, discrimination. If the problem of racial inequality is rooted in blacks' laziness or their inherent inferiority, it is hard to argue that scarce resources should be expended to rectify the resulting market disparities by providing preferential treatment to undeserving groups.

On another level, opposition to racial preferences can be understood if whites perceive that whites are hurt. The subtle logic here is that even if there is a rationale or justification for *some* remedy—for example, illegal discrimination, blocked opportunities, or the like—the specific remedy loses support from the majority group if that group believes that it is hurt by providing racial preferences to other groups.

Herein lies the reason for exploring race-neutral remedies. When race-conscious remedies are opposed—either because of perceptions that there is no good justification for remedying the racial inequality through state action or because of perceptions that the remedy hurts non-aggrieved third parties—race neutral remedies become attractive.

NOTES

1. This chapter draws on Myers, Samuel L., Jr., "Presidential Address – Analysis of Race as Policy Analysis," *Journal of Policy Analysis and Management*, 2002.

2. Government failure, explored in Brandl (1998, 135), is likened to market failure because both yield "inefficiency and unfairness." Also, see Brandl's APPAM presidential address (Brandl 1988).

3. For an example of tension between efficiency and equity in welfare policymaking, see Mary Joe Bane's APPAM Presidential Address (Bane 2001).

4. Myers does, in fact, examine this hypothesis and does not find consistent evidence that GSE behavior explains lender racial disparities in loan rejection rates.

5. Dunn (1994, 184) defines "error of the third type (EIII)" as "The formulation of the wrong substantive or formal representation of a problem when one should have formulated the right one. Type III errors should be distinguished from type I and type II errors, that is, rejecting the null hypothesis when it is true (EI) and accepting the null hypothesis when it is false (EII)." Raiffa (1968, 264) refers to EIII errors as "solving the wrong problem."

6. The details discussed drawn from: *Podberesky v. Kirwan,* 956 F.2d 52 (4th Cir. 1992); 38 F.3d 147 (4th Cir. 1994).

7. The key point of the appeals court, however, was that the district court erred in concluding that the University had proven present effects of past discrimination.

8. Lamberth argues that the state data do not differ substantially from the I-95 data.

9. http://www.aele.org/race.html.

10. Six other anti-racial profiling bills were introduced in the US House and Senate in 2001, including one bill introduced by Georgia Congressman Lewis banning racial profiling among international travelers.

Chapter 3

The Curious Case of Competitive Swimming and Racial Disparities in Drowning*

The Centers for Disease Control reports that drowning is the second leading cause of unintentional injury-related death for children between the ages of one and fourteen. African American children between the ages of five and nineteen are 2.6 times more likely to drown than their white counterparts. Almost every summer heartbreaking stories of African American drownings highlight this reality.[1]

Two families' day of fun quickly turned tragic when six teenagers at the gathering drowned in a Louisiana river on August 2. According to the *Associated Press*, the outing began as a typical family get-together with a large group of relatives and friends. The children waded in Shreveport, LA's Red River to beat the heat as adults were planning to prepare food. But tragedy struck before they were even able to fire up the grill. DeKendrix Warner, 15, one of the teens splashing around in the river, slipped off a ledge and plunged into water nearly 25-feet deep. As the teen struggled, a cousin attempted to rescue him but slipped on the same ledge. More relatives and friends tried to help in the rescue, but none could swim. The teens were thrown one life vest, but none could reach it (*Afro-American News*, August 7, 2010).

What makes the Shreveport drownings so poignant is the fact that the children were teenagers, not infants or toddlers. Between 2000 and 2007, the fatal unintentional drowning rate for African Americans across all ages was 1.3 times that of whites. The fatal drowning rate of African American

* Portions republished with permission of Nova Science Publishers, from "The Economics of Diversity: The Efficiency vs. Equity Trade-Off" in *Diversity Management: Theoretical Perspectives and Practical Approaches*, Sheying Chen, Editor. Nova Science Publishers, Inc. New York, 2011, pp. 55–70.; permission conveyed through Copyright Clearance Center, Inc.

children ages five to fourteen is 3.1 times that of white children in the same age range (CDC 2011).

According to the NCAA *2005–2006 Race-Ethnicity Report*, 107 African American non-Hispanic student-athletes competed in Division I competitive swimming, compared with 7,121 white non-Hispanics, 207 Asians, and 213 Hispanics. In other words, there are nearly seventy times more white non-Hispanic student-athletes than African Americans competing in Division 1 (NCAA 2006).

The USA Swimming Association, the primary organization of competitive swimming among age-group swimmers (those who have not yet reached high school or college) and the central pipeline in the United States for Olympic hopefuls, reported that .87 percent of its members were African Americans.

Blacks are disproportionately found among those who drown. They are severely underrepresented among those who are among elite swimmers. There is an obvious relationship between drowning and the ability to swim that has not escaped notice of the leadership of national swimming organizations such as the USA Swimming association. If there were ever a strong efficiency case for diversity, it would be the case for diversity in competitive swimming. Yet, diversity policies are difficult to embrace because efforts designed to make one group better off can be seen as unfair to other groups that may be made worse off.

Moreover, there is a widespread perception, even today, that blacks lack the *natural ability* to swim. Pseudo-scientific evidence has been offered over the years pointing to such myths as the lower buoyancy of blacks, their large feet, differences in bone density, and more recently the position of the center of mass above the ground. Bejan et al. (2010), for example, contend that the center of mass in blacks is 3 percent higher above the ground than in whites meaning that blacks hold a 1.5 percent speed advantage in running, and whites hold a 1.5 percent speed advantage in swimming, since swimming and running require different centers of mass for speed. Bejan et al. (2010) document that blacks dominate the record holders of the 100 meter sprint events in track and field but whites are almost exclusively the holders of the 100 meter freestyle events in swimming. Blacks dominate most (summer) Olympic events but, until recently, one of the last outposts of virtual total exclusion of blacks in Olympic sports is swimming. Both because of the widespread perception that there is a "natural" or genetic explanation for their underrepresentation in swimming and because of the view that there is no public policy problem to be solved, there is great resistance to remedying the problem of lack of diversity in swimming.

These phenotypic explanations for the inability of blacks to swim must be balanced against the long historical record of *racial barriers* to swimming. Historians have amassed enormous evidence of the excellent boating and swimming skills among coastal Africans and also the efforts of slave owners to routinely prevent their slaves from learning how to swim lest they escape. Moreover, even into the twentieth century segregated pools and the lack of access to public swimming pools became the norm for African American communities (Hastings 2006; Wiltse 2007). Somewhat ironically, segregation also coincided with the evolution of elite inner-city swimming programs in Atlanta, Washington, D.C., and Philadelphia. Powerhouse swimming teams at historically black colleges and universities (HBCUs) such as Howard University, Morehouse College, Morgan State University, and Florida AandM University routinely included highly visible graduates, such as former Atlanta Mayor Andrew Young, who promoted swimming as a life-long sport, and who served as lifeguards, water safety instructors, and role models to generations of inner-city youth. With the dismantlement of HBCU swimming programs and the exodus of many middle-class blacks from HBCUs to white colleges and universities, there is now a dearth of highly visible elite African American swimmers who can debunk the myth that blacks cannot swim.

One can issue any number of critiques of the thesis that blacks are not pre-disposed to elite swimming. For example, one could question the mechanical engineering studies putatively showing that blacks are not predisposed physically to swimming sprints. Bejian analyzes data on world record holders in the 100 meter freestyle in swimming and the 100 meter sprint in track to demonstrate the physical differences by race in the predisposition to swimming vs track. An immediate objection to the conclusion, however, is that the physical differences identified relate to the 100 freestyle. Had they investigated the true sprint event in competitive swimming—the 50 meter freestyle—they would have reached the conclusion that black male and female US Olympic swimming gold medalists qualified in this sprint. This conclusion unfortunately coincides with yet another racialist view, namely that blacks can only do sprints. Both conclusions, the explicit one of Bejian, et al. and the implicit one from looking at the evidence on which events blacks who have qualified for the Olympics have qualified miss an important element of the sport. Strokes are governed by the International Federal of Swimming (FINA) and the rules change over the years in response largely to the demands of the groups that participate.

There are many different strokes and competitive events in Olympic swimming. Fast breaststroke requires extremely strong thighs and calves and flexibility in the knees and ankles. Top freestylers who rely principally on a flutter kick that requires an upward movement of the legs are not necessarily great breaststrokers, which requires an outward and circular movement of the legs. Many of the top breaststrokers in the world, in fact, are short and stocky, whereas most of the top spring freestylers are tall and lanky. The butterfly requires extraordinary upper body strength and long arm spans. Among female butterflyers, one sees a wide range of body types and shapes, but relatively few with large breasts. Whereas large breasts are an impediment to streamlining on one's stomach and can create drag in the butterfly, the negative impacts are negligible when swimming on one's back. There are all sorts of body sizes and arm lengths and torso-to-leg proportions among the elite swimmers of the world in part because there are a large number of different strokes and techniques appropriate for different body types. Much of what counts for body shape is influenced by early childhood swimming experiences, which affect body development. Moreover, good coaches adapt drills and methods to a swimmer's body type. So, any realistic empirical analysis of racial disparities in elite swimming must account for these differences in early childhood exposure to good coaching and competitive swimming.

The efficiency aspect of seeking diversity in swimming rests largely on the evidence that blacks are overrepresented among those who drown. The logic is that if there were more highly visible black elite swimmers, there would be a larger pool of persons interested in becoming elite swimmers, which increases the demand for learning to swim programs, minority lifeguards, water safety instructors, coaches, and aquatic directors. Of course, with more minority elite swimmers, there would be a larger supply from which to hire lifeguards, water safety instructors, and learn-to-swim instructors, creating a cumulative impact that derives benefits not just to minorities but to everyone.

THE MINNESOTA CONTEXT: RACIAL
DISCRIMINATION WITHOUT RACISM

Minnesota is known for its tolerance and racial equality. When Dred Scott fled his slave owners in the 1830s, he escaped to slave-free Minnesota.[2] The state constitution specifically prohibits racial discrimination.[3] Interracial marriages are widespread.[4] To the extent that racial tolerance is indexed by the incidence of interracial marriages, Minnesota could be labeled one of the most tolerant states in the nation. Racial economic inequality, moreover, was far lower in Minnesota than elsewhere in the nation during most of the post–World War II era. Whereas the ratios of black-to-white income were .467, .502, and .599 in the United States in 1950, 1960, and 1970, they were .846, .776, .734 in Minnesota those years.[5] Thus, one prominent view is that racism and racial discrimination do not or historically have not existed in this state.[6]

Thus, recent findings of widespread racial gaps in lending, schooling, earnings, crime and incarceration, and other social and economic outcomes—including drowning rates—both alarm and confound Minnesota policymakers.[7] How can racial discrimination exist in a place where there are no racial discriminators?

One perspective, undoubtedly, is that things have changed. Perhaps there was one period early in the state's history when discrimination was less pervasive than elsewhere. The rest of the world has caught up with Minnesota or Minnesota has regressed toward the rest of the world. When other states refused to admit African Americans to their graduate and professional schools, Minnesota could boast of being one of the major producers of black professionals west of the Mississippi river.[8] The low numbers of African American and other minority students at the University of Minnesota in the 1990s is attributed to the overall decline in minority enrollments nationally and to well-known geographical and climatological disadvantages and not to perceived or real racism in the state, in this view. In other words, discrimination is relative.[9]

A second view is that racism and racial discrimination are alive and well in Minnesota, just as they are elsewhere in the nation. The dilemma is that the state is afflicted with a particular disease called "Minnesota Nice," which inhibits open and frank discourse about changing race relations or about racial discrimination. *Minnesota Nice* is defined in different ways: Mayor Sayles Belton once described it as "sweet and soft." Others have described it as "helpful, courteous and oddly apologetic," or "good neighborliness."[10] In the context of race relations this means that observed disparities in social or economic outcomes are not attributed to individual meanness or discriminatory behavior. They are neither talked about nor acknowledged. With the politeness of failing to disclose disparities, majority members of society are spared the discomfort of explaining the disparities.

A third and highly plausible view is that the aggregate disparities are an artifact of the unique geography and demography of the state. This aggregation issue can arise in many different contexts but reveals itself most starkly in data related to mortgage lending. In this view there may be an overall market disparity but, paradoxically, there is no individual lender disparity.

DROWNING RATES: THE MINNESOTA PARADOX, ONCE AGAIN

Of 249,182 members of the Unites States Swimming Association in 2005, there were 1,220 black females and 958 black males, or .87 percent of the total. Among young competitive swimmers, less than one percent of the total membership was African American. The national organization has actively promoted a wide range of diversity initiatives over the years, most with little success in significantly affecting the gross underrepresentation of blacks. The organization has embraced outreach activities, supported reduced membership fees for the disadvantaged, hosted outreach camps at it national headquarters, and made grants to local clubs so that the clubs can increase their outreach efforts. Earlier attempts to increase directly the numbers of minorities on the national teams have resulted in fierce opposition. One such effort was to stipulate differential qualifying times for inclusion in elite training camps, one of the principal stepping-stones to the US National Team and the Junior National Team. While most people favor "diversity" there is substantial opposition from coaches, parents, and athletes to efforts designed to achieve diversity.

Why then is this diversity argument so very difficult to embrace? A case in point is what might be called the Minnesota Paradox. Minnesota has the highest racial disparity in drowning rates in the nation. It also has the highest racial disparity in representation among age-group competitive swimmers. Nationally, there is a strong inverse relationship between drowning rates for African Americans and membership in competitive swimming.

Black youth are 2,700 times more likely to be in the Minnesota population than they are to be found among USA swimming registrants. Yet, virtually all of the ten and under state records from 1994 and 1995 until 2005 were held by two persons of African American heritage. One of these swimmers switched to basketball in high school and went on to a successful career in the National Basketball Association. The other went to the Olympic trials as a teenager and competed successfully at a top NCAA Division I university. In Minnesota, at least, there is the paradoxical conclusion that although blacks are severely underrepresented among all age-group swimmers, they are overrepresented among record holders. This has led many commentators to conclude that the problem is not about race or diversity at all.

Swimming is a good metaphor for understanding the equity vs efficiency conflict in diversity policies. There is a compelling state interest in remedying disparities in drownings, swim pass rates in the military, and eligibility for service in Special Forces and the Navy SEALs (Harrel 1999; Hastings et al. 2006; Tyson 2009). The efficiency grounds for diversity are clear. There are obvious distributional considerations evidenced by the illustration from the Minnesota Paradox, however. To get to the point of greater diversity in elite swimming—in an Olympic sport where only the top two finishers in most events in the Olympic trials have any chance of making the Olympic team—requires that there be some members of the predominant group who will not make the team. Majority group members instinctively argue that it is unfair to alter the rules for representation in the sport or to use any criteria other than speed or performance for assignment to elite teams. Diversity at the lower levels of the sport without diversity at the top may reduce motivation and aspirations further affecting the distribution of swimmers at the top. There is also the equity consideration that across many other competitive sports African Americans seem to dominate at all levels. Why can't whites have their own sport where they can reasonably expect to excel?

THE PUBLIC HEALTH RATIONALE FOR REDUCING
RACIAL DISPARITIES IN SWIMMING

In a recent series of publications, profound evidence of a public health rationale for reducing racial disparities in competitive swimming and employment of lifeguards emerges.[11] The research shows that there is a strong inverse relationship between black participation in competitive swimming and black drowning rates. This inverse relationship is particularly strong among young black males. Drowning is a leading source of accidental death among young black males and the research shows that there is a key correlate in helping to reduce these untimely deaths: participation in competitive swimming. But, why should we care about black swimmers? Why should there be specific interventions designed to reduce the gaps in participation in competitive swimming between blacks and whites? In this instance the answer is a public health response: increasing participation of blacks in competitive swimming will help reduce intolerably high rates of black drownings. This is one instance where the rationale for a race-based initiative is not simply one of equity or social justice. Black competitive swimmers become lifeguards and they save lives. They save black lives. New research confirms that the marginal effects of increasing black lifeguards on reduced black drowning rates are larger than the impacts of increasing the numbers of white lifeguards. Black lifeguards save black lives.

In the swimming world, there is little evidence of overt racism or discrimination. Swimmers are polite. Swimmers, who disproportionately come from middle and upper-middle income families, are courteous and refined. Unlike the rowdy antics of ice hockey, professional wrestling or auto racing—other conspicuously white sports—competitive swimming protocols generally frown upon shouting, screaming, yelling and boisterous cheering, particularly during the starts of races. The politeness of the sport makes it difficult to allege overt bigotry as the cause of the underrepresentation of blacks in the sport.

One reason for implementing a race-conscious remedy is to remedy discrimination or racial bias. In swimming, the rationale for the remedy rests elsewhere. The rationale is that rectifying racial disparities in competitive swimming—however generated or reproduced across generations—saves lives.

CONCLUSION

On its face, the problem we have identified as the *Minnesota Paradox* seems a plausible explanation for there to be discrimination when there are no discriminators. The very plausibility of the finding that there may be bias in estimates of market discrimination suggests that care should be taken to consider and account for this phenomenon in data sets with few minority observations. Examples of data sets where one is likely to encounter this problem are studies of labor markets where minorities are concentrated in particular industries or among a handful of employers; analyses of schooling and student performance where minorities are concentrated in particular school districts or schools; examination of arrests or convictions where minorities are concentrated in particular offense classifications or in particular adjudication jurisdictions.

Even where the *Minnesota Paradox* can explain away findings of racial disparities, there is still a larger question. If one finds market discrimination or disparities without discrimination or disparities by individual lenders, employers, schools, or jurisdictions, the appropriate question is, *Why are minorities concentrated in limited units to begin with?* The resolution of the resulting paradox rests with finding the historical factors that contributed to minority exclusion from units of society that yield the more favorable outcomes.

NOTES

1. This section is drawn on Myers, Samuel L., Jr., "The Economics of Diversity: The Efficiency vs. Equity Trade-Off," in *Diversity Management: Theoretical Perspectives and Practical Approaches*, Sheying Chen (ed.). New York: Nova Science Publishers, Inc., 2011, pp. 55–70.

2. See Harding, Vincent, *There is a River: The Black Struggle for Freedom in America.* New York: Vintage Books, 1981; also see, John Hope Franklin, *From Slavery to Freedom.*

3. The Bill of Rights states that "no member of this state shall be disfranchised or deprived of any of the rights or privileges secured to any citizen thereof..." In 1955, Minnesota Statute 363.03 was passed to prohibit discrimination based on race.

4. In 1988, of all the marriages in the US, .67 percent were interracial (black and white). In Minnesota the number was 1.2 percent, twice the national rate. Among all (Minnesota) black grooms from the 1980s, more than one-third listed white brides in marriage statistics. *Vital Statistics of the US*, US Department of Health and Human Services, 1988.

5. See Myers, Samuel L., Jr., *Widening Racial Economic Disparities: A Problem of 'Minnesota Nice'.* Technical Report, Humphrey Institute, University of Minnesota, December 1992.

6. For example, a 1996 Minnesota housing report blames ethnic secession, not racism for such gaps. The report states that too many blacks are "concentrated in certain housing areas that segregate them from much of the mainstream of population,

life, and opportunities in the greater Twin Cities." See Adams, John et al., *Minnesota's Housing: Shaping Community in the 1990s*, p. 102. Humphrey Institute, Center for Urban and Regional Affairs, 1996.

7. See Myers, Samuel L., Jr., *Widening Racial Economic Disparities: A Problem of 'Minnesota Nice'*. Technical Report. St. Paul, MN: Urban Coalition, December 1992; Ahlburg, Dennis et al. *Are Good Jobs Disappearing? What the 1990 Census Says About Minnesota*. Humphrey Institute, Center for Urban and Regional Affairs, 1995. Myers, Samuel L., Jr., "'The Rich Get Richer And...' The Problem of Race and Inequality in the 1990s," *Law and Inequality: A Journal of Theory and Practice* vol. XI, June 1993, No 2; Myers, Samuel L., Jr., and William Darity, "The Widening Gap: A Summary and Synthesis of the Debate on Increasing Inequality," prepared for the National Commission for Employment Policy, April 1995; Myers, Samuel L., Jr., and Tsze Chan, "Racial Discrimination in Housing Markets: Accounting for Credit Risk," *Social Science Quarterly* 76, 3, September 1995; "School system will try 'cycle' of improvement; Minneapolis experiment defines goals, strategies," Minneapolis *Star Tribune,* August 8, 1994, p. 1B; "Criminal justice: Minnesota's arrest, incarceration numbers are nation's highest in racial disproportion," Minneapolis *Star Tribune*, October 18, 1995 p. 14A.

8. The University of Minnesota Library Archives unofficially reports that the first African American to graduate with a Ph.D. was in 1934. The first graduate was in 1882, and the first post-graduate (a law degree) was in 1901. Alpha Phi Alpha, the first national black college fraternity was chartered with ten men on April 12, 1912, six years after its founding at Cornell University.

9. In a similar view one could agree that the low enrollments of minority students in Minnesota result from the low minority population in Minnesota.

10. See "It's time for all to take an oath," Minneapolis *Star Tribune*, January 5, 1994, p. 15A; "It doesn't take long for an out-of-towner to spot Minnesota nice," Minneapolis *Star Tribune,* September 29, 1993, p. 19A; and "Minnesotans munch to the beat of a different drumstick," Minneapolis *Star Tribune*, August 19, 1995, p. 1E.

11. Myers, Samuel L., Jr., Ana Cuesta, and Yufeng Lai, "Competitive Swimming and Racial Disparities in Drowning," *Review of Black Political Economy* 44, 77–97, 2017. DOI 10.1007/s12114-017-9248-y; Myers, Samuel L., Jr., and Yufeng Lai, "The Labor Market for Lifeguards and Racial vs. Ethnic Disparities in Drowning Rates," A paper prepared for presentation at the Western Economic Association and American Society of Hispanic Economist Meetings, San Diego, California, June 26, 2017.

Chapter 4

The Problem of Racial Disparities in Child Maltreatment*

There is no specific law, such as found in employment, housing, or public procurement and contracting, that prohibits discrimination by social welfare workers in the reporting of child maltreatment. The laws that prohibit discrimination in the placement of children, in fact, work against placing children in homes and with families of their same race. The investigation of whether there is discrimination in the child welfare system is fraught with defensive responses of child welfare workers, when they are presented with allegations that they discriminate.

Descriptive evidence of disparities and disproportionalities in reported child maltreatment is marred by several types of biases. First, in this chapter we illustrate an important bias called aggregation bias that further confounds discourse over whether observed disparities in reports of child maltreatment are attributable to racial discrimination and thus justify a race-conscious response. Second, we point out another type of bias—a hidden bias—that produces the very type of disproportionality that the statistical bias putatively resolves. The child maltreatment reports teach us that perceptions matter, even if there are solid statistical grounds for claiming that there is no problem to remedy. As we have argued earlier in this monograph, adopting remedies to racial inequality presupposes that stakeholders believe that there is a problem to remedy. In the case of racial inequality, many stakeholders are reluctant to embrace race-conscious remedies because the statistical evidence is ambiguous.

* Sheila D. Ards, Samuel L. Myers, Jr., Chanjin Chung, Allan Malkis, Brian Hagerty. "Decomposing Black-White Differences in Child Maltreatment." *Child Maltreatment* 8(2), pp. 112–121. Copyright ©2003. Portions Reprinted by permission of SAGE Publications.

MINNESOTA ONCE AGAIN[1]

In 1996, Minnesota led the nation in racial disproportionality in child maltreatment. In that year, for example, African American children were 7.4 times as likely to be in the population of maltreated children reported to the Minnesota child protective services as in the general population. Hispanic children were 3.2 times and American Indian children 4.4 times as likely to be in the population of maltreated children reported to authorities as in the general population.

Nationally, the racial disproportionalities in reports of child maltreatment have declined.[2] Whereas in 1996 African American and American Indian children were about twice as likely to be found in child maltreatment reports as they were to be found in the child population, by 2015, African American and American Indian were 1.56 and 1.59 times as likely to be found in child maltreatment reports as they were to be found in the child population nationally. But by 2015 in Minnesota, African American children were 2.15 times as likely to be in the population of children reported to the Minnesota child protective services as in the general population and American Indian children were 5.46 times as likely to be in the population of maltreated children reported to authorities as in the general population. Thus, despite improvements over time, African Americans and American Indians in Minnesota remain disproportionately among those reported to Child Protective Services (CPS) for maltreatment.

Before one rushes to conclude that child welfare workers in Minnesota discriminate against American Indian and African American children, one must acknowledge significant measurement issues, some of which are unique to Minnesota. In measuring racial disproportionality in Minnesota, one immediately confronts the problem of aggregation bias. Almost all black children reside in a relatively few counties where report rates are high. The appearance of disproportionality in reported maltreatment overall in the state may be an artifact of the uneven geographical dispersion of the child population.

We investigate whether the uneven geographic distribution of children of color in a few Minnesota counties creates the appearance of disproportionality where there is none. Moreover, it may appear that children of color are disproportionately counted in the child maltreatment data because they disproportionately live in areas of high substantiation of child maltreatment.

Using data for Minnesota from 2000, we show that measures of discrimination in maltreatment substantiation are inflated by a failure to disaggregate counties with large minority populations from those with small minority populations. The results reveal that common measures of disproportionality could plausibly inflate the degree of racial inequality because they fail to account for geographic distributions. This reasonable explanation for the observed disparities can affect decision makers' perceptions about whether there is a problem that needs to be remedied. In that sense, there may be a disconnect between the message conveyed to decision makers and the actual degree of racial inequality that we seek to remedy.

Definition of Terms

Minnesota law places responsibility for providing social services, including child protection services, with the eighty-seven counties in the state. To enable consistency in data collection, analysis, and interpretation, Minnesota initiated the Social Service Information System (SSIS), which captures data from all the counties into a single data system that can track officially reported cases of child maltreatment. In 2000, SSIS became the mandatory system for sharing data with the Minnesota Department of Human Services (DHS).

The SSIS data starts with an official receipt of a report of child maltreatment accepted for assessment. A report occurs when an individual or agency contacts a county CPS office about possible maltreatment of children. Assessment is the process of determining (substantiating) whether a reported incident meets the state's definition of child maltreatment. Some reports of child maltreatment are not accepted for assessment by the county CPS. The SSIS data include primarily those reports that have been accepted.

In most counties, data from reports are entered into SSIS after being originally captured on paper forms. In a few counties, the SSIS system serves as the primary filing system and data are entered there initially. At intervals, the entire SSIS dataset from a given county is uploaded into the statewide system for integration with data from other counties. At the end of the calendar year, DHS staff review the data, check for completeness and "cleanliness" of data, and produce mandatory reports for the federal and state government.

In the SSIS data system, a report of child maltreatment may include multiple children named as victims, multiple adults named as alleged offenders, and multiple individual allegations or occurrences of maltreatment on the same date. Each individual allegation of specific maltreatment of a particular child by a particular offender is called an event, while each report (which may contain multiple events) is referred to as an incident. In this paper, we will use report rather than incident to mean a set of one or more allegations of maltreatment (events). The distinction is critical, because the individual events are the units that are substantiated (i.e., the events have been determined to have actually occurred). Thus, a given report may contain more than one event, some or all of which may be substantiated by the assessment.

The SSIS data system contains 29,013 child-event pairs for the year 2000. These include several thousand cases in which the same child was alleged to be involved in more than one event. The final unduplicated number of children alleged to be involved in at least one event in the year 2000 was 21,560.

Our test of aggregation bias compares child maltreatment in the three metropolitan counties with the highest numbers of children of color in the state to the rest of the state: Hennepin, Ramsey, and Dakota. The remaining eighty-four Minnesota counties are called the non-study counties. "Children of color" is defined as all categories of children who are not white. We compute a conventional measure of disproportionality for all the states and then for the study versus non-study counties. We test whether there is a bias in the measurement of disproportionality by aggregating all counties and ignoring the fact that most of the children of color reside in just three of the counties.

Disproportionality in Minnesota

The basic statistics from the SSIS system in Minnesota and from reports to the National Child Abuse and Neglect Data System (NCANDS) show a persistent racial disproportionality in child maltreatment. These reports reveal wide racial disproportionalities between substantiations and representation in the child population in Minnesota for the years 1993 to 2000. The figures reveal that this disproportionality with respect to African Americans was largely stable over the decade.

The ratios range from 0.49:1 for Asians in 1995 to 6.3:1 for blacks in 1997. These results suggest that Asians were underrepresented among substantiated maltreatment cases, while African American children were over 6 times more likely to be found among substantiated cases as they are to be found in the child population. Across the decade of the 1990s, the ratios were surprisingly stable. Even the apparent dip in the black ratio in 2000 (based on SSIS data rather than the NCANDS data used in earlier years) shows higher rates of disproportionality among African Americans than any other racial group.

Table 4.1 shows measures of disproportionality in reports, computed in two ways. In the first column, the measure is based on child-event report pairs.[3] That is, it captures reported maltreatment events, which may include the same child on more than one occasion. In the second column, the report disproportionality measure is computed using unduplicated children. This method is replicated for all counties and then for the study counties and non-study counties. The second column shows the same ratio, using the number of unduplicated individuals in the numerator. There is little change in the report disproportionality when account is taken of the duplication of children. Whether one computes duplicated or unduplicated cases, one finds that the report disproportionality is greater in the non-study counties than the study counties for African Americans and Hispanics. For blacks, Asians and Hispanics, the overall report disproportionality in the state is larger than

Table 4.1 Racial Disproportionality Ratios, Minnesota, 2000

	$\delta^*(\rho)$, Duplicated Reports	$\delta^*(\rho)$, Unduplicated Reports	$\delta^*(s)$, Substantiated Reports
State	N = 31,973	N = 21,594	N = 9,736
White	0.63	0.70	0.94
Black	4.47	4.45	1.11
Hispanic	1.57	1.58	1.06
American Indian	4.65	4.53	1.07
Asian/Pacific	0.79	0.76	1.22
Islander	3.14	3.32	0.98
Other			
Study Counties	N = 17,449	N = 11,304	N = 5,317
White	0.51	0.51	0.93
Black	3.37	3.42	1.06
Hispanic	1.12	1.14	1.07
American Indian	6.54	6.10	1.10
Asian/Pacific	0.65	0.65	1.13
Islander	3.44	3.31	0.92
Other			
Non-Study Counties	N = 14,458	N = 10,290	N = 4,419
White	0.91	0.91	0.97
Black	4.09	4.27	1.19
Hispanic	2.09	2.09	1.03
American Indian	4.17	4.17	1.07
Asian/Pacific	0.50	0.53	1.38
Islander	2.35	2.10	1.10
Other			

Source: Authors' computations of Minnesota Social Service Information System and National Child Abuse and Neglect Data System data.

the disproportionality within the three counties where the largest number of children of color reside.

However, for American Indians, the reverse is true; the report disproportionality is larger in the three-county metropolitan area than in the non-study counties or in the state as a whole.

Nonetheless, our measures of report disproportionality for African Americans, Hispanics, and American Indians do not disappear when one disaggregates by study versus non-study counties. The third column of Table 4.1, however, reveals that substantiation-to-report disproportionalities are considerably smaller than report-to-population disproportionalities for black, Hispanic, and American Indian children. Although the substantiation-to-report disproportionality appears small, it is nonetheless significantly different from 1 for all groups. The underlying source of substantiation-to-report disproportionality ratios that exceed 1 are substantiation rates that differ between groups.

Differences in Substantiation Rates between Groups

Table 4.2 reports the results of t tests for differences in means between the substantiation rates for each race in study counties compared to non-study counties. It also provides t test results for comparison of nonwhite means to the white mean within each group of counties. The data reveal the complexity of the aggregation problem. In the three study counties, the majority of cases—68 to 69 percent—are nonwhite. In the state as a whole, only 47 to 48 percent of the cases are nonwhite, while in the non-study counties, about 24 percent of the cases are nonwhite. Thus, it is entirely possible for any statewide disparities in substantiation rates to be clouded by the uneven distribution of children of color within the state.

Table 4.2 shows that even this simple explanation of aggregation is not sufficient. White substantiation rates are nearly identical in the study and non-study counties: 43.2 percent for study counties and 41.7 percent in non-study counties. The difference is statistically insignificant.

Black substantiation rates are slightly lower in the study counties than they are in the non-study counties. The difference is not statistically significant.

Table 4.2 Substantiation Rates for Maltreatment Cases by Race of Victim T Tests between Races and Counties

Race of Victim	State Total	Study County	Non-Study County	pvalue) Study vs. Non-study
White	0.422	0.432	0.417	(0.1153)
[p value vs. White]				
{% of cases}	{53.01}	{31.78}	{76.3}	
Black	0.499	0.498	0.511	(0.5943)
[p value vs. White]	[<.0001]	[<.0001]	[<.0001]	
{% of cases}	{21.25}	{36.89}	{4.65}	
Asian Pacific	0.536	0.529	0.593	(0.2788)
[p value vs. White]	[<.0001]	[<.0001]	[.0014]	
{% of cases}	{3.21}	{5.42}	{0.79}	
Indian	0.488	0.526	0.457	(0.0103)
[p value vs. White]	[<.0001]	[<.0001]	[.0341]	
{% of cases}	{6.35}	{5.43}	{7.37}	
Other Race	0.429	0.416	0.480	(.0234)
[p value vs. White]	[0.5287]	[0.2888]	[.0134]	
{% of cases}	{9.01}	{13.73}	{3.83}	
Hispanic	0.477	0.511	0.441	(.0078)
[p value vs. White]	[<.0001]	[<.0001]	[.2111]	
{% of cases}	{6.74}	{6.65}	{6.84}	
Nonwhite	0.483	0.487	0.470	(.1375)
[p value vs. White]	[<.0001]	[<.0001]	[<.0001]	
{% of cases}	{46.99}	{68.22}	{23.7}	

Source: Authors' computations of Minnesota Social Service Information System and National Child Abuse and Neglect Data System data.

Blacks represent 37 percent of the cases in the study counties but only 5 percent in the non-study counties. Thus, in the portion of the state where blacks are most heavily represented, black substantiation rates are no higher than they are in other parts of the state.

Hispanic substantiation rates are higher in the study counties than they are in the non-study counties. Hispanics represent about 7 percent of cases in both study and non-study counties. The Hispanic substantiation rate is 51 percent in the study counties but only 44 percent in the non-study counties. This difference is statistically significant.

American Indians also have higher substantiation rates in the study counties than in the non-study counties. The difference is statistically significant. American Indians are more highly represented in non-study counties as opposed to study counties (7.4 percent vs. 5.4 percent).

To complicate matters further, Asian Americans who have higher-than-average substantiation rates (about 54 percent) and who are almost exclusively found in the study counties (5.4 percent vs. .8 percent) have slightly lower substantiation rates in the study counties than the non-study counties, although these differences are not statistically significant.

Still, each nonwhite group has substantiation rates higher than whites. This finding is true in the study counties, in the non-study counties and in the state as a whole. The descriptive evidence, therefore, does not bear out the aggregation hypothesis in any obvious or unambiguous manner.

PERCEPTIONS MATTER[4]

We conducted another test designed to uncover unconscious racialized perceptions about black versus white children. We wanted to know (a) whether child protective service workers *perceive* that blacks are more likely to be maltreated and thus act upon those beliefs, and (b) whether these racialized beliefs *explain* observed racial disproportionalities across counties in Minnesota.

Regression models of discrimination in the child protective services borrow from conventional economic methods to measure and detect discrimination (Blinder 1973; Gupta, Oaxaca, and Smith 2006; Oaxaca 1973). These methods derive from the premise that employers (or landlords or real estate agents or lenders or child welfare workers) are motivated by "tastes for discrimination" (Becker 1957). Refinements consider instances where agents do not engage in intentional discrimination but, when faced with limited information or uncertainty about such factors as employee productivity, risk of default, credit worthiness, or in the case of child welfare, "front-end risks," engage in actions that nonetheless can produce disparate outcomes (Aigner and Cain 1977; Arrow 1973). A recurring criticism of these economic models of discrimination, however, has been that they fail to explain or to detail the causal mechanisms that produce the underlying racial biases, beliefs or racialized perceptions that putatively produce observed discriminatory outcomes.

Recent experimental work in both social psychology and economics has produced valuable insights into the formation and prevalence of certain types of racialized perceptions that can produce observed disparities in markets and economically relevant outcomes. Included in this literature are tests about the impacts of names, skin color, and other signals about the race of participants in labor markets or consumer markets (Bertrand and Mullainathan 2004; Doleac and Stein 2010; List 2004; Nardinelli and Simon 1990; Nunley, Owens, and Howard 2010; Pope and Sydnor 2011; Ravina 2008). These field experiments can be criticized because, although they speak to the issue of whether racial discrimination exists, they leave largely unaddressed the question: how much of the observed racial disparities can be explained by the experimental measures of racial bias? There is almost no recent economic literature establishing a clear relationship between measures of racial animosity or individual beliefs about racial inferiority and observed racially disparate market or nonmarket outcomes.

The foundations for economic modeling of what might be called "racialized perceptions" can be found in the work of researchers examining stereotype threat models where the social stigma of intellectual inferiority borne by certain cultural minorities can undermine their performance (Aronson, Quinn, and Spencer 1998; Steele 1997; Steele and Aronson 1995). This is related to the work of social psychologists who use implicit association tests where subconscious beliefs about subgroups surface in rapid response tests that require pairing or making comparisons (Gawronski 2002; Greenwald, McGhee, and Schwartz 1998; Ottaway, Hayden, and Oakes 2001). These works point to a possible mechanism underlying racially disparate outcomes. Racialized perceptions can produce both the initial disparities and the self-confirming evidence that permits these disparities to persist through time.

Child neglect, unlike outcomes in traffic stops or rental markets or job interviews, comes within the framework of social workers. Historically, social workers have been white females whose work is driven by compassion, dedication to the disadvantaged, and commitment to equality. Yet, in child welfare we see wide racially disparate outcomes, just as one sees in other spheres of society, such as the criminal justice system, labor markets, housing markets, or credit markets. Moreover, one rarely sees the "smoking gun" of bigoted, racially offensive behavior on the part of CPS workers. Indeed, charges of racial discrimination or racial bias by such workers often produce great pain and anguish within the social work profession (Drake and Rank

2009). Elsewhere, Ards et al. (2012) produce compelling evidence that there is a relationship between indices of racialized perceptions and observed racial disproportionality in substantiated maltreatment across counties. Although it is helpful to produce new ways of measuring racialized perceptions, it is more important to be able to empirically establish whether there is any relationship between these perceptions, on one hand, and actual outcomes, on the other. We summarize the methodology and findings here. The interested reader is invited to consult the original journal publication.

Ards et al. hypothesize that black disproportionality in reported and substantiated child neglect hinges on how case workers visualize black versus white neglect situations. If things that "look black" are more likely to be perceived by caseworkers as reportable offenses, or to meet state definitions of child maltreatment than things that "look white," then it could be a pretext for locating larger fractions of black children among the reported and substantiated or out-of-home placements. They begin with the anecdotal finding derived from interviews with Minnesota child welfare workers about what constitutes a specific form of neglect. In the state of Minnesota, neglect refers to a failure to provide adequate food, clothing, or shelter that endangers a child's welfare. From caseworker interviews, Ards et al. unveiled a concept called "the messy room" (or apartment) phenomenon. Respondents in the interviews uniformly indicated that a filthy, messy, disorderly living environment is something they "know when they see it" and "it" usually signals a neglectful set of circumstances. Through focus groups and interviews with experienced CPS caseworkers and supervisors in Minnesota, researchers were able to create a stylized picture of a reportable child neglect situation that often results in substantiation and the decision to remove a child from the caretaker. This stylized picture was one of a "messy house" or a filthy, uninhabitable residence unsuitable for sheltering a child. From actual case files, researchers obtained pictures taken by law enforcement officials during a removal case and digitally superimposed alternately a black baby or a white baby. The experiment involved administration of an online exercise to all CPS caseworkers in Minnesota as a module within a regularly scheduled training session. Participants were not informed of the purpose of the exercise, which was embedded within existing training materials.

A total of 459 county child maltreatment intake, assessment, and caseworkers in eighty-two Minnesota counties participated in the web survey, concerning knowledge of the state assessment protocols. Included in the otherwise innocuous educational survey were the visual vignette of the messy room. The Minnesota Legislature's definition of child neglect and its reporting requirements were provided. A picture of a messy living room was shown. Then, a second picture of a bedroom appeared. Randomly distributed among the participants were pictures of a child placed on the bed; in other pictures no child was on the bed. Of those pictures with a child, the race of the child varied randomly.

After the caseworker was shown the two pictures, s/he was asked (a) whether the case depicted in the picture met the state definition of neglect; (b) if it was a reportable offense, based on state reporting requirements; (c) how often a similar situation results in an official report; and (d) how often a similar situation was encountered. The state definition of neglect is "Failure by a person responsible for a child's care to supply a child with necessary food, clothing, shelter, health, medical, or other care required for the child's physical or mental health when reasonably able to do so" (Minnesota Statutes Chapter 626, No. 556 Subdivision 2. Definition [Minnesota] (d) NEGLECT). The operable term in Minnesota is "when reasonably able to do so." In other words, there is greater flexibility in the Minnesota law that empowers caseworkers to interpret reasonable ability. It is likely that racialized beliefs manifest themselves when there is great discretion on the part of the decision maker, but not when the law makes explicit that there are no exceptions. The central finding of the experiment was that respondents who saw a black baby were more likely than those who saw a white baby, or no baby, to respond that the situation depicted in the picture coincided with the state definition of neglect and was reportable.

The researchers also estimated fixed effects linear probability and logistic models for the responses as to whether the situation in the picture meets the state definition and whether the offense is reportable. Independent variables included the respondent's age, gender, and race; whether the respondent was born in the Twin Cities metropolitan area (Minneapolis and St. Paul); majored in social work; was an intake worker; or worked in Hennepin County (of which Minneapolis is part). The regression results show that seeing the black baby adds 11.5 percentage points to the probability of agreeing that the situation meets the state definition of neglect and adds 10.1 percentage points to the probability that the respondent agrees that the situation depicted is a reportable offense. These results are robust across alternative model specifications and estimation methods and are statistically significant.

The researchers then created an index of these racialized beliefs. The metric reflects any differences in responses within a county to the reporting and definition questions between those viewing the black baby and those viewing no baby, or a white baby. The metric asks whether (a) the percentage of persons who viewed the black baby and responded that the situation meets the state definition of neglect, or is reportable and exceeds, (b) the response rate of those viewing the white baby, (c) the response rate of those viewing no baby, or (d) the response rate for those viewing the white or no baby. This metric is a dichotomous variable equal to 1 if the response rate for those viewing the black baby exceeds that of the other situations. This metric is equal to 1 when, at the county level, the average response among caseworkers differs when the picture seen is of a black baby[5].

This index of racialized perceptions was then used to predict racial disproportionality in child maltreatment reports, child maltreatment substiations, and out-of-home placements. Control variables included percentage of respondents who are white, share of county maltreatment cases that are sexual abuse cases, percentage of county population that is white, percentage of persons living in rural areas, county poverty rate, percent of the population between ages 18 and 34, mean household income squared, population density, and crime rate squared. These variables were chosen to control for demographic and socioeconomic characteristics in different counties in the state of Minnesota.

The results are striking. The researchers find consistently large and significant impacts of the racialized beliefs on substantiation rates. There are no impacts of CPS workers' racialized perceptions on the report disproportionality or on the out-of-home placement disproportionality. This finding is not surprising since caseworkers are not the primary source of reports. Among mandated reporters, law enforcement, and schools rank highest among sources of neglect reports. Moreover, some but not all of out-of-home placements originate from CPS offices. Many of these placements result from court orders (e.g., parents who are incarcerated or incapacitated).

Investigation and substantiation, areas over which caseworkers have the largest control, are most consistently correlated with racialized beliefs and perceptions. Racialized beliefs or perceptions of child protect service workers adversely affect county-level disproportionalities. Small differences in underlying perceptions about what constitutes a situation that meets the state definition of neglect or what signifies a reportable offense translate into sizeable differences in observed county-by-county substantiation rates. Thus, the link between almost inconsequential individual behavioral differences and aggregate differences in outcomes is apparent in these findings. This important discovery demonstrates that large racial disproportionalities in outcomes, such as substantiated child maltreatment rates, do not necessarily require comparably large disparities in perceptions and beliefs. Relatively minor differences in individual behaviors can generate large differences in outcomes in the aggregate.

IMPLICATIONS

We began with the premise that aggregation bias may be at the root of the disproportionate representation of children of color among the determined maltreatment population, justifying decision makers' beliefs that there is no racial disparity in child welfare outcomes justifying race-conscious remedies. As a practical matter, however, aggregation bias is far from the most compelling issue behind the numbers. Aggregation of African American cases at the state level understates how much independent variables explain the racial disparity in substantiation rates; yet, aggregation alone does not completely erase the disparity.

Disparities exist. Disproportionalities exist. Children of color in the child welfare system are treated differently than white children. The implications of these results are significant. Other researchers have examined the impact of neighborhood characteristics and other socioeconomic characteristics of the family on the likelihood that a case of child maltreatment is reported (Coulton, Korbin, and Su 1999). The results reported here support the finding of weak effects of geographical characteristics on child welfare agency decisions.

A second finding is that racialized beliefs of caseworkers, who must investigate and substantiate child maltreatment cases, have a decided impact on county-level disproportionality rates in maltreatment substantiations. The work of Ards et al. shows relatively small, but statistically significant, differences in responses to visual cues such as seeing a black baby versus a white baby. These small differences, however, translate into large and significant determinants of racial disproportionality at the aggregate level.

NOTES

1. This chapter relies on Ards et al. (2003).

2. Authors' calculations from US Department of Health & Human Services, Administration for Children and Families, Administration on Children, Youth and Families, Children's Bureau (2017). Child Maltreatment: https://www. acf.hhs.gov/cb/resource/child-maltreatment-2015 and https://www.acf.hhs. gov/cb/resource/child-maltreatment-1996.

3. The official reporting of child maltreatment is the end result of a process that begins with maltreatment of a child by a parent or caretaker. Let A^* be the actual number of child maltreatment occurrences, a measure that is generally unknown. Indicate the actual child population by P. Then the child maltreatment rate is $\frac{A^*}{P} = a^*$. For the kth and jth racial groups, the child maltreatment rates are given by; $\left(\frac{A^*}{P}\right)^k = a^{*k}$ and $\left(\frac{A^*}{P}\right)^j = a^{*j}$. Let an official report of child maltreatment be designated by R and let the official substantiation of child maltreatment be equal to S. Then, the ratio of substantiated reports to the child population is $\frac{S}{P} = \sigma$ and are the ratio of substantiated reports to the child population and the proportion of reports that are substantiated, respectively. For concreteness, we refer to as the substantiation-to-population ratio and s as the substantiation rate. These can be further defined for

races k and j. It is clear from Equation 1 that the substantiation-to-population ratio depends on the substantiation rate as well as upon the actual child maltreatment rate via the ratio of reports to actual maltreatment.

Equation 1

$$\frac{S}{P} = \frac{A^*}{P} \cdot \frac{R}{A^*} \cdot \frac{S}{R}$$

or

$$\sigma = a^* \cdot s \cdot \left(\frac{R}{A^*}\right)$$

Although A^*, the number of maltreated cases, and a^*, the maltreatment rate, are unknown, the substantiation-to-population ratio can be rewritten as a function of observables alone:

Equation 2

$$\sigma = s \cdot p$$

where

$$p = \left(\frac{R}{P}\right) = \frac{A^*}{P} \cdot \frac{R}{A^*}$$

We can interpret p to be the *report-to-population* ratio. The significance of Equation 2 is that the two terms R and P are reported regularly in official statistics. From these statistics, one can compute alternative measures of disproportionality.

The disproportionality between the kth group's representation in the reported population and the kth group's representation in the child population is expressed as
It is defined as the *report disproportionality*:

Equation 3

$$\delta^*(p) = \frac{p^k}{p} = \frac{R^k/P^k}{R/P} = \frac{R^k/R}{P^k/P}$$

The disproportionalities between the kth group's representation in the substantiated and the child population versus the kth group's representation in the reported population are given by

Equation 4

$$\delta^*(\sigma) = \frac{\sigma^k}{\sigma}$$

and

Equation 5

$$\delta^*(s) = \frac{s^k}{s}$$

Equation 4 defines the *substantiation disproportionality*, while Equation 5 defines the *substantiation-to-report disproportionality*. These varying measures of disproportionality ratios are computed for Minnesota in the next section of this article.

4. This section draws on Ards et al. (2012).

5. The researchers experimented with continuous variants of this metric but encountered data limitations because in smaller counties with fewer respondents there often were not enough cases to compute values other than zero or one.

Chapter 5

Public Procurement and Contracting

The Largest Affirmative Action Program of All

While affirmative action in college admissions and hiring are the source of most of the public debate about remedying racial and ethnic economic inequality, the largest affirmative action program of all is one directed not toward schooling or jobs but business ownership. State, local, and federal agencies allocate billions of dollars annually through targeted programs designed to increase the share of public dollars awarded to women and minority-owned business enterprises. The mechanism for these affirmative action awards is through the public procurement and contracting process, where government agencies require that prime contractors competing for federal, state, and local highway or bridge construction contracts, military contracts, transit system contracts, and billions of dollars in other contracting and procurement activities, meet affirmative action goals for subcontracting to disadvantaged-, women- and minority-owned businesses. The rationale for these affirmative action efforts is the ongoing disparity between the availability and utilization of disadvantaged businesses often resulting in huge disparities in the size of prime and subcontracts awarded to white male-owned firms compared to women- and minority-owned business firms.[1] As a response to the Kerner Commission Report[2] findings that civil unrest was linked to barriers to business ownership among minorities, the US Congress enacted Public Law 95–507 in 1978, requiring all federal agencies to set percentage goals for the awarding of contracts to small minority-owned businesses.

This initiative followed the authorization of minority set-asides in the 1977 Public Works Employment Act (PWEA), stemming from a floor amendment introduced by Maryland's Seventh District Congressman Parren Mitchell.[3] In *City of Richmond v. J. A. Croson Co.* (1989), the US Supreme Court ruled that minority business set-asides in public procurement and contracting generally are suspect and must meet a strict-scrutiny test to be constitutional.[4]

And, even when there is a factual predicate for implementing a race-conscious affirmative action program, there remains the question of whether minority business set-asides are effective in achieving improved performance among the intended beneficiaries.[5] The Clinton administration sought to find a middle ground in its effort to salvage this and other forms of affirmative action. The solution sought in the case of agencies receiving Federal Transit Authority (FTA) funds was to require that goals established to assist disadvantaged business enterprises (DBEs) be narrowly tailored, flexible, not overly inclusive and minimize the burden placed on other firms. To this end, the FTA guidelines require that the maximum feasible portion of any specified DBE goal be met through race-neutral means. Unfortunately, the guidelines do not provide much guidance on how to establish the portion of the goals that must be race-neutral. Myers and Ha[6] introduced a new methodology for establishing the race-neutral portion of a DBE goal, providing guidance on how to empirically compute the portion of race-neutral goals required. Many other jurisdictions, however, mistakenly have concluded that "maximizing the race-neutral goal" means creating a zero race-conscious goal, or, in effect, replacing the DBE goal with a new goal that is entirely race neutral.

The theoretical basis for replacing race-based remedies with race-neutral remedies stems from contentions that observed racial disparities in markets can be explained by place or class rather than by race.[7] Examples of class-based remedies include scholarships for low-income students and preferential admissions for the top 10 percent of graduates of inner-city schools. These remedies avoid the focus on race by examining factors highly correlated with race.

One approach to race-neutral implementation of DBE goals is to set aside contracts for bid only by firms that meet size and net worth criteria identical to the DBE criteria but without regard to race, gender or ethnicity of ownership. The New Jersey Department of Transportation (NJDOT) has implemented a version of this type of program called the Emerging Small Business Enterprise (ESBE) program. Other jurisdictions have implemented variants of the Emerging Small Business (ESB) program to fulfill their race-neutral goals. In Colorado, for example, projects with state funding or state and federal funding can apply ESB goals that provide financial incentives to prime contractors, protégé—mentor programs, bonding subsidies, and tuition credits for ESB firms that wish to increase their access to contracts through coursework and training. Oregon's ESB program provides exclusive bidding opportunities for firms often in the range of $50,000 or less. To the best of our knowledge, our publication[8] is the first to provide empirical evidence of the effectiveness of an ESBE program in expanding opportunities for DBEs. In this chapter, we discuss the methods of the race-neutral goals as well as disparity studies, which are normally conducted on a regular basis, to provide the comprehensive understanding of the market.

METHODS OF DISPARITY STUDIES

First- and second-generation disparity studies focus primarily on showing a disparity between the availability and the utilization of women/minority-owned firms. Third generation disparity studies add three additional components for analysis to meet the standards set by *Concrete Works of Colorado* (2003) and to overcome anticipated legal and econometric challenges. These three additional components calculate or address the presence of discrimination. They are agency discrimination analysis, passive discrimination analysis, and race-neutral remedies analysis. The first two components help determine whether any disparities observed can be attributed to impermissible discrimination. The third component determines whether it is possible to remedy any observed disparities without race-based initiatives. The analyses incorporate specific regression models that can evaluate whether any disparities are related to discrimination or are due to factors not related to race or gender. Other disparity study firms often do not provide a detailed analysis as to why discrimination exists.

As Nobel Laureate James Heckman[9] has pointed out in his critique of discrimination studies, the most popular methods of measuring discrimination (e.g., audit studies and disparity analyses) fail to convincingly establish a causal link between observed racial/ethnic or gender differences and market discrimination. The reason, Heckman argues, is that the measures often do not capture market participants who actually discriminate or who are the targets of discrimination. Thus, clever techniques such as "customized censuses" or special surveys designed to compare availability and utilization fail the Heckman test because they cannot measure discrimination on the margin, that is, discrimination experienced by actual victims and perpetuated by actual violators. Although Heckman is wrong in rejecting the importance of passive discrimination in markets where minority participation is constrained or limited and entry is blocked, he raises an important point that ongoing market discrimination requires information on actual participants in transactions.

The most important advance in recent years in the area of minority- and women-owned business development programs relates to race-neutral programs. Local governments, state, and local agencies have shifted to programs that do not directly target minority-owned business enterprises (MBEs) or women-owned business enterprises (WBEs) but instead target the characteristics that define MBEs and WBEs: size, net worth, and in some instances, location. These programs are sometimes called emerging small business enterprise (ESBE) programs, and the Roy Wilkins Center research team has produced a body of publications on the effectiveness of such alternatives to race-conscious programs. Another interesting trend is the use of set-asides based on the size of the contract. For example, some jurisdictions have set-asides only for bidding by SBEs on contracts under certain thresholds (e.g., $500,000 or $350,000). The logic of these programs is that MBEs and WBEs will be able to compete more effectively if the size of the contracts is below some threshold.

Fourth-generational approaches use modern econometric tools and mixed-methods techniques to establish that any observed disparity putatively due to discrimination cannot be due to any reasonably measured alternative explanation. The primary advantage of this type of approach is the ability to anticipate patterns and refute objections that might be raised by plaintiffs challenging the constitutionality of race-conscious programs.

Causality analysis includes the econometric procedure of testing for causality in regression models of discrimination. The procedure provides an empirical test of the hypothesis that the underlying results cannot be attributable to bias associated with endogenous variables. To perform this test, however, researchers must confront what is known as the identification problem. Identification means finding factors that explain an endogenous variable (e.g., prequalification score or credit rating) but that do not explain the outcome variable (e.g., contract award amount or bid success rates).

THE FTA GUIDELINES

In 1999, the FTA issued regulation 49 CFR Part 26, Participation by Disadvantaged Business Enterprises in Department of Transportation Programs; Final Rule,[10] which instructs state and local transit authorities on how to establish their disadvantaged business enterprise goals (DBE goals). Thus, FTA or FAA recipients, who expect to award contracts of $250,000 or more in the federal fiscal year must establish a DBE goal of at least 10 percent— the national aspiration goal. The government entity or agency must produce a goal based on

> demonstrable evidence of the availability of ready, willing and able DBEs relative to all businesses ready, willing and able to participate on your DOT-assisted contracts ("hereafter, the relative availability of DBEs"). The goal must reflect your determination of the level of DBE participation you would expect absent the effects of discrimination. You cannot simply rely on either the 10 percent national goal, your previous overall goal or past DBE participation rates in your program without reference to the relative availability of DBEs in your market.[11]

A two-step process is detailed for constructing the overall goal.[12] Step 1 requires the agency to establish a base figure of DBE availability in the specific industries and geographical market from which DBE and non-DBE contractors are drawn. Step 2 mandates that an adjustment be made to the base figure in light of other evidence regarding the market area. To comply with this rule, Step 1 can rely on DBE directories and Census Bureau data; bidder lists; data from disparity studies; goals from other DOT recipients in the same, or substantially similar, market areas; and/or any other alternative method that is based on "demonstrable evidence of local market conditions and . . . designed to ultimately attain a goal that is rationally related to the relative availability of DBEs in . . . [the] . . . market."[13]

The adjustment step, Step 2, considers the following types of evidence: the capacity of DBEs to perform work in the contracting program, as measured by the volume of work DBEs have performed in recent years; evidence from disparity studies conducted anywhere within the jurisdiction, to the extent it is not already accounted for in the base figure; differences in local markets and the contracting program; disparities in the ability of DBEs to obtain financing, bonding, and insurance; data on employment, and self-employment, education, training, and union apprenticeship programs. Adjustments can be made to the base goal using evidence of prior discrimination but such evidence "must be based on demonstrable evidence that is logically and directly related to the effect for which the adjustment is sought." Finally, the agency is to provide estimates of the portions of the overall goal it expects to meet through race-neutral and race-conscious measures.[14]

RACE-NEUTRAL GOAL STRATEGIES

In this section, we conceptually discuss the methods of the race-neutral goal-setting approach that we developed. Consider evidence from an agency that has a record of contracts awarded to DBEs and non-DBEs and for which there may be DBE subcontracts awarded by non-DBE prime contractors. The log-amount of the contract awarded is thought to be a function of the type of funding for the project (FTA vs. non-FTA), the type of industry or work to be performed (e.g., construction, professional services, supplies, and equipment), location and qualifications of the firm. To determine whether there is any discrimination against DBEs, one could estimate the independent impact of DBE status on the log-amount of contracts (or subcontracts) awarded. A Blinder–Oaxaca–Duncan residual difference decomposition can be performed to measure the portion of the gap in contract awards that cannot be explained by differences in characteristics of contracts and qualifications of firms.

Suppose that each contract is assigned a DBE goal from a previous fiscal year. Agencies that have, say, overall DBE goals of 15 percent, may assign goals of 0 percent on some contracts and perhaps goals of 100 or 50 percent on other contracts. The differential assignment of goals to contracts by procurement officers and agency officials may be based on the assumption that in order to fulfill the overall goal of the agency, high goals must be placed on contracts where there is a relatively good chance of meeting the goals, and low goals on contracts where there is little or no chance of meeting the goals. Some DBEs understandably receive their contracts via goals (e.g., a 100 percent goal established for a particular project). Other DBEs receive subcontracts through goals established on contracts awarded to non-DBEs. However, some DBEs received contracts where there were no goals and some non-DBEs subcontract to DBEs where there are no goals.

ARE GOALS NEEDED? THE CASE OF ASIANS

Billions of federal dollars require disadvantaged business enterprise (DBE) goals for contracting or subcontracting. A DBE is defined as a small business owned by one or more socially disadvantaged individuals. Persons who are rebuttably presumed to be socially and economically disadvantaged according to federal regulations are US citizens or permanent residents who are

1. "Black Americans," which includes persons having origins in any of the black racial groups of Africa
2. "Hispanic Americans," which includes persons of Mexican, Puerto Rican, Cuban, Dominican, Central or South American, or other Spanish or Portuguese culture or origin, regardless of race
3. "Native Americans," which includes persons who are American Indians, Eskimos, Aleuts, or Native Hawaiians
4. "Asian-Pacific Americans," which includes persons whose origins are from Japan, China, Taiwan, Korea, Burma (Myanmar), Vietnam, Laos, Cambodia (Kampuchea), Thailand, Malaysia, Indonesia, the Philippines, Brunei, Samoa, Guam, the US Trust Territories of the Pacific Islands (Republic of Palau), the Commonwealth of the Northern Marianas Islands, Macao, Fiji, Tonga, Kirbati, Juvalu, Nauru, Federated States of Micronesia, or Hong Kong
5. "Subcontinent Asian Americans," which includes persons whose origins are from India, Pakistan, Bangladesh, Bhutan, the Maldives Islands, Nepal, or Sri Lanka
6. Women
7. Any additional groups whose members are designated as socially and economically disadvantaged by the SBA, at such time as the SBA designation becomes effective (49 CFR 26.5)

There are also size and net worth criteria that must be met in order to be certified as a DBE. Recipients of Federal Transit Authority (FTA) funding must establish goals for the award of contracts to DBEs and must make good faith efforts to achieve those goals. As such, DBE goals are a form of diversity policy, designed to increase the representation of women- and minority-owned business enterprises among those receiving federally assisted transit contracts. This criterion is about equity. Both to remedy prior or ongoing discrimination against women- and minority-owned business enterprises and to correct for private marketplace inequalities, the goals program is designed to "level the playing field" in public procurement and contracting.

In the goal-setting process, however, recipients of federal funds are required to narrowly tailor their programs so that the maximum feasible portion of the goals is race- and gender-neutral (Roy Wilkins Center 2009). The logic is that the programs must not harm non-aggrieved parties or at least must minimize the harm to non-DBEs in the process of benefiting DBEs. This criterion is about efficiency.

The reason why the efficiency and the equity criteria are potentially in conflict is that federal regulations mandate that recipients of funding set goals for DBEs while prohibiting separate goals for different subgroups among disadvantaged business enterprises. The DBE program cannot be overinclusive, but it also cannot target subgroups within racial or ethnic categories.

One illustration of this problem is in a federal lawsuit challenging the DBE goals program of New Jersey Transit Authority (Myers 2007, 2008). Plaintiff's expert alleged, among other things, that the DBE program was overinclusive because it included Asian Americans, a group that apparently experienced great success in the award of contracts. In a 2002 disparity study of the availability and utilization of firms classified by their racial/ethnic and gender categories, it was found that overall DBEs were underutilized. Within the racial/ethnic groups, however, there was much variability in the ratio of utilization to availability. The share of contract dollars awarded to black, non-Hispanics was 3.8 percent, whereas blacks represented 4.5 percent of all willing, able, and qualified firms, resulting in a utilization/availability ratio of .84. The share of contract dollars awarded to Hispanics was 5.5 percent, but Hispanics represented 6.5 percent of ready, willing, and qualified firms, producing a utilization/availability ratio of .85. The share of contract dollars awarded to nonminority females was 7.2 percent, but nonminority females accounted for 26 percent of ready, willing, and qualified business enterprises, meaning that the utilization/availability ratio was .27. The share of contract dollars awarded to nonminority males was 77.8 percent, whereas nonminority males represented 64.9 percent of all ready, willing, and able contractors, producing a utilization/availability index of 1.20. For Asian Americans, however, the ratio of utilization to availability is greater than one. Asian Americans received 5.5 percent of contract dollars, but they represented 4.2 percent of all willing, able, and qualified firms. The result is a ratio of utilization to availability of 1.31. Even though the ratio of utilization to availability for DBEs as a group was less than one, the apparent "overutilization" of Asian Americans among DBEs prompted the expert for the plaintiff to argue that the DBE goal was overinclusive.

Further evidence in the lawsuit shows, however, that Asian American firms received lower contract awards than non-DBEs. The average contract award for a non-DBE was found to be $3,005,411 whereas the average contract award for an Asian American firm was only $362,900, a statistically significant difference. Thus, even though there does not appear to be a disparity between the availability and utilization of Asian-owned firms in New Jersey, there is indeed a major disparity in the contract amounts awarded.

Going a step further in examining the alleged overutilization of Asian-owned firms, the supplementary expert report for the defendant computed the representation in the year 2000 of minority-owned firms by nation of origin relative to white-owned firms (Myers 2010). The report computed odds ratios of self-employment, a measure of business ownership, from a regression model that included human capital and other characteristics. Odds ratios of less than 1 imply that there is an underrepresentation of businesses within a given subgroup. Odds ratios of greater than 1 mean that the group is over-represented relative to nonminority firms. The results showed odds ratios of .417 for African Americans as a group, with .385 and .318 for Haitian- and Jamaican-born blacks, the two largest black immigrant groups in New Jersey. The results showed odds ratios of .588 for Hispanics as a group, but for Hispanics of Puerto Rican and Dominican descent, the two largest groups of Hispanics in New Jersey, the odds ratios were .498 and .606. The results showed odds ratios of .715 for Asian Americans, with East Asian Indians, the largest group of Asians in New Jersey, showing odds ratios of .533 and with Chinese—the second largest group of Asians in New Jersey—showing odds ratios of .714. The odds ratio for Filipinos was .373. The odds ratio for Koreans, who represent a relatively small share of the total New Jersey population, was 2.025.

The tension between equity and efficiency arises in this illustration. The diversity objective of defining a broad class of socially and economically disadvantaged firms was adopted to achieve a social equity goal of leveling the playing field and opening up business opportunities for historically excluded groups. The equity goal mandated that racial and ethnic minorities as well as women-owned business enterprises be considered as a group, partly so as not to pit one subgroup against another. The efficiency criterion, however, mandates that only the best-qualified firms should receive public contracts, and thus, what amounts to affirmative action for women and minorities should not be overinclusive and should minimize the harm to qualified white male-owned firms. The distinction between equity and efficiency is made a bit more complex by that fact that Koreans, as a sub-group of Asians, are not found to be underrepresented among businesses in New Jersey, although Asian American-owned firms as a group are underrepresented. Moreover, Asian-owned firms as a group tend to receive lower than average contracts. Is it efficient to exclude Korean American-owned firms in the definition of the DBE program? Is it fair? Or, put differently, would the exclusion of Koreans from the DBE program help white small businesses? Would small, Korean-owned firms compete at the same rate without being designated as disadvantaged? The attempt to craft a diversity program for businesses to promote equity in public procurement and contracting is immediately confronted with these efficiency concerns.

DO NON-DBES BENEFIT FROM DBE PROGRAMS?

Who benefits from DBE programs? The conventional wisdom is that when prime contracts or subcontracts are awarded to women- or minority-owned firms through procurement and contracting goals programs, these firms benefit at the expense of other firms that do not receive preferential treatment. A very simple exercise using publically available data reported in mandated FTA and Federal Highway Administration (FHWA) reports submitted by the Minnesota Department of Transportation and New Jersey Transit reveals a consistent pattern: non-DBE prime contractors receive more dollars when there are DBE goals than when there are no goals. The net-benefit of goals to non-DBE primes often exceeds the net-benefits that accrue to DBE primes.

To see this, we have assembled data on prime contract awards to non-DBEs and DBEs with and without DBE goals. The information comes from reports provided by MnDOT for the years 2011–2014 and by NJT for the years 2009–2013. The available years chosen reflect years designed to capture stimulus funding from the American Recovery and Reinvestment Act of 2009.

Table 5.1 shows that during the period under review $1.6 billion FTA dollars were contracted by NJT to non-DBE prime contractors for projects with DBE goals while $283 million FTA dollars were contracted by NJT to non-DBE prime contractors for projects without DBE goals. The 81.8 percent difference can be viewed as the net-benefit to non-DBE prime contractors of participating in the DBE program.[15]

In Minnesota, an even higher benefit exists for participation in the program. Table 5.1 shows that during the period under review, 2.3 billion FHWA dollars

Table 5.1   Benefits to Non-DBE Prime Contractors from Participation in DBE Programs

	Total Dollars to Non-DBE Prime Contractors		Total Dollars to DBE Prime Contractors	
	NJT-FTA	*MN-FHWA*	*NJT-FTA*	*MN-FHWA*
Prime Contracts with DBE Goals	$1,552,980,908.71	$2,284,361,957.87	$12,006,245.09	$6,878,630.63
Prime Contracts without DBE Goals	$283,151,643.56	$53,950,010.21	$7,185,509.57	$337,981.40
Net-benefit of Goals	81.8%	97.6%	40.2%	95.1%

Source: NJT-FTA: July 1, 2009, through September 30, 2013.
    MN-FHWA: October 1, 2011, through September 30, 2014.

were contracted by MnDOT to non-DBE prime contractors for projects with DBE goals while $54 million FHWA dollars were contracted by MnDOT to non-DBE prime contractors for projects without DBE goals. The 97.6 percent difference can be viewed as the net-benefit to non-DBE prime contractors of participating in the DBE program in Minnesota.

Note that the net-benefits to DBE prime contractors of participating in the DBE program are smaller than the net-benefits to non-DBE prime contractors. In New Jersey, DBE prime contractors received $7.2 million in FTA dollars when there were no goals but $12 million FTA dollars when there were goals. Thus, there was only a 40 percent net-benefit of participating in the DBE program for DBEs versus an 82 percent net-benefit of participation in the DBE program for non-DBEs in New Jersey. Non-DBEs benefit more from the DBE program than do DBEs.

A smaller differential between the net-benefits of participating in the DBE program prevails in Minnesota. There, the net-benefits are 95.1 percent for DBE primes and 97.6 percent. This tiny difference, then, means that women and minorities do not benefit more from the preference program than non-disadvantaged businesses.

Of course, most DBE programs are structured as subcontracting programs. It is useful to examine whether non-DBE subcontractors benefit more than DBE subcontractors from preferential programs. The subcontracting data are provided in Table 5.2.

Table 5.2 shows that $60 million of FTA dollars were contracted to non-DBE subcontractors by NJT on contracts that had goals. Only $35 million of FTA dollars were contracted to non-DBE subcontractors by NJT on contracts that did not have goals. More dollars went to non-DBE subcontractors on contracts that had DBE goals than to non-DBE subcontractors on contracts

Table 5.2   Benefits to Non-DBE Prime Subcontractors from Participation in DBE Programs

	Total Dollars to Non-DBE Prime Subcontractors		Total Dollars to DBE Prime Subcontractors	
	NJT-FTA	*MN-FHWA*	*NJT-FTA*	*MN-FHWA*
Prime Contracts with DBE Goals	$60,031,253.94	$417,899,507.41	$70,055,092.02	$197,588,258.97
Prime Contracts without DBE Goals	$35,408,678.64	$2,237,732.42	$4,566,697.14	$410,702.04
Net-benefit of Goals	41.0%	99.5%	93.5%	9.8%

Source: NJT-FTA: July 1, 2009, through September 30, 2013.
    MN-FHWA: October 1, 2011, through September 30, 2014.

without goals. There was a net-benefit of 41 percent to non-DBEs in New Jersey. Understandably, since the DBE program operates in New Jersey as a subcontracting program, the net-benefits to DBEs of participating in the DBE program are greater than those found for non-DBEs. The total amount of subcontracting dollars equaled $70 million FTA subcontracting dollars for DBEs as compared to $60 million FTA subcontracting dollars for non-DBEs. The net-benefit to DBEs in NJT was a sizeable 93.5 percent because only $4.6 million of FTA subcontracting dollars accrued to DBEs on contracts where there were no DBE goals.

One cannot generalize from the New Jersey results that DBE subcontractors benefit relatively more than non-DBE subcontractors from the DBE program. In Minnesota, by way of contrast, the bulk of the subcontracting dollars—with or without goals—goes to non-DBEs. With DBE goals, non-DBE subcontractors received $428 million of FHWA dollars via contracts awarded by MnDOT. With DBE goals, DBE subcontractors only received $198 million of FHWA dollars via contracts awarded by MnDOT. Without goals, only a trivial number of dollars were awarded to subcontractors. The result is that the net-benefit of subcontractor participation on contracts with DBE goals is proportionally about the same for DBEs and non-DBEs on FHWA contracts awarded by MnDOT.

CONCLUSION

In a wide array of contexts, administrators of public programs are required to seek "race-neutral" means to address problems of racial disparities. Race-conscious programs in college admissions and scholarship awards, in hiring and promotion in technical and professional fields, and in the selection of private contractors to provide goods and services using public funds, generally must be narrowly tailored and must meet a strict-scrutiny test. To achieve these legal standards, administrators must also demonstrate that they have attempted to implement non-race-based (or race-neutral) remedies. The case of FTA requirements illustrates the tension between race-neutral and race-conscious remedies. On the one hand, the FTA rules require recipients of federal transit funds to set goals for the utilization of DBEs in procurement and contracting. On the other hand, these goals must be narrowly tailored and must maximize the use of race-neutral devices to achieve the goals. The regulations themselves offer little specific guidance to state and local governments on how to accomplish the race-neutral portions of the goals. This chapter suggests an empirical methodology that meets the legal standards outlined in FTA guidelines that also has the virtue of being transparent and easy to implement, using conventional econometric tools. The statistical methodology permits the local government or transit agency to predict the share of contract dollars that might be awarded to women- and minority-owned firms without numerical goals placed on prime contracts. This prediction becomes the basis for setting the race-neutral portion of the mandated FTA goals.

Two concerns, nevertheless, arise about the setting of these preferential goals. One is that some subgroups—for example, Asians—might appear to be unentitled beneficiaries of the preferential treatment. We investigate this claim using date from New Jersey and conclude that even when there does not appear to be a disparity between utilization and availability of subgroups within the larger class of firms covered by DBE program, these subgroups are still found to receive lower contract awards and face barriers to participation that justify their inclusion in the program.

A second concern is that DBEs benefit at the expense of non-DBEs. Evidence is provided in this chapter that refutes this overly simple claim. The evidence shows that the bulk of funding from federal programs such as FTA and FHWA goes to non-DBE prime contractors and subcontracts. Measuring the "net-benefit" of participating in a contract that has a DBE goal as the percentage difference between the dollars awarded on contracts with goals versus those without goals, we confirm that non-DBEs receive nontrivial "net-benefits" from participating in DBE projects. These net-benefits in some instances are more extensive than those that accrue to DBE firms. So, perhaps surprisingly, some of the biggest beneficiaries of preferential treatment in public procurement and contracting are not women or minorities but white males. The reasoning is that the preferential treatment program embodied in the federal DBE guidelines is one the designed to maximize the race-neutral portion of the goals and in doing so results in nontrivial benefits to businesses that are not technically disadvantaged.

NOTES

1. See Echaustegui et al., *Do Minority-Owned Business Get a Fair Share of Government Contracts?* Washington, D.C.: *The Urban Institute*, 1997.

2. On July 28, 1967, President Lyndon B. Johnson appointed the National Advisory Commission on Civil Disorders, also known as the Kerner Commission after its chair, Governor Otto Kerner, Jr. of Illinois, to investigate the causes of the 1967 race riots in the black neighborhoods of major US cities, including Chicago, Detroit, Los Angeles, and Newark. President Johnson asked the commission to answer three basic questions about the riots: "What happened? Why did it happen? What can be done to prevent it from happening again?" On February 29, 1968, the Commission's report concluded that the nation was "moving toward two societies, one black, one white—separate and unequal."

3. See LaNoue, G. R., "Split Visions: Minority Business Set-Asides. Affirmative Action Revisited," *Annals of the American Academy of Political and Social Science* 523, 104–116, 1992.

4. See Rice, M. F., "Government Set-Asides, Minority Business Enterprises, and the Supreme Court," *Public Administration Review* 51, 114–122, 1991.

5. See Myers, Jr., S., and Chan, T., "Who Benefits from Minority-Business Set-Asides? The Case of New Jersey," *Journal of Policy Analysis and Management* 15, 202–225, 1996.

6. See Myers, Jr., S., and Ha, I., "Estimation of Race-Neutral Goals in Public Procurement and Contracting," *Applied Economics Letters* 16(3), 251–256, 2009.

7. There are three publications for the details. (1) Heckman, J., "Detecting Discrimination," *Journal of Economic Perspectives* 12, 101–116, 1998. (2) Loury, G. C., "Discrimination in the Post-Civil Rights Era: beyond Market Interactions," *Journal of Economic Perspectives* 12, 117–126, 1998. (3) Cherry, R., *Who Gets the Good Jobs? Combating Race and Gender Disparities*. New Brunswick, NJ: Rutgers University Press, 2001.

8. See Davila, R., Myers, Jr., S., and Ha, I., "Affirmative Action Retrenchment in Public Procurement and Contracting," *Applied Economics Letters* 19(18), 1857–1180, 2012.

9. See Heckman, J., "Detecting Discrimination," *Journal of Economic Perspectives* 12, 101–116, 1998.

10. Refer to 64 FR 5126, 2 Feb 1999, as amended at 64 FR 34570, 28 June 1999; 65 FR 68951, 15 Nov 2000; 68 FR 35553, 16 June 2003.

11. See Electronic Code of Federal Regulations (e-CFR) current as of May 24, 2006; Title 49: Transportation PART 26.

12. See Myers, Jr., S. and Ha, I., "Estimation of Race-Neutral Goals in Public Procurement and Contracting," *Applied Economics Letters* 16(3), 251–256, 2009, for the technical details.

13. See Electronic Code of Federal Regulations (e-CFR) current as of May 24, 2006; Title 49: Transportation PART 26.

14. See Electronic Code of Federal Regulations (e-CFR) current as of May 24, 2006; Title 49: Transportation PART 26. See §26.51(c).

15. We note that the term *net-benefit* here is a misnomer. This simple calculation reported in the table is not the difference in the benefit to an individual firm of participating in the program versus the cost of participating. Rather, the calculation is the payments received by firms participating versus the payments received by firms that did not participate. An alternative term to describe the calculation might be "participation benefit."

Chapter 6

Markets, Market Failure, and Black-White Earnings Inequality

Race Neutrality and the Rising Tide Lifts All Ships Hypothesis

This chapter explores the concept of public value (or social value) as it is understood in conventional microeconomic analysis. It applies the efficiency criterion, a key microeconomics aspect of public value, to the problem of racial earnings inequality. Competing arguments are examined about whether racial inequality is a form of market failure (e.g., Bozeman 2007) requiring market intervention. A dominant view in the economics profession is that racial discrimination can arise as a form of short-term market equilibrium (e.g., Becker 1971) that disappears in the long run without government intervention. In the Becker Model, black-white income inequality is not considered to be a form of market failure, requiring special public initiatives to correct such failure. Instead, improvement in the relative incomes of blacks is best met through overall improvement in economic performance. This has led to a common refrain among mainstream economists that "a rising tide lifts all ships." This chapter provides evidence that refutes this claim and argues that unfettered markets cannot be relied upon to remedy black-white income disparities. The implication for research on public value is that criteria other than market efficiency must be relied on to justify government interventions designed to remedy racial and ethnic economic inequality (Myers 2011b).

Economists and public administration theorists share a concern about the ability of markets to solve resource allocation problems. Whereas the public administration concern about the appropriate criteria for assessing and evaluating potential interventions in the marketplace might be very broad, the economist's attention tends to be directed narrowly to the question of efficiency. This paper defines the market efficiency criterion and summarizes the range of circumstances when markets fail to allocate resources efficiently.

A particular point of departure in this chapter is the examination of markets and intergroup economic inequality with reference to the problem of black-white wage and salary income disparities.

For a variety of reasons, markets sometimes fail to provide the most efficient allocation of resources. There is public value in correcting or remedying these market failures. A dominant perspective, however, is that the solution to race-based inequalities should avoid race-based remedies. Instead, the preferred remedies should be race-neutral. Behind this reasoning is that "a rising tide lifts all ships." To understand this logic, one must understand the thinking about when or whether targeted market interventions should be undertaken by the government. This thinking revolves around discourse about whether observed racial inequalities are the result of market failures and whether the remedies to market failures should target special racial groups.

This chapter suggests that there has been a shift in thinking over the past decade about whether and how to intervene in the market place. This shift has been particularly evident in the area of remedying racial economic inequality. This shift means that there has been a change in the public value, perceived or real, associated with direct government efforts to reduce black-white earnings gaps.

This chapter presents evidence suggesting that there is no consistent pattern of narrowing racial gaps in earnings during periods of economic expansion and widening gaps during periods of contraction, as conventional wisdom would suggest. The "Rising Tide Lifts All Ships" metaphor that has guided recent efforts to respond to the deep recession is ill-founded. Top policy makers' lack of attention to escalating racial and ethnic economic inequality can be attributed to their desire to produce a recovery for all and a belief that such a recovery will lift all groups and lessen inequality. This chapter provides evidence that challenges the view that racial income gaps narrow during upturns and widen during downturns.

The chapter proceeds in the following manner. First, there is a summary of efficiency arguments in favor of using markets to allocate scarce resources. The idea that markets create public value is discussed. Then, the problem of market failure is detailed and classic examples of market failure are presented. We then provide an original contribution to the debate about the public value of direct market interventions designed to reduce black-white earnings disparities. It tests whether color-blind market changes, such as reductions in statewide unemployment rates, help to reduce black-white gaps in wage and salary incomes. In a concluding section, we discuss the implications for future research on public value and racial inequality.

MARKETS AND THE EFFICIENT
ALLOCATION OF RESOURCES

The towering accomplishment of microeconomic theorizing in the aftermath of World War II was the explicit mathematical proof that competitive markets with large numbers of buyers and sellers, with free entry and exit, and with full information available equally to all market participants produce an efficient allocation of resources. Economics Nobel Prize winners along a wide political spectrum have embraced this perspective. Paul Samuelson (1947), who in 1970 was the first American-born winner of the Nobel Prize in Economics, produced the most extensive and then widely read examination of the efficiency of market allocation in his 1947 *Foundations of Economic Analysis*. Important extensions and elaborations upon the modeling advanced by Samuelson include 1972 Economics Nobel Laureate Kenneth Arrow and Frank Hahn's (1971) *General Competitive Analysis*. The central tenets of what has come to be known as neoclassical economics have served as the cornerstone for both the reliance on markets and justification for government intervention in markets for much of the second half of the twentieth century throughout the non-communist world.

Not surprisingly, there is a broad literature critiquing the market efficiency concept of competitive markets. An important contribution to this literature challenges the very concept of "competition." The "competitive markets" in standard neoclassical economic theory reference a set of conditions under which buyers and sellers operate producing a static equilibrium. This differs from the notion of "competition" as a dynamic disequilibrium process, as it is understood by some critics of neoclassical economics (Mason 1995, 1999).

In a world of scarce resources, the desire to secure the most efficient allocation of those resources is often preeminent. In economics, "efficient" means that the resulting allocation produces the maximum feasible satisfaction (or utility) from consumers (constrained by their budgets) and the maximum technologically possible production from firms, given constraints on scarce inputs in the production process. The notion of "Pareto efficiency," or allocative efficiency has become the dominant guide to economic thinking and provides the analytical foundation for widely used public sector evaluative measures such as cost-benefit analysis. "Pareto efficiency" is achieved when an allocation cannot make one person better off without making another person worse off (Freedman 2002).

The foundational claims about the efficiency-producing effects of markets posit assumptions about consumer and producer behavior that are often not met in real-life markets. Some of these assumptions are: consumers and producers are rational; buyers and sellers face perfect information with no uncertainty; information is symmetric between buyers and sellers; mobility is costless; and firms are small relative to the market. Appropriate adjustments can be made to the underlying neoclassical model to produce the result of Pareto efficiency, but such a result is neither guaranteed nor assured. Indeed, the case for market regulation or government intervention in the market is often based on the argument that these key assumptions about the behaviors of market participants are not being met.

The foundational claim that markets can be or should be relied on to achieve efficiency is based on an assumption that the production of goods and services are directly produced by producers or consumed by consumers. However, not all market activities produce goods and services. Some market activities are related to exploiting uncertainty and information asymmetries that exist (e.g., futures markets and hedge funds). Indeed, some market activities, such as sophisticated trading schemes based on market uncertainties and information asymmetries, arose in the last decades of the twentieth century and appear *not* to be related to actual production or consumption of goods and services. Jadish Bhagwati (1982) labeled some activities of this sort DUP-ing behavior: directly unproductive activities that occur only because of the erstwhile failure of markets to achieve efficiency. Nonetheless, the general view among economists is that markets can or should be the primary vehicle for achieving efficiency.

Markets and the Creation of Public Value

In many respects, markets and market activities produce public value. The use of the term *public value* is conventional in economic literature and serves as a synonym for *social value* in a very narrow sense of producing efficiency.

The term differs from Bozeman's (2007, 132) more broadly conceived concept of "public value" as

a. the rights, benefits, and prerogatives to which citizens should (and should not) be entitled
b. the obligations of citizens to society, the state, and one another
c. the principles on which governments and policies should be based

In its conventional usage among economists, however, *public value* means net-benefits that accrue to society in general and not necessarily to individuals specifically. When total net-benefits received in society exceeds the sum of individual net-benefits, then there is public (or social) value. In this sense, the economic notion of public value is an efficiency measure.

Much economic literature historically has focused on how to maximize public value or social value from market activities. Markets, economists often argue, are a preferred source for organization of buyers and sellers for the purpose of maximizing public value as the term is used conventionally by economists. The reason is that markets can lead to a desirable allocation of resources improving upon the sum of individual net-benefits. Economists refer to this as the efficiency criterion. This does not mean that markets can or will do a better job than the government in allocating resources. What this condition means is that markets, under appropriate conditions, can achieve the desirable outcome of maximizing net social benefits and thereby result in efficiency.

Bozeman (2007, 134), however, explicitly rejects the normative criterion of efficiency for evaluating the appropriateness of various mechanisms for organizing all of society's transactions. He provides illustrations from the literatures on the sale of human organs and prostitution, noting that there is something entirely repugnant about selling one's kidneys or body for a profit. Unsurprisingly, a chorus of economists disagrees.

The conventional economic model suggests that the buying or selling of organs or of one's body can, under certain conditions, lead to market efficiency. The resulting market equilibrium, however, might include wide inequalities or substantial deviations from ethical or moral standards. The arguments against these types of market transactions rest on grounds other than efficiency grounds. In short, the Bozeman notion of "public value" must entail something more than simply the conventional economic concept of efficiency.

Whether one agrees or disagrees with the relevance and supremacy of the efficiency criterion for evaluation of resource allocation decisions, one can still question the effectiveness of markets in achieving this efficiency. A common by-product of attempts to achieve efficiency through market mechanisms is *inequality*. Inequality can arise within groups or between groups. Both sorts of inequality might meet the repugnancy test suggested by Bozeman and violate concepts of "rights, benefits, and prerogatives to which citizens should (and should not) be entitled; the obligations of citizens to society, the state, and one another; or principles on which governments and policies should be based." It is worth exploring briefly the classic instances where markets fail before proceeding to our discussion of racial inequality.

WHEN MARKETS FAIL—CLASSIC EXAMPLES

The textbook explanation for government regulation of industry and government use of industrial policies to remedy problems of inefficiency is the problem of "market failure" (Kahn 1988). Five classic examples of when exclusive reliance on markets fails to produce the desirable outcome of efficiency are (a) increasing returns to scale; (b) monopoly or market concentration;

(c) public goods; (d) information asymmetries; and (e) externalities (Kahn 1988). Each type of market failure justifies various degrees of government intervention in the form of incentives (taxes or subsidies), direct regulation, reallocation of property rights, or assignment of liability for harms created.

Public utilities represent the dominant illustration of market failure. Infrastructure industries—those providing power, water, and, at one point in history, communications technology—share an important operating feature: the average costs of production decline as a result of expansion of services. This feature of long-run declining average costs arises because of economies to scale. These industries are important to society because they provide the inputs for other industries and productive activities. Without power, energy, water, or communications, there will be no manufacturing, agriculture, education, or other services upon which the economy thrives.

The conventional solution to the market failure problem herein is to regulate the infrastructure industry, thus producing a quasi-public entity. The unique features of the public utility include the setting of rates, the determination of service levels, and the control of quality.

Monopoly is a second classic example of market failure. Some monopolistic activities derive not from the technological structure of the industry, such as the case with utilities, but from ruthlessness and aggressiveness in pursuing rivals in the marketplace. The irony here is that "competition" is supposed to produce efficiency, but eliminating rivals from the marketplace is a prelude to the creation of monopoly. A modern-day example is the practice of large, dominant airlines strategically pricing their tickets to and from the hubs of start-ups and smaller, lower-cost airlines in order to drive those airlines out of the market. The immediate impact of such pricing strategies is to benefit consumers, who pay lower prices for airfares to those hubs where dominant airlines compete with newer airlines. The longer-run impact is to drive the lower-priced airlines out of the market, to produce dominance in that market for the larger airlines, and thereby to drive prices up, reduce competition, and reduce service. The market fails. The original justification for regulating the airline industry by controlling both the service levels and routings as well as proposed mergers and acquisitions was to correct for this market failure.

A third form of market failure involves public goods. Some goods are public goods in the sense that once provided it is not possible to distinguish between those who pay and those who do not pay. There are wide benefits to acquisition of such goods and significant social costs in the event that the goods are not provided at all. Private markets fail in the presence of public goods. The most commonly offered example of a public good is national defense. We all benefit from having standing armed forces to protect us from attacks. No one, however, is willing to voluntarily bear the full cost of providing this service, and once provided, all benefit. Markets fail.

Information asymmetries still represent a fourth form of market failure. In this instance, buyers and sellers have different knowledge about the products being sold. The pioneering work of Akerlof (1970) illustrates this form of market failure by reference to the "Market for Lemons." In the used-car market, in the days before CarFax© and AutoCheck©, sellers knew more about the potential or existing mechanical defects of a given automobile than buyers. This asymmetry of information produces instances where buyers, whose beliefs about the quality of the automobiles prove to be erroneous, purchase "lemons." The market fails. The solution? Warranties. Improved consumer protection laws, and interestingly enough, information services such as CarFax© and AutoCheck©.

A final form of market failure arises in cases of what is known as externalities. An externality is understood to mean a transaction where the full cost or benefit is not transmitted through the pricing mechanism. An example is a smoke stack. A Beijing steel company produces iron rods that are sold to plants that manufacture smoke stacks sold to billions of consumers around the world. The smoke from the smoke stack pollutes the air making it nearly impossible for poor local residents living in the air drift of the smoke stack to breathe. Children develop severe cases of asthma. Adults suffer from chronic obstructive pulmonary disease (COPD) and develop various forms of lung cancer. The unpriced output of the smokestack produces costs to individuals and to society (Wong 2013). The market fails.

Absent from this list of classic examples of market failure is the problem of racial or ethnic economic inequality. The problem of market discrimination is not seen in most economic models as a form of inefficiency or market failure. Indeed, perfect price discrimination is a classic *solution* to some forms of market inefficiencies (Varian 1993). Inequality, in and of itself, is not necessarily viewed by economists as a problem of market inefficiency. Racial inequality or other forms of intergroup inequality may or may not coexist with markets that allocate resources efficiently.

IS RACIAL INEQUALITY A FORM
OF MARKET FAILURE?

It is tempting to classify intergroup disparities in markets as a form of market failure. Marcus Alexis (1973) and others have introduced models where racial animosity is a form of externality. Whether these intergroup disparities are based on race, ethnicity, gender, caste, tribal background, or other social constructs, they may arise in markets in the form of differences in wages, earnings, labor force participation, unemployment, assets, wealth, education, and a host of other economically meaningful outcomes. To the extent that these outcomes are related to market processes, there is the temptation to link intergroup disparities in these outcomes to market imperfections or to the failure of markets to allocate resources efficiently.

The temptation to make the connection between market failure and intergroup inequality arising from the underrepresentation of women and minorities among the tenured faculty of top science and engineering programs at first glance might be attributed to the failure of markets (or public schools) to signal to high performing students the advantages of taking advanced placement calculus and science courses in high school. These courses are virtual pipelines to college majors in engineering, biomedical and behavioral sciences, and other science and technology fields, where many women and minorities are severely underrepresented (Myers and Husbands Fealing 2012). It is tempting to classify the racial disparities in public procurement and contracting as a form of market or government failure as well. The inability of a vast array of public programs designed to improve access to bid opportunities and to produce larger shares of dollars awarded to disadvantaged business enterprises can be seen both as a failure of government and of the market.

These temptations should be avoided. Certainly market failure may be at work here: information asymmetry constitutes a market failure explanation. Inefficiencies in public agencies and the difficulties they face in implementing programs point to government failure. Distinct from the racial and ethnic inequality traceable to established forms of market or government failure is the racial inequality that exists and persists even when markets or governments are operating efficiently (Mason 1995, 1999). Market failure is a signal of inefficient allocation of resources. Racial and ethnic inequalities arise for reasons beyond simply inefficiency. Sometimes racial inequality persists in efficient markets because it serves a purpose, a stabilizing purpose. Sometimes racial inequality arises and persists because of the power of dominant groups, precisely the same groups that manage and operate efficient markets and governments (Darity 2005). The criteria of whether racial inequality detracts from public value rest among the range of items suggested by Bozeman, including the criterion of fairness and justice.

MARKETS AND INCREASING INTERRACIAL INEQUALITY: WIDENING GAPS IN UNFETTERED MARKETS

A common response offered during the post-recession years of the Obama administration was that "a rising tide lifts all ships." This response was proffered in the face of increasingly vocal and antagonistic complaints from some quarters within the African American scholarly community concerning the absence of a racially conscious policy designed to reduce black-white economic inequality. The opposition argued that little, if anything, was being done to assist black communities hit particularly hard by the recession of 2008. In most of the nation, unemployment rates for blacks were two to three times as high as they were for whites. In metropolitan areas such as the seven-county Minneapolis/St. Paul area, which historically has witnessed robust employment growth, black unemployment rates were four times as high as white unemployment rates in 2008. The tepid response from the White House was that all Americans would benefit from ongoing efforts to increase government spending on jobs programs, infrastructure investments, and small business tax breaks. The disparity has hardly improved in the post-recession years, leading many people to question whether a rising tide lifts even those ships that are sinking.

A widely held view is that overall economic growth contributes to the improved relative economic well-being of subgroups within the economy. This belief is particularly pertinent to labor markets. As the macro economy improves, unemployment rates for subgroups in society will decline. This theme has come to be known as the "rising tide lifts all ships" hypothesis (Hines, Hoynes, and Krueger 2001). Contested, however, is whether economic growth—"a rising tide"—also produces higher intergroup and intragroup inequality, and thus, higher relative disparities in incomes or earnings.

Much of the evidence in the United States supporting the rising tide hypothesis comes from the expansion years of the 1960s and 1970s when rapid economic growth coincided with the improved economic well-being of vulnerable populations. However, the responsiveness of wages to cyclical fluctuations reportedly declined during the 1980s and 1990s (Hines, Hoynes, and Krueger 2001), resulting in increased income inequality during those two decades (Hungerford 2011). The explanations for why the lowest earners may be less responsive to overall economic growth may rest with differential occupational distributions by gender, race and, ethnicity (Couch and Fairlie 2008; del Río, Gradín, and Cantó 2011) as well as educational differences (Couch and Fairlie 2008). The evidence from the United States is that not all people benefited from expansion of the economy during the boom years of the 1990s (Freeman 2001; Wray and Pigeon 2000).

Recent studies of the relationship between economic growth and overall inequality confirm that, in the short and medium terms, across a wide array of nations, rapid economic growth is associated with widening intragroup inequality (Chambers 2010). Within counties, the pattern of improvements in economic well-being varies across locations and within metropolitan areas. The pattern of improvement also varies between the central city and non-central city areas (Partridge and Rickman 2008), with central cities often lagging behind other locations when improvements transpire. Despite the concern about widening inequality that arises from rapid improvements in the macro economy, most estimates show a trickle-down effect to local areas where poverty rates fall when overall unemployment rates decline (Freeman 2003).

From 1970 to 2007, annual rates of growth in the United States averaged about 3.3 percent, with periodic swings up and down. Major downturns producing negative economic growth occurred in the United States in 1974–1975, 1980, 1982, and 1991 prior to the recession of 2008. Thus, the period of the 1990s, the Clinton years, is considered to be an atypical run of sustained growth. The downturn in 2001 did not produce negative economic growth, so the entire period from 1992 to 2007 can be regarded as boom years for the American economy. It is during years like these that one might expect to see evidence that "a rising tide lifts all ships."

However, Figures 6.1 and 6.2 reveal that black-white earnings disparities do not always respond to economic expansion in the manner predicted by the "rising tides" hypothesis. To produce these figures, we have computed, for each year and for each gender, the ratio of black-to-white wage and salary incomes from the Integrated Public Use Microsample (IPUMS) version of the Current Population Survey (CPS).

During the period when government affirmative action policies were most keenly pursued, from the late 1960s to the late 1970s, the ratio of black-to-white earnings increased among both males and females. Earnings disparities diminished during this era. Then, as white female employment opportunities

Figure 6.1   Ratio of black male to white male wage and salary income, 1970–2009.
Authors' computations from IPUMS-CPS (Flood et al. 2017).

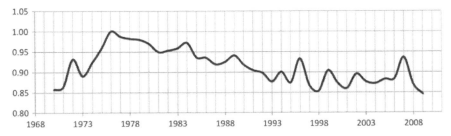

Figure 6.2   Ratio of black female to white female wage and salary income, 1970–2009.
Authors' computations from IPUMS-CPS (Flood et al. 2017).

expanded in high-skilled occupations, the ratio of black-to-white earnings saw a long-term decline, dropping from a peak for black females of 1.00 in 1977 to a low of .85 for black females in 1999. The ratio rose after the 2001 recession and fell again after the 2008 recession. Thus, for females, there is the appearance of long-term declines in black-white earnings ratios, consistent with the "rising tides" hypothesis.

Among males a different picture emerges. Figure 6.3 superimposes the dates of the recessions since 1970 on the mapper of earnings gaps to capture the effects of recessions on earnings disparities. Recession years are defined as December 1969 (IV) to November 1970 (IV); November 1973 (IV) to March 1975 (I); January 1980 (I) to July 1980 (III); July 1981 (III) to November 1982 (IV); July 1990 (III) to March 1991(I); March 2001(I) to November 2001 (IV); and December 2007 (IV) to June 2009 (II). Post-recession years occur in the two quarters following the end of a recession. All other years are those that are not recession or post-recession years. The conventional wisdom is that these gaps should widen during the downturn and narrow during the recovery, but the figure shows that, in four of the past six recessions, earnings disparities narrowed among males during the downturn. This evidence is not consistent with the "rising tides" hypothesis.

The gray shading denotes the recession quarters from 1970 to 2010. During the 1973 recession racial earnings gaps narrowed for males; during the 1980

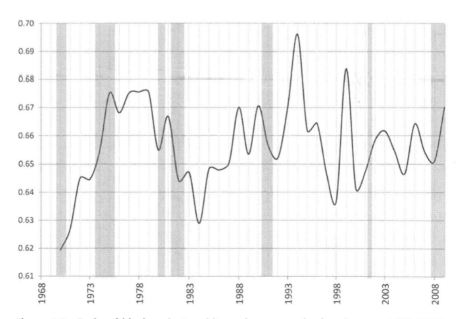

Figure 6.3 Ratio of black male to white male wage and salary income, 1970–2009.
Authors' computations from IPUMS-CPS; Recession months defined by the NBER's Business Cycle Dating Committee, noted in gray bars.

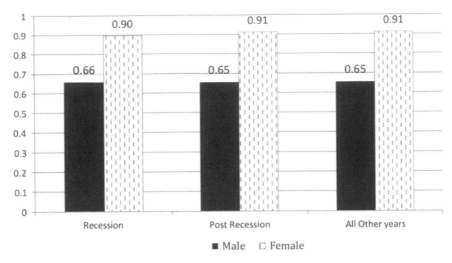

Figure 6.4   Ratio of black/white wage and salary incomes. Authors' computations from IPUMS-CPS.

recession, earnings gaps narrowed; during the 2001 recession, earnings gaps narrowed; during the second part of the recent recession, earnings gaps narrowed. Of course, earnings gaps are based on data for those who work, and if there are differential exits from the labor market during the recession, with the lowest earners selectively withdrawing from the market, the result could be the observed pattern found in Figure 6.3. However, for this explanation to make sense there would have to be greater withdrawals among black males than white males during the downturn. In the recent downturn, we do observe larger drops in labor force participation among white males than black males, but not always at the lower end of the occupational distribution. Thus, the descriptive evidence alone is insufficient for testing the "rising tide lifts all ships" hypothesis.

Figure 6.4 shows the average ratio of black-to-white wage and salary incomes for the recession, post-recession and all other years. The ratios of black-to-white wage and salary incomes across the span of the years 1970–2009 are virtually identical during the recession years, the post-recession years, and all other years. This result is true both for males and females.

Further evidence that the "rising tide lifts all ships" hypothesis fails comes from a more detailed regression analysis. The model estimates the impacts of economic expansions and contractions on earnings inequality controlling for human capital factors, family/household structure, industry and occupational variables, location-specific measures, and overall unemployment in a state. Variables in the model include age, education, occupation, industry, household head, number of children in the household, household in an urban area, and region. Current Population Survey data (March Supplement) are used to estimate black and white earnings equations for each year and for each gender as a basis for estimating the impacts of state unemployment on earnings. One can compute the impacts of changes in unemployment on earnings inequality and test whether upturns result in narrowing inequality and downturns produce widening inequality: the central prediction of the "rising tides lifts all ships" hypothesis.

Figures 6.5 and 6.6 present results of estimating the effects of unemployment on earnings inequality from 1980 to 2009. The values reported

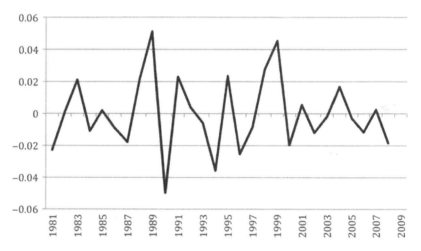

Figure 6.5   Effect of change in state unemployment on black-white earnings inequality, females. Authors' computations from IPUMS-CPS.

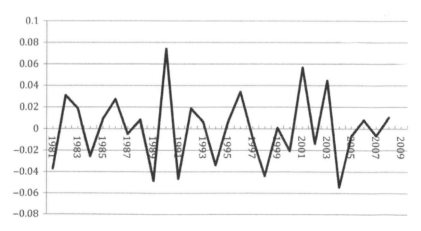

Figure 6.6   Effect of change in state unemployment on black-white earnings inequality, males. Authors' computations from IPUMS-CPS.

Chapter 6

are the estimated changes in black-white inequality when unemployment increases. When this value is positive, increases (reductions) in unemployment increase (reduce) inequality. When this value is negative, increases (reductions) in unemployment reduce (increase) inequality. The rising tide hypothesis assumes that the values will be positive: that inequality moves in the same direction as unemployment changes. For males, Figure 6.6 shows the computed value of the change in inequality with respect to state unemployment is positive and greater than .01 in only 10 of the 28 paired years. In another five years, the value is close to zero but non-negative. In another five years, the value is close to zero but negative. Finally in nine of the years, the value is negative and greater than .01 in absolute value. The underlying coefficients on the state unemployment variable are all

Table 6.1　Estimated Coefficients of State Unemployment in Earnings Equation

Year	White Male	White Female	Black Male	Black Female	Males	Females
1981	−0.0029	0.0061	−0.0250	−0.0247	−0.0373	−0.0228
1982	−0.0048	0.0032	0.0104	−0.0049	0.0308	0.0006
1983	0.0049	−0.0069	−0.0107	−0.0156	0.0186	0.0211
1984	−0.0056	−0.0050	−0.0398	−0.0348	−0.0256	−0.0108
1985	−0.0149	−0.0078	−0.0235	−0.0268	0.0092	0.0018
1986	−0.0120	−0.0055	−0.0298	−0.0263	0.0273	−0.0091
1987	−0.0147	−0.0125	−0.0598	−0.0242	−0.0049	−0.0179
1988	−0.0137	−0.0137	−0.0539	−0.0076	0.0081	0.0217
1989	−0.0150	−0.0164	−0.0633	−0.0319	−0.0484	0.0512
1990	0.0035	0.0105	0.0036	−0.0562	0.0738	−0.0498
1991	0.0284	0.0128	−0.0453	−0.0041	−0.0465	0.0230
1992	0.0324	0.0254	0.0052	−0.0145	0.0185	0.0042
1993	0.0277	0.0259	−0.0180	−0.0182	0.0062	−0.0061
1994	0.0243	0.0277	−0.0276	−0.0103	−0.0340	−0.0356
1995	0.0216	0.0341	0.0037	0.0317	0.0061	0.0235
1996	0.0171	0.0272	−0.0069	0.0013	0.0341	−0.0254
1997	0.0248	0.0124	−0.0333	0.0119	−0.0085	−0.0086
1998	0.0080	0.0093	−0.0416	0.0174	−0.0439	0.0277
1999	−0.0004	0.0129	−0.0061	−0.0067	0.0007	0.0453
2000	0.0048	0.0173	−0.0016	−0.0476	−0.0206	−0.0197
2001	0.0026	−0.0006	0.0168	−0.0458	0.0567	0.0053
2002	0.0213	0.0091	−0.0212	−0.0414	−0.0139	−0.0120
2003	0.0113	0.0038	−0.0173	−0.0347	0.0445	−0.0019
2004	0.0122	0.0063	−0.0609	−0.0303	−0.0546	0.0167
2005	−0.0037	−0.0043	−0.0222	−0.0575	−0.0070	−0.0029
2006	−0.0018	−0.0073	−0.0133	−0.0576	0.0079	−0.0117
2007	−0.0091	0.0059	−0.0285	−0.0327	−0.0065	0.0023
2008	0.0035	0.0122	−0.0095	−0.0287	0.0101	−0.0185
2009	−0.0017	0.0005	−0.0248	−0.0219		

Source: Authors' computations from IPUMS-CPS.

statistically significant. The conclusion, then, is that only in 35 percent of the paired years does the evidence favor the hypothesis that a rising tide lifts all ships among males.

For females, the measure of the change with respect to state unemployment is positive in eight of the years, and greater than .01. In nine of the years, the measure is close to zero. In the remaining ten years the value is negative. The overwhelming evidence is not consistent with the view that reductions in overall state unemployment rates works to reduce black-white earnings inequality among females.

Both figures reveal that the slope of the black-white inequality index with respect to state unemployment is as often below zero as it is approximately equal to zero or greater than zero. This erratic fluctuation in the impact of state unemployment on black-white earnings disparities does not seem to follow any particular pattern across the business cycle itself. In some instances the negative values are associated with post-recession years; in other instances the negative values are associated with recession or non-recession years (see Table 6.1).

SUMMARY AND CONCLUSION

Because black-white inequality generally is not considered by adherents to the Becker Model to be a form of market failure, economists have paid insufficient attention to the intergroup inequality problem; the inattention is often justified by the belief that "a rising tide lifts all ships." In this chapter, evidence is provided showing that race-neutral remedies like overall macro-economic stabilization policies might not work in reducing racial inequality. The evidence suggests that black-white earnings gaps are just as large during the downturn as they are during recovery. While one can argue for economic growth and stabilization on other grounds, the argument that "a rising tide lifts all ships" is insufficient to remedy racial gaps in wage and salary incomes.

One plausible reason why President Obama resisted the temptation to advocate race-conscious policies that would target African Americans and other racial minority groups is that he genuinely believed that by focusing on economic growth and addressing the multiple facets of the great recession that racial minority groups would benefit disproportionately. The logic is that if during the recovery the worst off groups gain the most, then racial and ethnic disparities should narrow. Without specifically targeting racial minority group members, the strategy of speeding the economic recovery has the effect of disproportionately benefiting racial minority group members. There is something extremely attractive in this logic: reduce racial inequality without specifically addressing the underlying causes of that inequality and perhaps arousing opposition and animosity among groups that believe targeted remedies hurt whites. But, as the evidence presented in this chapter demonstrates, the rising tide may lift all ships but it does not assure reductions in racial disparities in earnings.

Chapter 7

Deterrence as a Race-Neutral Strategy

The Case of Racial Disparities in Lending

Discrimination is illegal.[1] Why do we need a race-conscious remedy for discrimination if market forces can work to reduce discrimination? Media exposure is one market force that highlights the behavior of market participants. And there is always the expectation that government enforcement of anti-discrimination laws should also suffice to reduce discrimination. In this chapter, we explore the effects of public and private deterrence on racial disparities in loan denial rates. The analysis uses data on HUD enforcement activities and information about media accounts of allegations of discrimination in mortgage lending, combined with Home Mortgage Disclosure Act (HMDA) loan application records (LARS) for 1994–2003, to test the hypothesis that public and private enforcement efforts reduce lending discrimination. We find that there are year-to-year differences in the deterrent effectiveness of HUD enforcement activities and of media exposure. The years with the most robust impacts on reducing lender discrimination through media exposure were 1998 and 1999, when 100 percent and 77 percent of the media accounts of interaction with race are negative and statistically significant for blacks, and 44 and 55 percent are negative and significant for Hispanics. The peak year for the effectiveness of HUD enforcement efforts appears to be 1998 for blacks and 1997 for Hispanics.

We also find that media accounts of allegations of discrimination more consistently produce reduced discrimination for blacks than for Hispanics. The estimates of the deterrent impacts of media accounts are slightly more robust among blacks than are the estimates of HUD enforcement efforts. Among Hispanics, HUD enforcement efforts are more robust than are the effects of media accounts.

THE PROBLEM

There are wide racial disparities in loan denial rates. Fair lending advocates claim that these disparities arise from inadequate enforcement of the anti-discrimination laws and from overall discrimination by lenders and GSEs. Lenders and secondary market institutions such as Freddie Mac and Fannie Mae contend that their efforts to expand opportunities for low-income and minority families are affected by poor access to credit for many minority families. These same institutions have implemented new credit screening devices, however, that could arguably increase the adverse impacts of poor credit availability for low-income and minority families. Fair lending advocates such as ACORN expressed alarm about the new technological advances in mortgage lending and contended that the introduction of new credit scoring devices and other automated underwriting techniques had adverse impacts on minority borrowers. Extensive media accounts of these allegations, as well as the filing of lawsuits against specific lenders or GSEs to whom lenders sell their loans, could have deterrent effects on discrimination, as much as direct government enforcement efforts are expected to have deterrent effects on mortgage discrimination. Are these private enforcement efforts and the implied threats effective in reducing discrimination? Do threats to enforcement with widespread media exposure have deterrent effects?

THE HOMEOWNERSHIP CONTEXT

There is an historic underrepresentation of minority households among American homeowners. Only 18.7 percent of African American households owned their own homes in 1890. Among whites, 53 percent of households owned their own homes. In 1890, the ratio of black-to-white homeownership was .35. The white homeownership rate dropped after 1890 falling to 45 percent in 1940. The black homeownership rate increased steadily rising to 50 percent in 1940. Thus, the racial gap in homeownership narrowed considerably from .35 to .50 over the first half of the twentieth century. By 1950, the racial gap had narrowed even further, with the ratio of black-to-white homeownership rates reaching .60. After World War II, however, the racial gap in homeownership rates barely changed. In 1985, for example, the ratio of black-to-white homeownership rates was .64, and in 2000, the ratio of black-to-white homeownership rates was still .64. Even though black homeownership rates hit all time highs (registering 47.6 percent in 2000, based on Current Population Survey estimates), black homeownership rates in 2000 were lower than white homeownership rates were in 1890.

There are substantial gaps in homeownership between Hispanics and whites, as well. In 1985, the ratio of Hispanic-to-non-Hispanic white homeownership rates was .60, lower than the black-white ratio in that year. In 1990, the ratio of Hispanic-to-non-Hispanic white homeownership rates was .59. After dipping in the recession years of the early 1990s, the ratio rose steadily to .63 in 2000. Thus, over a decade and a half, the gap had narrowed only slightly. In 2000, Hispanic homeownership rates were 46.3 percent. Hispanic homeownership rates were lower at the start of this century than white homeownership rates were at the beginning of the previous century: in 1900, white homeownership rates were 48.3 percent.

THE FAIR LENDING CONTEXT

Mortgage lending is the primary source of funding for homeownership. Thus, one of the usual suspects in analysis of racial disparities in homeownership is racial disparities in access to credit. The Equal Credit Opportunity Act prohibits discrimination in various types of lending, including mortgage lending, and the enforcement of this Act is one of the primary tools for reducing disparities in credit access.

Public Perceptions and Media Accounts
of Lender Fair Lending Activities

In 1992, the Boston Federal Reserve published a pioneering study "Mortgage Lending in Boston: Interpreting HMDA Data" that established the existence of racial discrimination in mortgage lending (Munnell et al. 1992, 1996). Initially, the study received widespread media exposure, supporting the view that the wide disparity in loan rejection rates was attributable to unequal treatment of equally qualified loan applicants. The Boston study, unlike any before it, controlled meticulously for virtually every conceivable alternative explanation for why blacks (and Hispanics) might be more likely to be denied loans. The study focused explicitly on various measures of credit worthiness and likelihood of default. The conclusion was inescapable: even after controlling for credit risk, blacks and Hispanics were more likely to be denied loans than equally qualified whites.

The Boston study, however, caused considerable consternation among Boston area lenders and underwriters, national banking regulators, and the Federal Reserve Board's research staff. Soon after it was published, there was an avalanche of denunciations. These groups had hoped that the Federal Reserve study would "convincingly demonstrate that race was not a determining factor in loan decisions" (Goering and Wienk 1996, 15). The study found, however, that "race was indeed a fairly powerful influence in lending decisions" (Goering and Wienk 1996, 15), and it confirmed earlier data that "revealed that the rejection rates for African Americans were twice as high as those for whites—rates comparable to those found over twenty years earlier (Listokin and Casey 1980, 58) and virtually identical to the disparities found in 1994 HMDA data" (Goering and Wienk 1996, 13).

This finding was opposite of what the lending industry had been preaching. A cottage industry of sorts evolved, mainly financed by the American Bankers Association and various lender and mortgage lending associations, to discredit the Boston Federal Reserve's findings.

Criticisms of the Boston Federal Reserve study continued to abound, most of which centered on the question of whether the Boston Federal Reserve adequately controlled for all measures of credit risk. An illustration of such criticism came from work on student loans. Boyd (1997) contended that blacks had a higher rate of default than whites in the Stafford Loan Programs. He found that blacks are more likely to be studying for degrees that yield lower incomes; they are less likely to graduate; and ultimately, they are less likely to be able to repay their student loans. The dominant cost of the high default rates on these loans is the higher risk that blacks impose on lenders when they apply for future loans. In a nutshell, this view contended, blacks are not discriminated against in the mortgage market. Instead, the race of the loan applicant captures prior defaults. The problem then is risk, not race, in this view.

Another conventional explanation for why there is no discrimination against blacks in the loan market, despite the showing of wide racial gaps in lending, was that blacks are more likely to default on Federal Housing Authority (FHA) loans. This finding, stemming from work of Berkovec, Canner, Gabriel, and Hannan (1994), contended that if there were discrimination against blacks, only the very best risks would be allowed access to loans. Thus, only the very best risks among blacks would be observed in default and thereby their default rates should be lower than average. Since their default rates are higher than average, so this reasoning went, blacks are not being discriminated against. The higher loan denial rate is justified by the higher risk of default. Blacks, bankers contend, are simply worse risks.

Still, strong counter findings supported the original results of the Boston Federal Reserve. One careful and detailed replication of the Federal Reserve analysis found "an African American is still more than twice as likely as a white to have his home mortgage loan application rejected" (Carr and Megbolugbe 1993). Another more exhaustive evaluation concluded: "Compared to their white counterparts, African American and Hispanic home seekers are shown far fewer houses and apartments (and indeed sometimes excluded from available housing altogether), given far less assistance in finding the house or apartment that best fits their needs, and in finding a mortgage, and are steered to neighborhoods with minority concentrations or low house values" (Yinger 1995, 5).

In other words, even in the face of skepticism about the Boston Federal Reserve study, there were those who believed that discrimination plays a significant role in determining loan outcomes for blacks. This view, however, was prevalent neither among social scientists nor economists. The conventional wisdom continued to be that blacks have worse credit than whites.

One survey, designed to determine the underlying causes of poor credit conducted on behalf of Freddie Mac, the Freddie Mac Consumer Credit Survey (CCS), showed that "having a poor credit record is a relatively common problem in today's society," and "credit problems persist across income groups." (Freddie Mac 1999) Still, the study concludes, "minority borrowers are more likely than white borrowers to experience credit problems" (Freddie Mac 1999). Forty-eight percent of African Americans were deemed to have bad credit, while only 27 percent of whites were. Table 7.1, produced from the Freddie Mac press release, shows these results.

Blacks and Hispanics are more likely to have bad credit; they are less likely to have good credit; and they are more likely to have indeterminate credit than are whites, according to Freddie Mac's press release. While the majority of whites and Hispanics have good credit, the release contended that the majority of blacks are likely to have indeterminate or bad credit.

This conclusion caused outrage among members of Congress and journalists. Two quotations from the *Washington Post* reflect this response:

> A Freddie Mac study concluding that far more black people have bad credit than white people, even when both have the same incomes, has come under attack in Congress, and some experts have questioned whether it oversimplifies a complex issue. (Cohn 1999, B1)

> I strongly reject Freddie Mac's assertion that the reason African Americans own fewer homes than whites is that they have "bad credit." (Waters 1999)

This type of negative publicity can have adverse impacts on the stock market prices of GSEs' traded stock. It can have effects on management. It can effect decisions to improve fair lending activities. Although not directly tied to official government enforcement efforts, it arguably can work as a deterrent to discrimination, just as public enforcement effort is expected to be a deterrent to discrimination.

We can make an analogy here to allegations of racial profiling in police departments. Some departments are known to have reduced minority traffic stops once major newspaper reports claimed that these departments were

Table 7.1   Freddie Mac Press Release on Credit Ratings by Race

Credit Record	White (%)	Black (%)	Hispanic(%)	Chapter 8 Combined (%)
Bad	27	48	34	30
Indeterminate	12	16	15	13
Good	61	36	51	57

Source: Freddie Mac News Release [On-line]. September 2, 1999.

discriminating.[2] This type of media-induced deterrent effect is the impetus for the current analysis.

Of course, there are public enforcement efforts as well. The Equal Credit Opportunity Act (ECOA) prohibits lenders from discrimination in credit transactions on the basis of race, color, national origin, religion, sex, and other specified grounds.[3] This Act was passed in 1974 as an amendment to the much broader Consumer Credit Protection Act, passed in 1968.[4] The ECOA is broader than the Fair Housing Act (FHA) since the ECOA covers virtually all lenders, while the FHA covers only real estate-related lending. Housing lenders are subject to both statutes.

The ECOA stipulates that any creditor is subject to one of three enforcement actions (Walter 1995). First, the enforcement agencies may take action in response to complaints. Second, individuals or the Department of Justice may bring civil court actions. Third, the banking agencies periodically examine every bank for evidence of discrimination. The agencies take remedial or punitive action if evidence of discrimination is found.

Federal efforts to ensure compliance with fair lending laws have not always been energetic. Prior to the DOJ's first major fair lending investigation in 1989 of Decatur Federal Savings and Loan, federal efforts to deter, detect, and punish instances of mortgage discrimination were quite limited.[5] However, in 1988 and 1989, Congress amended FHA and HMDA, respectively, to both expand the scope and breadth of the laws and to strengthen FHA's enforcement provisions. The DOJ also began an intensive fair lending enforcement campaign. Other federal agencies with oversight responsibilities in fair lending enforcement began, at about the same time, to respond to the increasing calls for accelerated fair lending enforcement efforts (GAO report 1996). But, partly because of the less than energetic fair lending enforcement by public institutions, private advocacy organizations embraced media approaches to expand the calls for enforcement actions. Examples include the publication by the National Community Reinvestment Council's "Best and Worst Lender" guide and ACORN press releases on HMDA disparities.

This chapter reports results that show that public and private deterrent effects are nontrivial, rendering this type of race-neutral remedy relatively effective. We identified all home mortgage loans in 1994 and 2000 in the fifty largest MSAs in the United States. We collected information on allegations of mortgage discrimination from newspapers in these fifty largest MSAs as well as HUD enforcement information from its ten regional offices linked to the fifty MSAs. We then measured whether public or private enforcement efforts influence lender's behavior and thereby reduce racial disparities in loan denials.

THEORETICAL BACKGROUND

Theorists commonly distinguish between two types of deterrence: general deterrence and what has been variously called special (Antunes and Hunt 1973), specific (Tittle and Logan 1973), primary (Bankston and Cramer 1974) or individual (Walker 1965) deterrence. The threat, which aims toward general deterrence, typically accompanies a legal order commanding a group of unnamed individuals not to engage in a particular activity. The threat often specifies the punishment that might be applied if members of the groups are caught violating the command. To the extent that members of the group eschew the forbidden activity from fear of punishment, there is a general deterrent effect (Lempert 1982, 514). Deterrence is not the only process by which a legal command, including the portion that threatens, may order behavior. At least in theory, a law can affect behavior directly through its moral-educative effects (Bowers and Salem 1972; Silverman 1976) and, indirectly, through its general effects on community solidarity (Erickson 1966). Empirically, it is difficult to separate deterrent effects from associated processes of legal ordering (Gibbs 1975).

One can distinguish among three types of enforcement that might exhibit deterrent effects in mortgage credit markets: actual enforcement activities, threats of enforcement, and lender beliefs of enforcement. Actual enforcement includes government reviews of lenders, filing of suits against lenders, fines, penalties, and administrative proceedings.

In the area of ECOA enforcement and fair lending, focus must also be placed on threats. Unlike criminal law where arrests and prosecution dominate as the form of deterrence, in fair lending—for better, or for worse—few lenders are ever "arrested" or prosecuted for alleged racial discrimination. Rather, a dominant form of action is a threat. A threat is understood in this context to be any public or private action designed to convey to a lender that there may be enforcement action taken against it. Threats include letters sent saying, "If you do not cease and desist from engaging in these actions, we will be forced to file suit." Threats also can derive from activities of advocacy groups and local legal aid societies, for example, "if you fail to improve your minority lending, we will bring charges against you."

Plaintiffs include actual loan applicants as well as representatives of a class of applicants.

Beliefs are centered on the lender's assessment of likelihood of enforcement. If there is a threat from a plaintiff, the lender forms opinions about the credibility of the threat. Lender beliefs about enforcement may depend on threats but also on prior enforcement activities. One can hypothesize two different impacts of prior enforcement activities. When there has been little or no enforcement, some lenders may assume that the current administration does not place a high priority on fair lending or ECOA enforcement. Thus, the lender believes that the probability of being punished is low. Alternatively, lenders may assume that there is always a risk of being challenged for their fair lending activities and, after a long period with no investigative action or public or private challenge, perceive that their chances of being challenged may increase. Their beliefs or perceptions about the risk of enforcement action may also be influenced by media disclosures about disparate impacts of technological innovations, such as desktop underwriting and automated credit scoring procedures. While lenders themselves may not intentionally discriminate by adopting new technologies that putatively have disparate impacts on racial minority group members, their attorneys nonetheless may express caution. This type of belief about enforcement efforts may be just as powerful as actual enforcement or threats of enforcement.

Of course, it is not possible to directly observe lenders' beliefs or perceptions about enforcement. However, media accounts of allegations of lender discrimination and threats from advocacy groups, both of which affect the unobserved lender variable are assumed to affect beliefs about enforcement. Since public knowledge of fair lending is minimal, media accounts of allegations about discrimination should be a good measure of public threats to lenders.[6]

We also know the actual enforcement efforts of HUD. The actual enforcement is measured at the MSA level. The lender's decision to reject a particular loan is a function of the characteristics of the borrower, characteristics of the loan, characteristics of the neighborhood, characteristics of the lender, and the race of the borrower, and two possible deterrent variables: HUD enforcement and media exposure of alleged discrimination. The key hypothesis is that controlling for deterrence variables, measured discrimination ought to decline.

Note that some of the loan or borrow characteristics are known to the lender but unknown to the data analyst. Such factors as the credit score, or the terms of the loan, are normally not included in public data sets, and, thus, the coefficient on R is not an unchallenged measure of discrimination. It is a better measure, however, than the simple disparity in loan denial rates.

Nonetheless, the analyst might collect information for each market about the level and intensity of media exposure to allegations of racial discrimination in lending or HUD enforcement efforts. Such allegations could be in the form of specific filings of lawsuits, settlement of cases, or related official acts. Or, they may take the form of broad and unspecified charges. A search of newspaper databases permits one to codify the occurrence of different types of threats and allegations by public and private parties. Alternatively, the enforcement efforts might be measured by numbers of filings alleging discrimination relative to loan applications, or actual findings of discrimination by HUD investigators.[7]

The model developed for the descriptors above is estimated using data from individual LARS assembled for given years for individual lenders. The information on media accounts and HUD enforcement efforts comes from MSA and regional office locations. Conventional maximum likelihood estimators of the coefficients in a logistic model of the loan denial equations will fail to account for the location-specific homogeneity of enforcement efforts and media accounts. Therefore, fixed effects estimators are used to obtain the coefficients and their associated standard errors.

We use HMDA data merged with the Cleveland Federal Reserve's lender files for 1993 to 2004. For each lender and each MSA, we merged data from a Lexis/Nexis search of local newspapers in the top fifty MSAs. The largest two daily newspapers were selected for review and all articles citing discrimination or allegations of discrimination in mortgage lending were photocopied, read, and coded. The conventional method for analyzing the presence of deterrence in news media is content analysis where the key search terms are *racial discrimination, mortgage lending,* and *allegation.* This study analyzed a sample of 280 news articles in 77 news publications across 15 categories. Next, we detail the procedures.[8]

Our data included a total of fifty-seven independent variables; however, only nine action-specific variables are selected for analysis. Private enforcement using adverse publicity is measured by the percentage of articles that identified a threat action or allegation. The variables selected for analysis are as follows:

Action-specific:

a. Class action lawsuit (dichotomous variable)
b. Threat (dichotomous variable)
c. Type of threat (categorical variable)
d. Allegation (dichotomous variable)
e. Type of allegation (categorical variable)
f. Reason for alleged disparate or differential treatment (dichotomous variable)

g. Source for alleged disparate or differential treatment (categorical variable)
h. Alleged treatment (dichotomous variable)
i. Alleged type of treatment (categorical variable)

RESULTS

Our initial search strategy produced a total of 281 news articles. After eliminating articles that did not meet the search criteria, the sample size for the media accounts was 175. Six percent of the news articles identified a threat action toward a lending institution by an individual or group. Over half of the articles retrieved included an allegation against a lending institution made by an individual or group. Out of these articles, 26 percent alleged racial discrimination on the part of the lending institution. Twenty-seven (15.4 percent) articles referred to class action lawsuits against lending institutions. Seventy-one percent of the articles cited either disparate or differential treatment experienced by minority loan applicants. Of those, a majority of articles cited either denial of their mortgage loan or received a higher interest rate by lending institutions. Alleged mistreatment by lending institutions made up 57.5 percent of the articles. When decomposed, 43 percent of the articles pointed to differential treatment.

The central questions we explore in this analysis are as follows:

1. Does a HUD enforcement effort reduce loan denial rates for protected group members?
2. Does media exposure reduce loan denial rates for protected group members?
3. Are there differential effects of HUD enforcement efforts over media exposure?
4. Do HUD enforcement and/or media exposure reduce discrimination against protected group members?

But, deterring discrimination might also come at the expense of increasing lender exposure to high credit risks. Lenders faced with threats of lawsuits based on allegations of discrimination might increase loan approval rates for protected groups without necessarily reducing market discrimination. In our model, this would occur when there is a reduction in loan denial rates for specific racial groups as a result of enforcement efforts or media exposure without a corresponding reduction in the adverse impacts of race on loan denial or a reduction in discrimination due to enforcement of media exposure.

Thus, we also ask in the analysis below whether there are adverse impacts of enforcement efforts.

Figure 7.1 shows the basic patterns of percentage racial gaps in loan denial rates over the decade. In 1994, when white, black, Hispanic, and other loan denial rates were 10.19, 18.35, 16.29, and 13.24 percent respectively, the black-white gap was 80.08 percent, the Hispanic-white gap was 59.89 percent, and the other-white gap was 29.93 percent. These percentage gaps narrowed throughout the mid-1990s reaching a low for other-white of −10.33 percent in 1998, when the loan denial rates for Asian Americans and American Indians were lower than the loan denial rates for whites. The black-white gap hovered around 60 percent during the late 1990s and then widened considerably to the point where the black loan denial rates were more than twice that of the white loan denial rates. The Hispanic-white gap and the other-white gap also increased steadily during the early 2000s, reaching proportions that exceeded anything seen during the previous decade. By 2003, when the loan denial rates for whites, blacks, Hispanics, and others were 8.36, 18.11, 15.55, and 11.74 percent, percentage gaps between the nonwhite groups and whites soared to 116.64, 86.04, and 40.48 percent. The widening gap by 2003 over 1994 clearly came about because of falling white loan denial rates and not rising nonwhite loan denial rates.

Table 7.2 collects the estimated coefficients on the interaction terms between race and media exposure and HUD enforcement. There are two different media account measures and four HUD enforcement measures so we estimate a total of twelve regressions that include one or both media

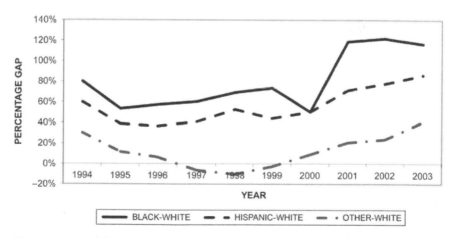

Figure 7.1   Racial gaps in loan denial rates, 1994–2003. Authors' computations based on Freddie Mac News Release [On-line]. September 2, 1999.

Table 7.2   Estimation of Deterrent Impacts of Media Exposure and HUD Enforcement, Micro Analysis

	Media Exposure (%)	Enforcement Efforts (%)
Blacks		
1994	22.22	16.67
1995	0.00	25.00
1996	22.22	25.00
1997	44.44	41.67
1998	100.00	66.67
1999	77.78	33.33
2000	0.00	33.33
2001	55.56	33.33
2002	0.00	8.33
2003	55.56	25.00
All Years	**37.78**	**30.83**
Hispanics		
1994	0.00	25.00
1995	11.11	25.00
1996	22.22	41.67
1997	11.11	41.67
1998	44.44	25.00
1999	55.56	25.00
2000	0.00	33.33
2001	0.00	50.00
2002	0.00	0.00
2003	0.00	0.00
All Years	**14.44**	**26.67**

Source: Authors' computations from the annual Federal Reserve HMDA Loan Application Register files (FR HMDA-LAR).
The bold is the average percentage for all years in the list above.

accounts and HUD enforcement measures. A thirteenth equation provides the coefficients on Hispanic and black when interaction terms are not included.

There are nine different ways that media account interactions with race can enter into the equations. There are twelve different ways that HUD enforcement interactions can enter into the equations. Thus, there are 90 different race-media account interactions and 120 different race-HUD enforcement interactions that can be observed over the ten-year period under analysis. We compute for each year the percentage of coefficients on the interaction terms in the underlying equations that are negative and statistically significant. A negative and statistically significant coefficient on the race-media account or race-HUD enforcement variables indicates that there is a deterrent effect from exposure to the media of HUD enforcement. The negative coefficient signals that discrimination against blacks or Hispanics falls when these deterrents take place. Or put differently, the overall impact of race on loan denials is lessened as a result of media exposure regarding lending disparities and/or HUD enforcement activities. Larger numbers of statistically significant coefficients on the race-deterrent interaction terms suggest that the impacts are robust across different model specifications and different measures of deterrence. A finding that almost all of the coefficients in a given year are negative and statistically significant suggests that at least for that year the impacts are robust.

Table 7.2 is convenient for illustrating two important conclusions revealed in the detailed regressions. First, there are year-to-year differences in the deterrent effectiveness of HUD enforcement activities and of media exposure. The years with the most robust impacts of media exposure on reducing lender discrimination are 1998 and 1999 when 100 percent and 77 percent of the media accounts of interactions with race are negative and statistically significant for blacks, and 44 and 55 percent are negative and significant for Hispanics. The peak year for the effectiveness of HUD enforcement efforts appears to be 1998 for blacks and 1997 for Hispanics.

A second central conclusion is that media accounts more consistently produce reduced discrimination for blacks than for Hispanics. Collecting the statistically significant and negative coefficients over the entire ten-year span reveals that for blacks media account interactions with race are statistically significant and negative in 37 percent of the specifications whereas they are only negative and statistically significant in 14 percent of the specifications for Hispanics. The estimates of the media account deterrent impacts are slightly more robust among blacks than the estimates of the HUD enforcement efforts. Whereas 37 percent of the coefficients on the media account interactions are negative and significant, only 30 percent of the coefficients on the HUD enforcement interactions are negative and significant among blacks. Among Hispanics, the HUD enforcement efforts are more robust than the media accounts effects.

We have also estimated impacts of the enforcement efforts and media accounts on loan denials in the pooled 1994–2003 MSA data. The results are summarized in Table 7.3. The effects are estimated separately by race/ethnicity. There are no unintended impacts of enforcement efforts or media exposure of allegations of discrimination on the loan denial rates of blacks, whites, or Hispanics. We do find that there are statistically significant declines in the loan denial rates of others as a result of media exposure of lending discrimination. We find in contrast that higher numbers of HUD allegations in an MSA relative to loan applications increase loan rejection rates for others. The combined impacts of HUD enforcement and media accounts are generally significant for others.

Table 7.3   Summary Table: Pooled MSAs 1994–2003, Significant Negative Impacts at 5 Percent Level

		Whites	*Blacks*	*Hispanics*	*Others*
Media *Exposure*					
Media 1	Any allegation of racial discrimination in lending, flipping, loan steering, or redlining	No	No	No	Yes
Media 2	Specific discrimination allegation against a named lender	No	No	No	Yes

HUD
  Enforcement
  Efforts					

Enforcement 1	Probability of any type of closing or no finding	No	No	No	No
Enforcement 2	Probability of a finding of discrimination, consent order or settlement	No	No	No	No
Enforcement 3	Probability of finding of discrimination, no closing	No	No	No	No
Enforcement 4	Number of complaints/ Number of loan applications in MSA	No	No	No	Yes
Combined					
	Eight Different Pairs	No	No	No	Yes

Source: Authors' computations from the annual Federal Reserve HMDA Loan Application Register files (FR HMDA-LAR).

Thus, with the exception of Asian Americans and American Indians, there are no unintended impacts of media exposure or HUD enforcement efforts on loan outcomes. The finding that there are unintended impacts on other races (Asian Americans and American Indians) merits further exploration and analysis.

CAVEATS AND LIMITATIONS

The Home Mortgage Disclosure Act of 1975 (HMDA) was designed by Congress to focus on mortgage lending so that the public and regulators could better determine whether or not individuals or specific neighborhoods were being unfairly denied access to mortgage loans. When the HMDA micro-data was first released in 1991, reports showed a remarkable disparity in the loan denial rates among racial and ethnic groups.[9] Ross and Yinger (2003) point out that findings of discrimination using HMDA data can be challenged on many grounds. We describe some of the challenges below.

Omitted Variables

HMDA data do not include information on credit histories, debt burdens, loan-to-value ratios (LTV), and other factors considered in making mortgage decisions. Some argue that the Boston Fed study, which attempts to address this limitation of the HMDA data, still omits key explanatory variables (Day and Liebowitz 1996; Horne 1994; Liebowitz 1993; Zandi 1993; Zycher and Wolfe 1994). For example, Day and Liebowitz (1996) and Carr and Megobolugbe (1993) included "unable to verify" and "meets guidelines" in the loan denial equations. The inclusion lowered the minority status coefficient by 27 percent and 15 percent respectively. The coefficient of one variable (minority status) will be biased if the estimating equation omits variables that are correlated with that variable, and that help explain the dependent variable (loan denial). If these omitted variables have a positive impact on loan denial, and are positively correlated with minority status, then their omission will bias upward the coefficient of the minority status variable, or lead to an overstatement of discrimination (Ross and Yinger 2003, 108).

There also exist defenders of the Boston Fed Study (Browne and Tootell 1995; Carr and Megobolugbe 1993; Glennon and Stengel 1994; Ross and Yinger 2003). Carr and Megobolugbe (1993) recommend not using "meets guidelines" and "unable to verify" variables, especially "meets guidelines." These two variables were not recorded in the original loan files. They involve the after-the-fact judgment of the individual completing the HMDA data forms. "Meets guidelines" was answered roughly one year after the loan approval decision. Some unsuccessful applications were coded as not meeting credit history guidelines even though those applicants had no credit problems. Ross and Yinger (2003, 111) argue that the "Boston Fed study's equations contain a remarkably complete set of explanatory variables, and most claims concerning omitted-variable bias are implausible or have been shown to be incorrect."

The "unable to verify" and "meets guidelines" may be endogenous and their inclusion as exogenous variables in the underwriting model may lead to biased results. But no consensus has yet emerged on the magnitude of the impact that these variables have on the minority status coefficient, or on the appropriate way to treat these two variables in a loan denial equation.

SUMMARY AND CONCLUSION

In this chapter, we provide estimates of the impacts of public and private enforcement efforts on measured discrimination in home mortgage lending. Using data on media accounts of allegations of discrimination (which we argue serve as a proxy for perceptions that lenders will be sued or at least serve as a threat not to discriminate) and data on actual HUD enforcement efforts, we find that lenders discriminate less when there are threats or perceptions of adverse outcomes to lenders. However, we do not find a similar pattern with respect to Hispanics. This may be a reflection of the higher visibility of African Americans in many of the large media areas, or it may be a result of lender insensitivity or lack of responsiveness to media accounts when making loan decisions relating to Hispanics.

We also find that the deterrent effectiveness of media exposure is slightly more robust than the deterrent effectiveness of actual HUD enforcement efforts. Accordingly, policies designed to increase the media awareness of actual HUD enforcement efforts are likely to enhance the overall effectiveness of HUD efforts.

We test for the possibility that there are unintended impacts of enforcement efforts, whereby increased enforcement leads to increased exposure to lender risk (through lower loan denial rates to protected groups unaccompanied by reductions in discrimination). We do not uncover such unintended impacts and conclude that increased enforcement efforts achieve precisely the intended impact: reductions in discrimination.

NOTES

1. This chapter is based on the report, "Final Report: The Deterrent Effects of Media Accounts and HUD Enforcement on Racial Disparities in Loan Denial Rate." supported by the US Department of Housing and Urban Development. Able research assistance was provided by Stephannie Lewis, Andrew Tehmeh, and Bosu Seo. The source data used for this study was collected between 1993 and 2004, prior to the Great Recession.

2. See Myers, Samuel L., Jr., "Analysis of Racial Profiling as Policy Analysis," Curriculum and Case Notes, *Journal of Policy Analysis and Management* Vol. 21, No 2, Spring, 287–300, 2002.

3. ECOA and Fair Housing Act, enacted in 1974 and 1968, respectively, comprise the federal civil statutes applicable to extensions of credit by banks and other lending institutions. These "fair lending laws" prohibit discrimination in all forms of credit transactions, including consumer and business loans as well as mortgage loans. To support the enforcement of the fair housing laws, the Home Mortgage Disclosure

Act (HMDA) provides for disclosure, to the regulatory agencies and the public, of information about mortgage loan applicants and borrowers (GAO report 1996; U.S. Commission on Civil Rights 1994).

4. For more detail for historical change, see Board of Governors, Consumer Compliance Handbook (1995).

5. It should be noted that the impetus of the Decatur investigation was a series of articles in the *Atlanta Constitution*.

6. For more on lack of knowledge in the public about fair housing laws, see Abravanel, Martin D., "Public Knowledge of Fair Housing Laws: Does it protect against housing discrimination?" *Housing Policy Debate* Vol. 13, No 3, 2002.

7. The key question we can answer by estimating this equation is whether the coefficients on R decline as a result of accounting for the impacts of private enforcement efforts. Therefore, we compute

$$\frac{\partial^2 \Pr(denial)}{\partial R \partial Z} = p(1-p)\pi$$

The interpretation of the cross-partial derivative is that the value will be less than zero when public or private enforcement efforts reduce discrimination. Or, put differently, if media accounts of discrimination or HUD enforcement efforts have a deterrent effect on lender behavior, one would expect the marginal effects of race on lender decisions to be smaller in those locations with higher levels of public or private enforcement efforts.

8. Search methodology

Examining the effects of media exposure on the lending industry as a whole would yield a smaller sample size, given that few news reports of mortgage discrimination reach national attention. Moreover, news reports that receive national attention are disproportionately published by news publications with national coverage such as the *New York Times* and the *Washington Post*. To reduce selection bias, we selected the nation's fifty largest metropolitan statistical areas (MSAs) in which to examine the level and intensity of media exposure on lender behavior.

We then selected two major news publications within each MSA for analysis. We defined a news publication as "major" if its daily edition had the highest annual revenue and circulation when compared to other news publications within the same MSA for the year 2003. This information was gathered by utilizing the online business and industry tool, Hoover's online. As a result of our search, we drew seventy-seven major news publications for the fifty MSAs.

We conducted a guided news search using LexisNexis (our primary media index) for each selected newspaper from 1994 to 2003. In conducting our search in LexisNexis, we selected "US News" as a search category. We then selected news sources based on the geographic location of the publication and the news publication itself. Racial discrimination, mortgage lending, and allegation were the search terms to retrieve articles for content analysis.

9. The history and developments of HMDA data are in chapter 1 in Ross and Yinger (2003).*Chapter 7*

Chapter 8

Compliance as a Race-Neutral Strategy

The Case of Reverse Discrimination Litigation

Surprisingly little is known about how state agencies that receive federal funds allocate these funds to racial and ethnic minority group members when complying with federal rules and mandates.[1] One federal mandate, promulgated during the Clinton administration, requires that recipients of federal transportation funding set goals for allocating funds to women, minority, and disadvantaged business enterprises (DBEs). More than $7 billion dollars was distributed to DBEs through the US Department of Transportation funding in 2009 and 2010 alone. The programs designed to set and implement DBE goals, however, have been challenged by white-male-owned business enterprises alleging that these forms of targeted support for women and minorities amount to reverse discrimination.

This chapter examines whether reverse discrimination litigation reduces compliance with the federal mandates through lower DBE goal settings. Reverse discrimination claims pose a significant implementation challenge to state and local decision makers. On the one hand, agencies may lose federal funds by failing to comply with rules that require them to make efforts to distribute funds equitably to women- and minority-owned business enterprises. On the other hand, litigation, or the threat of litigation, may cause rational actors to limit their affirmative action programs. Deterrence theory is the basis for the prediction that greater litigation will reduce goal-setting efforts. Alternative theories, such as prospect theory, predict the opposite. Thus, the chapter also provides a basis for the testing of deterrence theory and its application to federal rule compliance.

The chapter is organized as follows. First, we reiterate background information on public procurement and contracting and the federal rule mandating DBE goals. Then, we discuss the competing theoretical foundations for the model we estimate, stating that the DBE goal is a function of reverse discrimination litigation. Next, we detail the data used for the model estimation. Finally, we provide an assessment and interpretation of the results relevant to the larger debate about compliance with federal rules.

BACKGROUND

Billions of dollars are awarded each year by the federal government to state departments of transportation, which use these funds to contract with private construction companies, and to procure such professional services as architectural design, surveying, engineering, and technical support. The contracts range from the construction and repair of bridges, highways and tunnels, to the design of information accounting and report systems. In fiscal year (FY) 2012, for instance, the US Department of Transportation's (DOT) Federal Highway Administration (FHWA), Federal Transit Administration (FTA), and Federal Aviation Administration (FAA) requested, respectively, $70.5 billion, $22.35 billion, and $18.66 billion to fund construction and professional services for all states.[2] These requests increased annually. The three agencies' requests in FY 2012 were approximately 70 percent, 84 percent, and 20 percent higher than FY 2010. The sheer magnitude of these requests contrasts with other non-defense spending was in decline during the same period.

White males historically have dominated the ownership of private construction industries. The use of public funds for construction projects passively contributes to historic disparities arising in the private market place (Echautegui et al. 1997). As a result, the US DOT has mandated programs and policies to remedy historic or ongoing disparities in the award of contract dollars to women- and minority-owned business enterprises. One of the most visible and perhaps most controversial areas of federal mandates involves the requirement that recipients of FTA, FHWA, and FAA funding institute percentage goals specifically for DBEs. These goals are designed to create a level playing field for minority-owned and women-owned businesses in DOT-assisted public procurement and contracting. The Code of Federal Regulations Title 49 Part 26, "Participation by Disadvantaged Business Enterprises in Department of Transportation Financial Assistance Programs," requires that recipients of US DOT funding establish realistic DBE goals annually and report them to the US DOT for review and approval.

Early affirmative action efforts in federal procurement and contracting date back to 1969, when the Small Business Administration created a special 8(a) program to provide historically disadvantaged firms with opportunities to participate in federal contracts, and to facilitate capacity-building and successful graduation of such firms from the program once self-sufficiency had been developed (Leiter and Leiter 2002).

Congress enacted Public Law 95–507, as an amendment to the Small Business Act and Small Business Investment Act of 1958, which authorized minority set-asides and required all federal agencies to submit annual percentage goals for minority business utilization. Defense contractors, for example, were required to achieve at least 5 percent minority business participation within three years, according to the National Defense Authorization Act. The Public Works Employment Act required that 10 percent of federal construction grants be reserved for minority-owned enterprises. The Federal Acquisition Streamlining Act encouraged federal agencies to promote race-conscious procurement activities (Colamery 1998).

The US Supreme Court decisions in *Croson v. City of Richmond* (1989) and *Adarand Constructors v. Pena* (1995) found that race-conscious set-asides in government procurement and contracting are generally suspect and must meet a strict-scrutiny test, the most stringent level of judicial review. The Clinton administration, maintaining that "affirmative action in federal procurement is necessary, and that the federal government has a compelling interest to act on that basis in the award of federal contracts,"[3] sought to find a middle ground in an effort to salvage such programs. The solution sought was to require that goals established to assist DBEs be narrowly tailored, flexible, not overinclusive, and must minimize the burden placed on other firms. The US Department of Justice issued further guidance on applying the *Adarand* decision to government procurement and contracting programs. In the case of DOT contracts, Federal Rule 49 CFR Part 26 requires recipients to set DBE goals based on the availability of willing, able, and qualified women- and minority-owned firms and to meet the maximum feasible portion of any specified DBE goal through race-neutral means.[4]

In *City of Richmond v. Croson* (1989), Justice O'Connor commented that "where there is a significant statistical disparity between the number of qualified minority contractors willing and able to perform a particular service and the number of such contractors actually engaged by the locality or the locality's prime contractors, an inference of discriminatory exclusion could arise."[5] Federal, state, and local agencies will have to be able to demonstrate a compelling interest to justify the installation of a narrowly tailored program that uses not rigid quota schemes, but statistical evidence and scientific disparity studies to reflect an actual need for minority business participation in the government-assisted contracting process (Halligan 1991; La Noue 1993; Rice 1993).

Some state transportation agencies, consequently, have sought support for data collection and analyses (Rice 1992), whereas others have failed to conduct the adequate and systematic research required to meet the mandate. The Transportation Research Board of the National Academies reports that there are wide variations in how states meet their *Croson* requirement of establishing a compelling interest for their race-conscious procurement and contracting programs.[6] Relatively little is known about the degree to which state agencies comply with 49 CFR Part 26 in general. Some jurisdictions attempted to comply with the rule, but fearing litigation, responded by eliminating their race-conscious DBE goals and replaced them with race-neutral goals (Myers and Ha 2009). The question we examine in this chapter is whether threats of litigation systematically affect goal setting itself.

DETERRENCE AND COMPLIANCE

The area of public procurement and contracting remains largely understudied in applied economics and policy analysis. One body of existing literature examines historic reasons that justify the use of race-based contracting policies by government agencies. Transformations of urban economic structures (Bates 1984) and persistent racial disparities in financial markets (Blanchflower, Levine, and Zimmerman 2003; Boston 1999; Cavalluzzo and Cavalluzzo 1998; Fairlie and Meyer 2000; Fairlie and Robb 2008; Munnell et al. 1996) make it all the more important for public sector contracting programs to create a level playing field for minority firms (Feagin and Imani 1994). Another group of studies mainly investigate the effectiveness and policy impacts of affirmative action programs in government contracting (Bates 1981; Black 1983; Echautegui et al. 1997; La Noue 1994, 2008; Myers and Chan 1996; Rice 1991). Some case studies of DBE programs in the post-*Croson* era, for example, suggest that such narrowly tailoring adjustments may have led to reduced shares of contracting dollars awarded to minority businesses (Bates 2009; Davila, Ha, and Myers 2012).

Deterrence theory predicts that benefits and costs of rule compliance or noncompliance vary with the certainty and severity of punishment as well as measures of the consequences of compliance. An individual or organization will choose to comply with laws and regulations when the expected benefits of compliance are perceived to exceed the related costs (Becker 1968; Braithwaite and Makkai 1991; Ehrlich 1972; May 2005; Tittle and Logan 1973). This theoretical framework has been used in studies of federal rules and regulations (Braithwaite 1985; Hutter 1997; Langbein and Kerwin 1985; Scholz and Gray 1997; Whitford 2005; Winter and May 2001). In the case of DBE goals in public procurement and contracting, one consequence of compliance is the risk of litigation from aggrieved third parties. By way of contrast, 49 CFR Part 26 does not require that state recipients of DOT funds actually meet their DBE goals, suggesting that the cost of noncompliance may be trivial. However, failure to submit goals for review, as well as failure to make good faith efforts to implement the goals, could potentially result in the withholding of critical federal dollars required for the completion of important highway, airport, or transit projects. Thus, there are possible net costs associated with compliance but also uncertain losses associated with noncompliance.

There are three main compliance enforcement mechanisms available to the federal funder: (a) referral to the US Department of Justice for possible litigation; (b) withholding of federal funds; and (c) delay in approval of proposed goals and/or delay in release of federal funds. It is the third compliance mechanism that is most often utilized, and thus, the net costs of noncompliance arguably are relatively small.

The first two mechanisms were rarely used in the pre-Obama years. The third is rather common, and has the same practical effect as the withholding of funds. Projects are delayed; the public inconvenienced.

We turn to the costs associated with compliance. The main cost of rule compliance is the threat of legal challenges from white male-owned firms, alleging that the DBE goals, per se, or the goal-setting process, contributes to discrimination against non-protected group members. Such challenges typically involve the filing of lawsuits in state or federal courts, and the expensive, distracting, and protracted pre-trial discovery process intended to induce government agencies to abandon their DBE goals, lower the DBE goals, replace them with race-neutral goals, and/or compensate non-DBE firms for the harm that they experience from implementation of DBE goals. Some litigation is pursued based on principle, with the ultimate intention of going forward to the United States Courts of Appeals or the US Supreme Court in an attempt to establish the unconstitutionality of the DBE goals.

Anecdotal evidence supports the view that some public agencies with highly successful DBE programs aggressively pursue their DBE goals when confronted with the threat of lawsuits, precisely to make the point that their programs matter more than the occasional discontented non-DBE. These programs are located in states with large minority populations and/or large DBE populations.

Formalizing these arguments suggests that it is an empirical question of whether net costs from compliance are high enough in order to reduce overall DBE goals.[7] The rational choice model under uncertainty predicts that as the risk of litigation increases, there should be a reduction in the overall goal. Surprisingly, a simple illustration suggests this might not be the case. The 9th Circuit Court of Appeals (Alaska, Arizona, California, Hawaii, Idaho, Montana, Nevada, Oregon, Washington) ruled in *Western States Paving Co., Inc. v. Washington State Dep't of Trans* (2005) that the DBE programs were not sufficiently narrowly tailored. The initial reaction in Washington state was the elimination of race-conscious goals but in subsequent years, many of the states affected by this ruling have increased their overall goals—perhaps to compensate for elimination of the DBE goals. These states have large, vocal, and politically active DBE populations. Whereas the race-conscious portion of the goal is limited by the court decision in this jurisdiction, the actual size of the overall goal can increase in the face of opposition to the race-conscious goal.

The rational choice theory assumes, furthermore, that state government administrators face incentive structures and decision mechanisms permitting them to respond like rational decision makers under uncertainty.

Prospect theory (Kahneman and Tversky 1979) helps to explain why behavior might differ when facing increases in losses compared to reductions in gains. Prospect theory posits that agents are more sensitive to increases in losses than changes in their gains. From this perspective, one expects there to be asymmetric and possibly non-transitive impacts of litigation on goal setting and goal attainment. Put differently, under prospect theory, one expects that reverse discrimination litigation will reduce DBE goals, but the absence of reverse discrimination litigation will not increase goals.

Complex models building on the work of Herbert Simon (1991), Kahneman and Tversky (1979), and others in what might be called the behavioral economics literature suggest inertia, framing effects, and other aspects of bounded rationality with alternative predictions of the impacts of litigation on federal rule compliance. Under inertia, also known as incrementalism in the public administration literature, small increases or reductions in net losses neither increase nor reduce overall goals. A similar prediction emerges under Simonian bounded rationality.

By way of contrast, framing suggests that high degrees of DBE support for goals would result in little retreat from goal setting, or even possibly increases in DBE goals when faced with litigation threats. Sometimes this reaction is called "the best defense is a good offense." The data from these observations about framing effects come from FHWA (highway) funding projects by State Departments of Transportation. Stakeholder groups affect the framing of risks. The main stakeholder group for FHWA projects is highway users whose preferences differ from state to state. One can assume, for example, that more liberal states with large DBE populations will show greater support for DBE programs and will set higher goals. In the framing perspective and relying on prospect theory, however, reverse discrimination claims will have a smaller impact on goal setting than the larger issue of support for affirmative action in the state.

DATA AND MEASUREMENT

The models we estimate use unique pooled cross-section, time-series data obtained through the Freedom of Information Act (FOIA) request to the US DOT. Upon request, DOT provided copies of the "Uniform Report of

DBE Awards or Commitments and Payments Form," the data for which was reported to DOT's Office of Civil Rights by each of the fifty state DOTs, between FY 2001 and 2010. We have acquired separate annual reports for FTA and FHWA, two of the three federal agencies within US DOT. These yearly reports contain the race-neutral and race-conscious portions of DBE procurement and contracting goals proposed by each state transportation agency, as well as the actual percentages of contracting dollars awarded to DBE firms.[8] Our final analyses are based on the FHWA reports.[9] These original data allow us to examine the impact of litigation efforts upon agency DBE goal setting and attainment.

Dependent Variable

Our dependent variable is the relative DBE goal. All state and local highway administrations receiving above a certain threshold in federal funds are required to establish annual (triennial after FY 2010) DBE goals. The goals are supposed to be set according to a three-step methodology: (a) estimation of a base goal; (b) adjustments to the base goal; and (c) partitioning of the adjusted goal into race-conscious and race-neutral portions. The base goal is determined by the availability of DBEs in the relevant geographic market area. The required filings to US DOT provide access to the overall DBE goals and the race-neutral and race-conscious portions of the goals that state agency recipients of FHWA funding formulate each year. A DBE goal of 8 percent indicates that the state transportation agency plans on allocating 8 percent of the coming year's public contracting dollars specifically to firms certified as DBEs. Overall DBE goals submitted by states between 2001 and 2010 range between 3 percent (Nevada) and 32 percent (Washington, DC). Naturally, such goals are more likely to be lower in states with fewer DBE firms. In order to examine goal setting primarily as a function of legal challenges, we compute the relative DBE goal as overall goal divided by availability of DBE firms. The availability data comes from women and minority business enterprise shares reported in the Survey of Business Owners by state. Thus, higher relative goals mean aggressive upward adjustment of the goals from the base goals, or better predictions of the availability of women- and minority-owned firms. Clearly, states with active DBE programs and/or with well-represented women- and/or minority-owned firms on agency bid lists or certification lists will have higher relative goals.

Independent Variables

Legal Challenges. Our independent variables mainly center on litigation activities. The Westlaw online legal database provides full access to

comprehensive lists of lawsuits in which preferential affirmative action programs or policies were involved. For the purposes of this chapter, to examine
race-based DBE goals and attainment, we have narrowed the list by selecting
cases in which discrimination or reverse discrimination claims made were
primarily race based.[10] For each case coded, we record information on the
race/ethnicity of the plaintiff, the outcome of the lawsuit,[11] whether or not
the plaintiff was represented by a nonprofit legal foundation, and whether the
defendant was a transportation agency in particular, which may have a more
direct bearing on DBE-related decision-making. Moreover, we identify the
level of the judiciary at which the case was decided, as well as the case history, and whether the case was appealed and at which level of court. Detailed
case histories are listed in Appendix A.1. We create four dummy variables
for state supreme court, federal district courts, federal courts of appeal, and
the US Supreme Court to specify at which level of court the lawsuit occurred.
We expect the decisions of state supreme courts and federal district courts to
have a stronger impact on state DBE programs than Courts of Appeals and
US Supreme Court rulings.[12]

We collected and reviewed sixty-nine cases and a total of 104 lawsuits at
all levels of court. Fourteen of these cases were filed against a state departments of transportation to specifically challenge existing DBEs plans. There
were sixteen lawsuits at the state level. Forty lawsuits were received in federal
district courts, forty-four in federal courts of appeals. There were eight individual court decisions in which the race-based public programs in question
immediately failed the judicial strict-scrutiny test and eight decisions in which
affirmative action was upheld. More than half of the cases were dismissed or
rejected due to lack of standing or evidence, or declared moot. A majority of
the reverse discrimination claims that challenged government-installed affirmative action programs were eventually denied in courts. We return to the
implication of this data artifact in our discussion of the results.

For each year, and for each state and the District of Columbia we coded
the following variables:

x1 if there is any lawsuit in prior year(s)
x2 if there is any lawsuit in current year
x3 if there were no lawsuits in the current year or previous years
x4 lawsuit at federal circuit court of appeals in prior or current year
nx1 any white plaintiff in prior years
nx2 any white plaintiff in current year
nx3 never any white plaintiff in current year or previous years
nx4 white plaintiff at federal circuit court of appeals in prior or current year
defendant if the state transportation agency was a defendant in a reverse dis-
    crimination complaint

Political Factors. Our next set of independent variables measures the political party compositions of state legislatures and the political party affiliation of governors. This partisanship information is obtained from the annual statistical abstracts published by the US Census Bureau. We create dummy variables for Republican- and Democrat-controlled state legislatures, and Republican and Democratic governors. We hypothesize that state DBE goal setting may also be at least partially affected by a state's political climate. There is a well-established literature on the influence of political branches on public policymaking. In particular, studies have shown that compared to Republican-controlled legislatures, legislatures controlled by the Democratic Party are more likely to favor redistributive programs (Erikson 1971; Winters 1976), and more likely to enact racial and gender-related programs (Barrilleaux and Miller 1988; Dye 1984; Garand 1985; Meier et al. 1996; Nice 1982). Therefore, we also propose to test the effect of partisanship on state DBE programs by controlling for the presence of a Democratic governor and legislature.

Public Attitudes. Public attitudes toward race-related policies may also affect a state's general racial policy environment and, thus, DBE program implementation. Public opinion studies suggest low support for race-conscious policies (Kinder and Sanders 1996). White attitudes toward affirmative action in public employment, education, and contracting tend to fall between uncertain and negative, and reflect a widespread belief that such programs amount to reverse discrimination (Alvarez and Brehm 1997; Kemmelmeier 2003; Schuman et al. 1998; Steeh and Krysan 1996).

To measure racial attitudes, we use an index of citizen ideology first proposed by Berry et al. (1998). On a scale of 0 to 100, this measure denotes the ideological positions of a state's citizens and will more or less reflect the degree to which race-related federal policies such as the DBE programs are perceived at the state level. Meanwhile, we also utilize another possible measure of racial attitudes by taking into account the fact that anti-affirmative action ballot initiatives have been introduced at the state level (Hajnal, Gerber, and Louch 2002; Kellough 2006). These data are collected from the online ballot measures database through the National Conference of State Legislatures website.[13] We create a dummy variable, coded as 1 if the state ballot initiative or referendum aiming to ban affirmative action was successful, and 0 if it eventually failed. A list of both successful and failed ballot measures between 2001 and 2010 is found in Appendix B.1. Under the assumption that state bureaucracy does not intend to deviate dramatically from the preferences of its constituents, we expect to see a decline over the years of state DOTs' overall DBE goals and, in particular, the race-conscious portions, in states with more conservative citizens.

RESULTS

Figure 8.1 reveals that DBE goals were consistently higher for states and years where there was litigation than otherwise. Whether the litigation variable was defined as litigation in the current year, previous years, in federal courts, or with white plaintiffs, the results are the same: the DBE goal reported by the state DOT was always higher in instances where there was litigation. These effects are all statistically significant.

These results are tempered by the fact that litigation also occurred in states where there were large numbers of minority firms. When one examines Figure 8.2, which shows the relative DBE goals (the ratio of the goal to the percentage of women or minority firms in the state), the effects are no longer statistically significant. The ratios average from .24 to .25 for states without litigation to .26 to .27 for states with litigation. The differences are statistically significant only when litigation is measured as prior years.

Table 8.1 reports the results of ordinary least squares estimates controlling for circuit court, political representation, and the percentage of the DBE goal that is race neutral. The effects are generally positive when there is litigation (or negative when there is no litigation) but statistically significant only in three out of eight models: any litigation in previous years, white plaintiff in previous years, and never a white plaintiff in current or previous years. These results do not support a general deterrence theory predicting *lower* DBE goals when there is litigation.

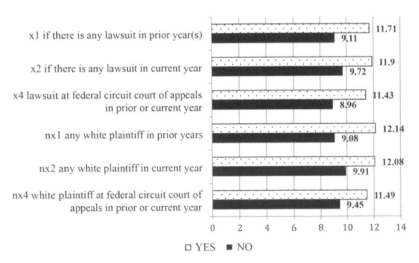

Figure 8.1   Differences in DBE goals by litigation type. Authors' computations of US DOT, FTA, and FHWA data.

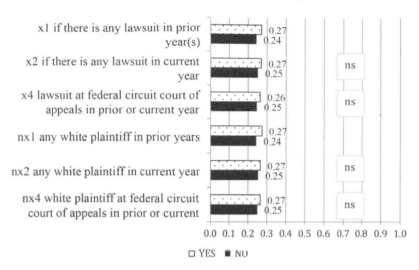

x1 if there is any lawsuit in prior year(s) 0.27 0.24

x2 if there is any lawsuit in current year 0.27 0.25 ns

x4 lawsuit at federal circuit court of appeals in prior or current year 0.26 0.25 ns

nx1 any white plaintiff in prior years 0.27 0.24

nx2 any white plaintiff in current year 0.27 0.25 ns

nx4 white plaintiff at federal circuit court of appeals in prior or current 0.27 0.25 ns

0.0 0.1 0.2 0.3 0.4 0.5 0.6 0.7 0.8 0.9 1.0

□ YES ■ NO

Figure 8.2   Differences in relative DBE goals by litigation type. Authors' computations of US DOT, FTA, and FHWA data.

A Hausman-Wu test for endogeneity suggests the weak possibility that current litigation is a function of past or current DBE goals. However, prior litigation cannot be predicted by current DBE goals and thus the argument that the positive coefficients are simply an artifact of simultaneous equation bias is not supported. To see this further, the second row in Table 8.1 reports the two-stage least squares (2SLS) estimates of the litigation coefficients. Instruments include ideology, ideology squared, Democratic house of representatives, Democratic governor, whether affirmative action program in question was invalidated by court, Federal District 1–8, Federal District 10–11, year 2003–2009. The 2SLS produce estimates that are all negative for current or previous litigation or positive for no litigation. None of the effects, however, are statistically significant, undermining the suggestion that the causal path is from the setting of goals to litigation and not litigation to goal setting.[14]

Table 8.1 also reports feasible generalized least squares (FGLS) estimates. None of the coefficients on the litigation variables are statistically significant. We cannot conclude, therefore, that litigation has an adverse impact on DBE goal setting.

Prospect theory suggests that the risk of losses should have a larger impact on DBE goals than the absence of losses (e.g., gains). Prospect theory predicts a negative coefficient on the litigation variable that represents losses and a positive coefficient on the litigation variable that predicts gains. The absolute value of the loss coefficient should be larger than the absolute value of the gain coefficient. The problem here, however, is that the ordinary least squares

Table 8.1   Effects of Reverse Discrimination Litigation on Relative DBE Goals

ESTIMATOR	Any lawsuit in Prior Year(s)	There is Any Lawsuit in Current Year	Never any Lawsuit in Current Year or Previous Years	Lawsuit at Federal Circuit Court of Appeals in Current or Prior Year	White plaintiff in prior years	White Plaintiff in Current Year	Never any White Plaintiff in Current or Previous Years	White Plaintiff at Federal Circuit Court of Appeals in Prior or Current Year
OLS	0.129***	0.0343	-0.0622	0.0318	0.121***	0.0256	-0.0946**	0.0413
Robust standard errors	(0.0406)	(0.0424)	(0.0478)	(0.0539)	(0.0417)	(0.0547)	(0.0441)	(0.0440)
N	276	276	276	276	276	276	276	276
2SLS	-0.0858	-0.160	0.0994	-0.0405	-0.0634	-0.357	0.0958	-0.0419
Robust standard errors	(0.304)	(0.645)	(0.336)	(0.242)	(0.275)	(1.1210)	(0.353)	(0.252)
N	297	297	297	297	297	297	297	297
FGLS	0.0240	-0.0161	-0.0464	-0.0113	0.0426	-0.00215	-0.0750	0.00665
Robust standard errors	(0.0367)	(0.0255)	(0.0917)	(0.100)	(0.0366)	(0.0342)	(0.0840)	(0.0812)
N	276	276	276	276	276	276	276	276

(Robust Standard Errors in Parentheses).
Dependent variable: relative goal in ([dbe total goal percent]/[mbe+wbe percent]).
The significance for ** is 5% and for *** is 1%.
Source: Authors' computations of US DOT, FTA, and FHWA data.

Table 8.2   Estimates of Specific Deterrent Effects of Litigation

Estimator	Coefficient	Std Error	t	P>|t|
OLS, No Covariates	−0.0025	0.082	−0.03	0.98
OLS, with Ideology	0.0081	0.0817	0.1	0.92
OLS, Full Set of Covariates	−0.0604	0.0463	−1.31	0.19
2SLS	−0.5008	0.6364	−0.79	0.43
FGLS	−0.0286	0.1074	−0.27	0.79

Source: Authors' computations of US DOT, FTA, and FHWA data.

(OLS) estimates are all positive for the loss variable and negative for the gain variable, in direct contradiction to the predictions of the prospect theory.

Table 8.2 examines the impacts of lawsuits against the state department of transportation. The difference here is that the effect is a specific deterrent rather than a general deterrent. The estimates obtained using OLS with no covariates, OLS controlling only for ideology, OLS with a full set of covariates, 2SLS and FGLS all produce the same substantive result: there is no specific deterrent effect of litigation on DBE goal setting.

The only statistically significant determinants of the relative DBE goals turn out to be those that are most closely aligned with the framing model. In jurisdictions such as the 11th Circuit Court of Appeals, where the Western Paving case was decided, virtually banning race-conscious programs, and the 5th Circuit Court of Appeals, where there is a long-standing run of anti-affirmative action cases, the *framing* of the policy of setting DBE goals is more important than whether there are litigants challenging the goals, another factor that is consistently significant is the ideology variable. DBE goals are set higher in more liberal states.

CONCLUSION

We find no evidence in this chapter supporting the deterrence theory, wherein reverse discrimination claims hinder the setting of race-conscious goals and thwart the intent of the federal mandates regarding affirmative action for DBEs in the state programs receiving federal highway funding. No support is found for specific deterrence, whereby defendants in reverse discrimination litigation reduce their DBE goals, or general deterrence whereby any type of anti-discrimination litigation reduces DBE goals. We also test for the possibility of framing effects and do find limited support for this proposition. We test the prediction of prospect theory and reject the hypothesis that losses have a larger impact than gains on outcomes.

The results are consistent with inertia, incrementalism, and bounded rationality models where small changes in threats do not have a major impact on goal setting. It is not surprising that alternative methods of estimating the coefficients of the litigation variables in a model predicting the natural log of the relative DBE goal that the effects are statistically insignificant for all but previous litigation measures. Whereas there is limited support for the idea that high goals produce litigation, the consistent finding of our analysis is that litigation does not measurably affect relative goals.

An important qualification of our results is that we do not test for other types of costs and benefits or gains and losses from reverse discrimination litigation. Expanded parameters will require additional data to which we do not have access at this point. Such gains and losses involve the budgets of the state agency and levels of support or opposition from elected officials.

Another qualification is that we have not yet interviewed state agency heads or procurement officials to determine whether other factors could explain the unexpected finding that DBE goals were higher in states with litigation than in states with no litigation. A plausible explanation is that there is endogeneity in the model suggesting that reverse discrimination claims are more likely to arise in states with high goals, although the Hausman-Wu tests do not support this proposition.

A final qualification is that the theory suggests *threats of litigation* should also act as deterrents to goal setting. We have yet to collate and assemble court filings and related pre-trial hearings that typically precede the final outcomes of litigation. The typically long and expensive legal processes associated with these threats might encourage agencies being sued to reach settlements. Such settlements would not be located using the data we have assembled on litigation. These threats might affect agencies and counterpart governmental departments in a state from pursuing race-conscious plans. Future analysis will explore these issues.

APPENDIX A.1

State	Year	Case	Issue	Outcome	History
AL	2006	*Robert Rogers v. Michael Haley*	Department of Corrections Reverse discrimination on basis of race	Dismissed	
	2008	*Timothy D. Pope v. State of Alabama*	Reverse discrimination on basis of race	Dismissed	
AK					
AZ	2005	*John Killingsworth v. State Farm Mutual Automobile Insurance Company*	Reverse discrimination on basis of race and age	Overruled	2007: Circuit Court
AR	2008	*Donna Humphries v. Pulaski County Special School District*	Reverse discrimination on basis of race	Overruled	2009: Circuit Court
CA	2001	*Ward Connerly v. State Personnel Board*	Challenged affirmative action	Partially invalidated affirmative action plan	
	2001	*L. Tarango Trucking v. County of Contra Costa*	Discrimination on basis of race and gender	Overruled	
	2002	*Jaxon Enterprises v. DOT*	Challenged DBE plan	Upheld DBE plan	
	2002	*Donald Bruce Crawford v. Huntington Beach Union High School District*	Challenged racial balancing for public schools	Invalidated affirmative action plan	
	2004	*C&C Construction Inc. v. Sacramento Municipal Utility District*	Challenged affirmative action	Invalidated affirmative action plan	
	2007	*Coral Construction Inc. v. City and County of San Francisco*	Challenged DBE plan	Invalidated DBE plan	2010: State Supreme Court

(Continued)

State	Year	Case	Issue	Outcome	History
	2010	Coalition to Defend Affirmative Action v. Arnold Schwarzenegger	Challenged anti-affirmative action initiative	Dismissed	
CO	2003	Concrete Works of Colorado Inc. v. City and County of Denver	Challenged affirmative action	Upheld affirmative action	
CT	2001	Board of Education of the City of Norwalk v. Commission on Human Rights and Opportunities	Challenged racial discrimination ruling	Overruled	2003: State Supreme Court
	2002	Sheryl Broadnax v. City of New Haven	Fire Department discrimination on basis of race	Dismissed	2004: State Supreme Court
	2007	Josephine Smalls Miller v. Praxair Inc.	Discrimination on basis of race	Dismissed	2009: District Court
	2009	Gilbert Cortez v. State of Connecticut DOT	DOT discrimination on basis of race	Overruled	
	2010	Lorraine Gariepy v. State of Connecticut	Reverse discrimination on basis of race	Overruled	
DE					
FL	2003	NAACP v. Florida Board of Regents	Challenged anti-affirmative action laws	Upheld claim	
	2004	Hershell Gill Consulting Engineers Inc. v. Miami-Dade County, Florida	Challenged DBE plan	Invalidated DBE plan	
	2004	Florida A.G.C. Council Inc. v. State of Florida	Challenged DBE plan	Invalidated DBE plan	
GA	2001	Melvin Reid v. Lockheed Martin Aeronautics Co.	Discrimination on basis of race	Dismissed	
HI	2003	John Doe v. Kamehameha Schools/Bernice Pauahi Bishop Estate	Reverse discrimination on basis of race	Overruled	2005: Circuit Court (Invalidated affirmative action plan)

(Continued)

State	Year	Case	Issue	Outcome	History
IA	2007	*Glynn Jones v. Cargill Inc.*	Discrimination on basis of race	Overruled	
	2007	*Fred Gilbert v. Des Moines Area Community College*	Discrimination on basis of race	Overruled	
ID					
IL	2001	*Builders Association of Greater Chicago v. County of Cook*	Challenged DBE plan	Invalidated DBE plan	2003: State Supreme Court
	2003	*Jeffrey Horan v. City of Chicago*	Reverse discrimination on basis of race	Dismissed	
	2004	*Northern Contracting Inc. v. State of Illinois DOT*	Challenged DBE	Upheld DBE plan	2005-2007: Circuit Court
	2006	*Carl Qualis v. Steve Cunningham et al.*	Discrimination on basis of race	Overruled	
	2006	*Bernard Mlynczak v. Samuel W. Bodman (US Department of Energy)*	Reverse discrimination on basis of race	Overruled	
	2010	*Darryl W. Jackson v. Paul Cerpa*	DOT discrimination on basis of race	Overruled	
IN	2006	*Mary Wallskog v. Indiana Department of Correction*	Discrimination on basis of race	Overruled	2006: Circuit Court
	2006	*Gabe Keri v. Board of Trustees of Purdue University*	Discrimination on basis of race	Overruled	
KS	2002	*Klaver Construction Inc. v. Kansas DOT & US DOT*	Challenged DBE plan	Dismissed	
KY	2004	*Gerald Arthur Theisen v. Kentucky State University*	Reverse discrimination on basis of race	Upheld claim	

(Continued)

State	Year	Case	Issue	Outcome	History
	2004	Glenn E. Bone v. City of Louisville	Reverse discrimination on basis of race	Overruled	
LA	2001	Charles Albright v. City of New Orleans	Reverse discrimination on basis of race	Overruled	2003: Circuit Court
	2008	Terry R. Lewis v. City of Ruston, Louisiana	Discrimination on basis of race	Overruled	
	2008	Harrell Sharkey v. Dixie Electric Membership Corporation	Reverse discrimination on basis of race	Overruled	
ME					
MD	2002	Associated Utility Contractors of Maryland Inc. v. Mayor and City Council of Baltimore	Challenged DBE plan	Dismissed	
	2005	Carmen Thompson v. US Department of Housing and Urban Development	Discrimination on basis of race	Overruled	2006: State Supreme Court
MA	2002	Winifred N. Cotter v. Massachusetts Association of Minority Law Enforcement Officers	Reverse discrimination on basis of race	Overruled	
	2006	William Brackett v. Civil Service Commission	Reverse discrimination on basis of race	Upheld affirmative action plan	
MI	2001	David Sharp v. City of Lansing	Reverse discrimination on basis of race	Overruled	
	2002	Crawford v. Department of Civil Service	Reverse discrimination on basis of race	Overruled	
	2003	Cindy A. Pilon v. Saginaw Valley State University	Reverse discrimination on basis of race	Overruled	

(Continued)

State	Year	Case	Issue	Outcome	History
	2004	*Coalition to Defend Affirmative Action v. Board of State Canvassers*	Discrimination on basis of race	Upheld claim	
	2006	*Coalition to Defend Affirmative Action v. Regents of University of Michigan*	Challenged anti-affirmative action initiative	Overruled	2007, 2008: State Supreme Court
MN	2001	*Sherbrooke Turf Inc. v. Minnesota DOT*	Challenged DBE plan	Overruled	2003: Circuit Court
MS					
MO	2005	*Michael Martinez v. City of St. Louis*	Reverse discrimination on basis of race	Upheld claim	
	2009	*Kansas City Hispanic Association Contractors Enterprise v. City of Kansas City, Missouri*	Discrimination on basis of race	Overruled	
MT					
NE	2006	*Michael Pritchard v. City of Omaha, Nebraska*	Reverse discrimination on basis of race	Invalidated affirmative action plan	
NV					
NH					
NJ	2002	*Dr. Andrew C. DeSanto v. Rowan University*	Discrimination on basis of race and gender	Overruled	
	2007	*Jeanne Klawitter v. City of Trenton, New Jersey*	Reverse discrimination on basis of race	Upheld claim	
	2009	*Geod Corporation v. New Jersey Transit Corporation*	Challenged DBE plan	Upheld DBE plan	2010: Circuit Court
	2010	*Vulcan Pioneers of New Jersey v. City of Newark*	Discrimination on basis of race	Overruled	

(Continued)

142

Chapter 8

State	Year	Case	Issue	Outcome	History
NM					
NY	2005	*Jana-Rock Construction Inc. v. New York State Department of Economic Development*	Discrimination on basis of race	Dismissed	
NC	2003	*H. B. Rowe Inc. v. W. Lyndo Tippett et al. (DOT)*	Challenged DBE plan	Upheld DBE plan	2007, 2008, 2010: Circuit Court
ND					
OH	2002	*Kathryn Ogletree v. Ohio Wesleyan University*	Discrimination on basis of race	Overruled	
	2006	*Gordon P. Koehler v. Ohio Civil Rights Commission*	Reverse discrimination on basis of race	Overruled	
	2007	*Regina Russell v. University of Toledo*	Discrimination on basis of race	Overruled	2008: Circuit Court
OK	2001	*Kornhass Construction Inc., TAO Inc. & Daco Construction Company v. State of Oklahoma, Department of Central Services*	Challenged affirmative action plan	Invalidated affirmative action plan	
OR	2002	*Marilyn A. Robinson v. Spencer Abraham (Department of Energy)*	Discrimination on basis of race	Overruled	2004: Circuit Court
PA					
RI					
SC					
SD					

(Continued)

State	Year	Case	Issue	Outcome	History
TN	2002	*West Tennessee Chapter of Associated Builders and Contractors Inc. v. City of Memphis*	Challenged DBE plan	Dismissed	2004: District Court
	2006	*Walt Ruffin v. Gerald F. Nicely (TN DOT)*	DOT discrimination on basis of race	Dismissed	
TX	2001	*Rothe Development Corporation v. US DOD & Department of Air Force*	Challenged DBE plan	Upheld DBE plan	2004, 2007, 2008: Circuit Court
	2007	*Johnny B. Crawford v. City of Houston Texas*	Discrimination on basis of race	Overruled	
UT					
VT					
VA					
WA	2001	*Parents involved in Community Schools v. Seattle School District*	Challenged racial balancing in public schools	Upheld affirmative action plan	2003: State Supreme Court; 2005: Circuit Court; 2007: US Supreme Court (invalidated affirmative action plan)
WV					
WI					
WY					
DC	2006	*Marilyn Vann v. Dirk Kempthorne (US Department of the Interior)*	Discrimination on basis of race	Dismissed	2008: Circuit Court
	2007	*Dynalantic Corporation v. US DOD*	Challenged DBE plan	Dismissed	

APPENDIX B.1

State	Year	Initiatives and Referenda	Status
AZ	2010	Prop. 107: Preferential Treatment or Discrimination Prohibition	Pass
CA	2003	Prop.54: Classification by Race, Ethnicity, Color or National Origin	Fail
CO	2008	Amendment 46: Discrimination and Preferential Treatment by Governments	Fail
MI	2006	Prop. 06-2: Proposal to Amend the State Constitution to Ban Affirmative Action Programs	Pass
NE	2008	Initiative 424: Affirmative Action Ban	Pass

NOTES

1. This chapter is based on a paper prepared with Yuan Gao of the University of Missouri-Columbia for the presentation, "The Deterrent Effects of Reverse Discrimination Claims on Federal Rule Compliance" at Law and Society Association Annual Meetings, Minneapolis, MN, May 30, 2014, and is based on data collected from 2010 to 2012. Earlier versions of this paper were presented at the Western Economic Association International (WEAI) Annual Conference, Seattle, WA, June 29, 2013, and at the APPAM International Conference, "Collaboration among Government, Market, and Society: Forging Partnerships and Encouraging Competition," Fudan University, Shanghai, China, May 25–27, 2013.

2. See http://www.dot.gov/sites/dot.dev/files/docs/fhwa_%20fy_%202012_budget_estimate.pdf and http://www.dot.gov/sites/dot.dev/files/docs/faa_%20fy_%202012_budget_estimate.pdf.

3. See DOJ, Proposed Reforms to Affirmative Action in Federal Procurement, p. 26,050.

4. See 49 Code of Federal Regulations Part 26 "Participation by Disadvantaged Business Enterprises in Department of Transportation Financial Assistance Programs."

5. See 488 US at 509 (1989).

6. See National Cooperative Highway Research Program (NCHRP) Report 644: "Guidelines for Conducting a Disparity and Availability Study for the Federal DBE Program." Transportation Research Board of the National Academies.

7. Consider the outcome variable (Gt), the DBE goal required to be submitted to the US Department of Transportation annually since 2000. This value should be approximately equal to the relative representation of DBEs in the geographic market area, subject to a possible upgrade adjustment that requires evidence of ongoing discrimination against DBEs. The relative representation of DBEs in the market place is the base goal, denoted as (g(t)). The adjustment to the base goal can be denoted by ($\alpha(t)$), so that the submitted goal is:

Equation 1:

$$Gt = g(t)\big[1 + \alpha(t)\big]$$

For example, if minority and women's businesses account for 10% of the relevant market, and if the agency determines that about half of the disparity in contract awards to DBEs versus non-DBEs is due to discrimination, then the resulting Gt submitted should be about 15%. Compliance with the federal rule suggests that the submitted goal is about equal to the base goal plus an adjustment.

The cost of submitting a high goal with a possibly large adjustment, C1, may result in costly litigation (L) from aggrieved white male-owned firms on the grounds of reverse discrimination. The cost of submitting an unrealistically low goal or failing to submit one at all, C2, may lead to federal sanctions and/or loss of federal funds (F). The expected utility from the goal-setting, therefore, can be given by:

Equation 2:

$$EU(Gt) = U\big[Gt \geq g(t)(1+\alpha(t); C1(g,\alpha,L)\big]p(C1) + U\big[Gt < g(t-1)(1+\alpha(t); C2(g,\alpha,F)\big]p(C2)$$

This equation depends on the probabilities of incurring either of these costs as well as the potential sizes of these costs, L and F. For simplicity, we can denote that the social benefits to the state come through setting the goal. The benefits of a goal equal to or greater than the base goal are assumed to be greater than the benefits of a lower goal or goal of zero to the state. Therefore, equilibrium for the risk-neutral decision-maker occurs when the expected net benefit of compliance exceeds the expected net benefit from noncompliance. The probability of compliance depends on the cost of compliance C1 which comes from the base goal and the adjustment along with possible litigation costs (L), and the probability that these costs are incurred $(p(C1))$, versus the cost of noncompliance C2 which comes from the base goal and the adjustment along with possible federal sanctions (F), and the probability that these sanctions will occur $(p(C2))$. Consequently, increases in certainty and severity of federal sanction are expected to increase compliance, whereas increases in the certainty and severity of legal challenges are expected to reduce compliance. Specifically, the theory suggests that reverse discrimination lawsuits produce expected costs that exceed the expected social benefits of the goals and thus result in a lowered goal. In short, one expects that reverse discrimination litigation will have a deterrent effect on state DOT compliance with federal rule 49 CFR Part 26.

8. The forms differ slightly across years. Race-neutral goals were not reported in 2001. In earlier years, entries existed for the partitioning of the DBE attainment by race and gender.

9. There are many missing values in the FTA reports. A great number of the fifty states did not properly report DBE goals between 2001 and 2004.

10. The cases that we exclude dealt with issues related to gender, age, disabilities, national origins and other categories to which affirmative action programs typically do not? apply.

11. Value of 1 signifies that the affirmative action program in question was invalidated by court. Other outcomes, such as anti-affirmative action claims, being dismissed or rejected are coded as 0.

12. Our preliminary examination of state DBE reports suggests that a federal circuit court's decision may not significantly influence decision-making of the agencies within the circuit. For example, the 9th Circuit Court of Appeal (Alaska, Arizona, California, Hawaii, Idaho, Montana, Nevada, Oregon, and Washington) ruled in *Western States Paving Co., Inc. v. Washington State DOT* (2005) that the DBE programs were not sufficiently narrowly tailored. Nevertheless, the state of Washington made only small reductions in their DBE goals, whereas many other states affected by this same ruling have actually increased their overall goals.

13. See http://www.ncsl.org/legislatures-elections/elections/ballot-measures-database.aspx.

14. OLS: Other controls include: percentage DBE goal that is race neutral, Democratic House of Representatives, Federal District 10, Federal District 6, Federal District 9, Federal District, 8, Federal District 11, Federal District 4, Federal District, 5, Federal District 2.

2SLS: instrumented variable x1, instruments ideology, ideology^2, Democratic House of Representatives, Democratic Governor, Whether affirmative action program in question was invalidated by court, Federal District 1–8, Federal District 10–11, year 2003–2009.

Pooled FGLS estimator or population average estimator: percentage DBE goal that is neutral, Democratic house of representatives, Democratic governor, unsuccessful ballot initiatives/referendums banning race-based affirmative action, citizen ideology, whether the affirmative action program in question was invalidated by court, Federal District 2–11, year 2004–2010.

Chapter 9

Alternatives to Race-Neutrality*†

If not race-neutrality, then what? In previous chapters we explored three explicit forms of race-neutral remedies: general economic growth, anti-discrimination enforcement, and compliance. These remedies are race neutral in the sense that they focus on maximizing efforts to remedy racial disparities by doing things other than directly targeting protected group members and providing them with preferences. Instead, they focus on non-protected group members or persons of all races and attempt to assure that there is no adverse impacts on these majority groups. We demonstrated that anti-discrimination enforcement does not always benefit racial minority group members as much as it benefits non-protected groups. We showed that a rising tide does not always lift all ships. And, compliance alone does not always do what it is intended to do.

Alternatives to race-neutral remedies beyond the conventional race-conscious remedy of affirmative action include reparations and racial reconciliation. Before examining these alternatives to race-neutral remedies, we return to the theme of the first chapter about problem structuring and remedies. In order to understand why there is so much disagreement about reparations and lack of understanding about racial reconciliation, one must remember that remedies differ in their underlying logic. They differ in the problem(s) they attempt to solve.

A convenient analytical framework for evaluating remedies requires that one first raise the following questions:

* Portions republished with permission of Taylor & Francis, from If Not Reconciliation, Then What? Review of Social Economy, 58(3), 361–380 (2000).

† Portions republished with permission of American Economic Association, from "The Political Economy of Antiracism Initiatives in the Post-Durban Round," AEA Papers and Proceedings 93(2) (May 2003) 330–333.

- What is the problem the remedy is designed to solve?
- Why are we attempting to solve the problem (justification for the remedy)?
- Is the remedy fair?
- Is the remedy efficient?
- Are there other criteria to evaluate the remedy? (constitutionality; administrative feasibility; sustainability)?
- Are there other remedies that achieve the same results that are more fair/efficient?

Types of remedies to racial inequality depend on the presumed causes of that inequality. Three broad classes of explanations exist to understand racial inequality: (a) discrimination; (b) past wrongs or atrocities; and (c) blocked opportunities.

DISCRIMINATION

Discrimination can be evaluated on three different dimensions. The most obvious is *current discrimination* or ongoing discrimination. This type of discrimination might arise when there is differential treatment of otherwise identically situated individuals, or in the form of disparate impacts of race-neutral decisions. An example of the former type of current or ongoing discrimination is when a lender decides not to make loans to persons who are African American. An example of the latter type of discrimination is when a lender decides not to make loans in neighborhoods where African Americans disproportionately live. Both forms of discrimination are illegal under the Equal Credit Opportunity Act and conventional anti-discrimination laws are designed to combat these types of discrimination (see Figure 9.1).

A second type of discrimination is termed *passive discrimination*. This type of discrimination is not necessarily overt or conscious discrimination, but nonetheless can result in racially disparate outcomes. An illustration of passive discrimination is where a state department of transportation repeatedly contracts with prime contractors that benefit from discrimination against or to the exclusion of disadvantaged business enterprises in the private sector. The public sector procurement or contracting activity is not directly discriminatory in the sense that the state agency treats DBEs differently from non-DBEs. Rather, the public sector activity indirectly and passively contributes to the private market discrimination by engaging prime contractors in public activities that benefit from discrimination in their private sector activities. These private sector activities include prime contractor refusal to subcontract to DBEs; lender discrimination against DBEs through denial of business loans or less favorable credit terms; inability to start a business in particular industries because of licensing restrictions, bonding, or business insurance

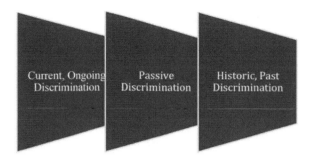

Figure 9.1   **The problem to be remedied: discrimination.** Authors' analysis.

discrimination. By participating in market activities where there are firms that routinely benefit from private market discrimination, the public agency is passively contributing to that discrimination.

A third form of discrimination that is more difficult to remedy is sometimes called "general societal discrimination" and is understood to mean the lingering effects of past discrimination or exclusion from opportunities. Swimming disparities is a great illustration. It is hard to imagine the USA Swimming association or NCAA actively discriminating against African American swimmers in terms of placement in competition heats or in award of medals or in the selection for the few slots on Olympic relay teams. The rules are clear and the rules are presumably enforced without regard to race or ethnicity (although they do differ with respect to age, gender and disability). So, the wide racial disparities in competitive swimming participation probably are not due to ongoing, current discrimination. After all, as we have argued in earlier chapters, swimmers are not racists. It is also unlikely that the causes of observed racial disparities in swimming are due to passive discrimination since the swimming world is a more or less continuous, seamless and connected world—literally from preteen to adult. Rather, what is likely is that there are lingering effects of past discrimination or exclusion: absence of competitive swimming teams in many minority communities; inadequate access to learn-to-swim programs; and segregated swimming pools generations ago. One might also point to the fact that many black women don't know how to swim and thus they do not emerge as the first instructors for their young children curious about swimming. These impacts are neither aspects of current discrimination nor passive discrimination. Rather, these are examples of lingering impacts of past discrimination and qualify to be classified as *general societal discrimination*.

PAST WRONGS AND ATROCITIES

The removal of American Indians and Australian Aborigines from their homes and forcibly raping them and preventing them from speaking their native languages are among past wrongs that remedies to inequality are occasionally designed to address. Other atrocities and denial of basic human rights, rooted in religious beliefs or economic expediency include slavery, exploitation and fundamental abuses of individuals simply because of their skin color, their tribal or caste affiliation, or country of origin. Included in this classification are infamous lynchings in southern US states of black men who dared to speak to white women or to "talk back" to white overseers (see Figure 9.2).

Crimes of Atrocity have come to be understood under international law as referencing: genocide, crimes against humanity and war crimes. The legal meaning is found in the 1948 Convention on the Prevention and Punishment of the Crime of Genocide and subsequent treaties and encompass the crime of ethnic cleansing. In particular, genocide is that component of atrocity crimes that target individuals simply because of their group membership. The United Nations states:

> Genocide, according to international law, is a crime committed against members of a national, ethnical, racial or religious group. Even though the victims of the crimes are individuals, they are targeted because of their membership, real or perceived, in one of these groups. (United Nations 2002)

In India, for example, "crimes of atrocity" means hate crimes committed by non-scheduled castes/tribes against scheduled castes/tribes in India. The actions referenced are considered to be shockingly cruel and inhumane and include rape, murder, and infliction of pain and suffering. The Scheduled Castes and Tribes (Prevention of Atrocities) Act of 1989 and its revisions in 1995 detail the specific acts perpetuated by non-scheduled castes/tribes against scheduled castes/tribes that would merit prosecution and include such indignities as forceful drinking or eating of inedible or obnoxious substances, sexual exploitation, injury or common annoyances.

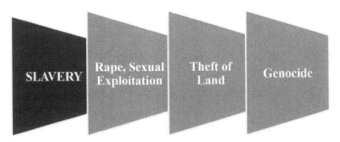

Figure 9.2   The problem to be remedied: past wrongs or atrocities. *Source*: Authors' analysis.

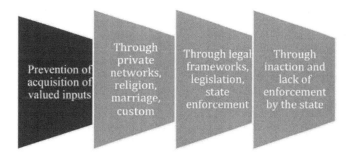

Figure 9.3   The problem to be remedied: blocked access to opportunities. Authors' analysis.

A particularly noteworthy aspect of atrocities and past wrongs is theft of land and property. The long-run consequences of losing one's productive assets are often more severe than the consequences of current or ongoing discrimination that many remedies are designed to redress. Loss of productive assets means the inability inter-generationally to transfer wealth and resources required for achieving mobility. Without these assets entire communities are unable to acquire education, start and nurture businesses, and thrive without dependency on the state or the generosity of their former oppressors. Theft of land or even blocked access to land and other forms of wealth all fall under the category of past wrongs. Current barriers to credit, savings, and accumulation of wealth are often rooted in historic barriers to accumulation of wealth, which include state enforced restrictions on intergenerational transfers of assets or religious, customary, or private barriers to transfers of assets. These wrongs are often difficult to comprehend in the current era because history is often silent on how these barriers manifested themselves.

Note that there can be lingering impacts of past wrongs or atrocities long after these wrongs have been rectified on the surface. For example, although slavery in the United States was officially abolished through the Thirteenth Amendment, well into the 1950s the predominant occupation of African American women was servant, maid or sharecropper, precisely the occupations black women held during slavery. And, the sons and daughters of servants and maids in the current generation as well as the sons and daughters of the parents who employed the servants and maids have little understanding of the linkages between these historic wrongs and current inequalities (see Figure 9.3).

BLOCKED ACCESS TO OPPORTUNITIES

The majority of Americans believe that lack of education is the cause of racial inequality. The General Social Survey (GSS) does not go very deep into

Table 9.1   On the Average (Negroes/Blacks/African Americans) Have Worse Jobs, Income, and Housing Than White People. Do You Think These Differences Are

	Yes		No		Total	
	N	%	N	%	N	%
Mainly due to lack of education	907	52.6	818	47.4	1725	100
Mainly due to discrimination	759	44.0	966	56.0	1725	100
Mainly due to lack of will	745	43.2	980	56.8	1725	100
Mainly due to inborn disability	145	8.4	1580	91.6	1725	100

Source: Authors' computations, General Social Survey, 2016.

explaining precisely what constitutes lack of education but a conventional understanding of lack of education is that it blocks access to opportunities.

Table 9.1 reports the results from 2016 GSS question: "On the average (Negroes/Blacks/African Americans) have worse jobs, income, and housing than white people. Do you think these differences are . . ." The results show that the majority of respondents—excluding those who responded "don't know," "no answer" or "not applicable"—say the problem is lack of education. The majority of respondents said "no" when considering discrimination as the cause. Although a nontrivial number of respondents said the problem was mainly due to lack of will (43.2 percent), most said the problem was mainly due to lack of education (52.6 percent). In some respects, this modal response reflects a safe answer to the question and absolves the respondent of any guilt or responsibility in contributing to racial inequality.

The "blocked access to opportunities" explanation for racial inequality includes many of the features of historic wrongs or discrimination explanations. This explanation incorporates the understanding that there were barriers to acquiring valued inputs (e.g., education, training, housing, employment, or assets). The blocked access might have come through institutions or private networks and could be maintained through formal or informal mechanisms, such as the caste system in India or colorism in the United States. The blocked access might arise through state enforced restrictions and prohibitions, such as laws prohibiting interracial marriage or rules mandating redlining or segregated housing. The blocked access might be through inaction or lack of enforcement by the state. Examples include the failure to enforce fair lending laws by limited reviews of racial disparities in loan denial rates by agencies like the Federal Trade Commission or the regional Federal Reserve Banks. Although these aspects of blocked access resemble many of the features of discrimination or historic wrongs mentioned earlier, the key feature of "blocked access" is that it pinpoints the nature of the racial inequality problem among "opportunities" and not directly within the institutions or government structures that produced the observed inequalities.

Momentarily, we will argue that these three explanations for racial inequality suggest widely differing remedies. The clarification of the problem that

Table 9.2   Three Broad Categories of Problems and Remedies to Racial Inequality

The Problem to be Remedied	Justification for Remedy	Type of Remedy Implied	Criteria for Evaluation
Current Discrimination Passive Discrimination General Social Discrimination	Reduce Disparities	Anti-Discrimination Affirmative Action Diversity	Enforceability Constitutionality Efficiency, Administrative Feasibility
Prior Wrongs and Atrocities	Right Wrongs, Atone for Sins	Acknowledgment, Apology, Redress, *Reparations*, Guarantee of non-recurrence, *Reconciliation*	Fairness, Legality, Cost, Administrative Feasibility, Implementation
Blocked Opportunities	Reduce Disparities, "Level the playing Field"	Equal Opportunity	Cost, Fairness, Effectiveness

Source: Authors' analysis.

one hopes to solve in some respects provides the justification for the remedy that will solve the problem.

THE PROBLEM TO BE REMEDIED AND THE JUSTIFICATION FOR THE REMEDY

Table 9.2 summarizes the relationship between the three broad categories of problems that remedies to racial inequality are expected to resolve: discrimination, prior wrongs and atrocities, and blocked opportunities. The interpretation of blocked opportunities as the cause of the observe racial disparities in economic outcomes is that the historical reasons for why opportunities were blocked is less important than the fact that the current generation has an obligation *out of fairness* to level the playing field with the hopes of reducing observed disparities. The implied remedy is equal opportunity and this remedy can be evaluated based on criteria of costliness, fairness, and effectiveness. The effective criterion means that the remedy does what it is supposed to do. In the instance of blocked opportunities effectiveness means to level the playing field. The reason that cost enters the equation is that leveling the playing field might entail massive expenditures to overcome years of neglect and failure to remedy the problem. Fairness or equity is central to evaluation of equal opportunity because it reflects what Myrdal and others have characterized as the American ideal.

What is apparent about the remedy of equal opportunity is that is can be implemented without guilt or acknowledgment of wrong doing by current generations. And, equal opportunity can be implemented as a race-neutral mechanism for reducing disparities. Note that the outcome envisioned in the remedy of equal opportunity is never the elimination of disparities. Rather it is the effort or the intent to reduce disparities, even if those disparities are never eliminated or diminished. Often, equal opportunity is not enough.

The remedies of anti-discrimination, affirmative action, and diversity share an important concern about addressing discrimination, whether current, passive, or general societal discrimination. These remedies share aspects of evaluation criteria of efficiency, constitutionality, enforceability, and administrative (and political) feasibility. Surely, one would want to reduce discrimination if illegal discrimination is the cause of observed racial disparities. However, much of the litigation and public outcry about remedies designed to reduce discrimination arises from disagreements about whether observed economic disparities are, in fact, due to discrimination. Are black-white disparities in earnings, educational attainment, homeownership, public procurement and contracting, child maltreatment, or even competitive swimming due to discrimination or due to something else? That something else often is attributed to individual choices, defects among groups, or legally and economically relevant factors such as ability, aptitude, experience, qualifications, or behaviors. Now, clearly, some of these factors are rooted in prior inequalities. But, the current, passive, or general societal discrimination explanation fails to ask the question of *why* these disparities exist and as such place heightened weight on remedies that are often challenged on grounds of feasibility, efficiency, constitutionality, and enforceability.

Quite distinct from the problems of discrimination or blocked access is the problem of prior wrongs and atrocities. When a remedy is attempting to confront discrimination and blocked access, the justification for the remedy is often simply to reduce racial disparities. When a remedy is attempting to confront problems of racial hatred, hate crimes, past wrongs, or atrocities, then justification for the remedy goes far beyond merely reducing disparities. The justification is to right the wrongs. The justification is to atone for the sins committed. The theme of equal opportunity, anti-discrimination, affirmative action, and diversity remedies attempts to reduce disparities against the disadvantaged groups without necessarily harming the advantaged group. The theme of remedies to past wrongs and atrocities is to right the wrongs, even if in righting the wrongs the oppressor group must bear much of the burden for the harm inflicted upon the aggrieved parties.

The implied remedy to the problem of prior wrongs and atrocities is far more complex than current anti-discrimination or affirmative action policies. The implied remedy must entail acknowledgment of the wrongs. Acknowledgment opens the door for a genuine and heartfelt apology. Contrition. Not, "I am sorry you feel the way you feel." But, "I am sorry for the grievous harm my ancestors brought upon you and that I have benefited from." The remedy must assure that that there is never a recurrence and that there is redress and compensation for the wrongs. And, then and only then can there be reconciliation and forgiveness.

The remedies to prior wrongs and atrocities are unabashedly race conscious. It is nearly inconceivable to embrace a solution to the problem of theft of land, removal of indigenous children from their mothers, or perpetuation of slavery, denial of basic human rights, and restrictions on movement and access to property or economic resources of a racial group without directly targeting members of the aggrieved group. Ta-Nehisi Coates (2014) has eloquently summarized the case for reparations. But as Darity (1997, 2008) and others have conceded, the costs of implementing these race-conscious remedies—particularly reparations—often are enormous and can entail massive implementation hurdles.

RACIAL RECONCILIATION[1]

The alternative to anti-racism or racial healing and racial reconciliation is a counterpoint to other race-conscious remedies in that it seeks not one or two steps along the pathway toward remedying prior wrongs or atrocities. It requires the full range of steps from acknowledgment, to apology, to redress, to reparations, to forgiveness. The most visible national effort in the United States to address racial healing came not from the first African American president but from President Bill Clinton. The journey in understanding racial reconciliation as a remedy to racial inequality begins by acknowledging that racial inequality is rooted in white privilege. It is because of the failure to strike at the heart of white privilege in America that efforts to eliminate racial economic inequality have failed. Past policies were based on the disadvantage model. They sought to reduce deficiencies of blacks and other minorities without addressing racism and white privilege.

The dominant Eurocentric view of racial inequality is called the disadvantage model. This view, particularly prevalent among American and Australian neoclassical economists, posits that it is the human capital deficiencies and educational defects that underlie the poor market outcomes of blacks and other racial minority group members. These deficiencies and defects translate into lower earnings, lower incomes, higher unemployment, and generally greater social and economic inequality. Racial inequality, in the disadvantage model, seeks the source of the inequality within the least well-off group.

Racial inequality can also be understood through a theoretical construct called white privilege. In contrast to the disadvantage model, the white privilege model seeks the source of inequality within the best-off group. For there to be an underclass, there must be an overclass; understanding how the underclass got to be at the bottom requires understanding how the overclass got to be at the top. The white privilege model does not seek to make blacks or other racial minority group members white, as the disadvantage model does. Rather, it seeks to acknowledge and to confront the process by which inequality arose in the first place, seeking an empowering notion of remedying racial inequality. Acknowledging the theft, unfair and discriminatory treatment, separation and forceful removal of children, and the disproportionate numbers of deaths among those in custody does more than ease the sorrow and despair of those at the bottom. It squarely places the burden on the shoulders of those at the top, whose positions arose out of ill-earned advantage. Research on US racial inequality clearly demonstrates that the overclass has maintained its superiority in the marketplace, not because of the disadvantage of those at the bottom, but because those at the top consistently exhibit discriminatory behaviors. These behaviors adversely affect people who are not like them generally, but provide advantages to people who are like them specifically.

In 1998, Americans were confronted with a new national policy of racial healing, called racial reconciliation.[2] This public policy response followed an apparent failure of alternative means of remedying racial and ethnic economic inequality. President Clinton's call for racial reconciliation in the United States came at a time when affirmative action and race-based initiatives for redressing past wrongs against African Americans and other racial minority groups were under vicious attack. Attacks included challenges to affirmative action in admissions to public universities, litigation regarding DBE programs, and opposition to race preferences in hiring and promotion in public sector jobs.

To understand the unlikely rise of racial reconciliation under the Clinton administration, one must understand the attacks on race-conscious programs like affirmative action. The attacks came in three parts. The first was related to the belief that affirmative action was no longer needed because the problem we were attempting to remedy—racial discrimination and the lingering vestiges of government-sanctioned slavery and segregation—was no longer a significant problem. Yes, much racial inequality remains, according to this view, but that inequality is not the result of ongoing racism or racial discrimination. Instead, it is rooted in defects within racial minority communities themselves. Either these defects are manifestations of such prior policies as affirmative action or welfare that have unintentionally led to a perverse form of dependency upon the government or these defects are genetic, environmental, or even the lingering legacy of prior periods of social deprivation. Only the last of the effects can justly be remedied by government action and race-based initiatives do not assure that.

The second part of the attack contended that even if discrimination lingered from the past and even if racism or racial discrimination continued, race-conscious affirmative action did not solve the underlying problem.

The contention, for example, was that well-meaning efforts to promote racial minority group representation among students in elite colleges and universities resulted in a mismatch causing lower graduation of minority group members from those institutions. Special funding for scholarships, summer programs, and admissions of minorities could not be justified because of the apparent ineffectiveness in increasing representation. Critics of affirmative action—even those who admitted something needed to be remedied—pointed repeatedly to the dismal failure of prior affirmative action efforts to remedy racial inequality.

The third, and most compelling, argument against race-based initiatives to remedy racial and ethnic economic inequality was that these initiatives were unfair. The view was that in a constitutional democracy, where the majority rules, any effort that consciously benefits a minority group—solely based on their race—at the expense of the majority is suspect. The legal and constitutional logic of this reasoning came from post–Civil War constitutional amendments prohibiting states from passing laws that would disenfranchise newly freed slaves. The language of the equal protection clause in the Fourteenth Amendment does not speak specifically to the preferred status of one race over another, but within the historical context of the times, it was understood that laws could not be passed that harmed former slaves, while leaving whites harmless. This three-pronged attack on affirmative action, suggesting that race-based corrective actions were no longer needed, hopelessly ineffective, or simply unfair in a democratic society, combined with a general dismantlement of the civil rights apparatus of the 1960s to represent a new ideological mindset. The new approach was either seen as a negative resurgence of racism—what might be called new racism—or a positive manifestation of a new quest for remedying racism.

The positive force accompanying the unfortunate ugliness of retrenchment efforts away from affirmative action compelled policymakers to confront the need to acknowledge the deeply rooted pain and hurt associated with prior racism. Further, they were compelled to reconcile these wrongs. Seen from the perspective of Australians who were struggling with their Aboriginal reconciliation efforts, or seen from the perspective of the Maori, the indigenous people of New Zealand who through the Waitangi Treaty efforts nearly completed their reconciliation, and seem through the lens of the South African Truth and Reconciliation efforts, one can appreciate the initiatives of President Clinton to seek healing.

Racial reconciliation rests on three prongs: first is acknowledgment of prior wrongs; second is an official apology for those wrongs; and third is compensation for the wrongs. Much work remains within the economics community to address the technical aspects of the compensation question: How much? For how long? In what form of payment? To whom? The Australian experience shows how compensation can go awry.

The Australian government authorized $64 million to provide psychological counseling and to assist in locating lost Aboriginal relatives who had been removed from their homes. While the effort may help repair some of the damage associated with those wrongs, the money did not go directly to the victims. In fact, the scheme appeared to benefit the libraries, archives, location services, and psychological counselors (who received compensation for these services) more than the victims. Market economists would argue it would have been better to give the money directly to the victims—who may well have chosen to spend the money on psychological counseling or, perhaps, relative location. As it stands, the stolen generation did not receive any real economic benefits from the expenditure. If anything, the program created a new industry that thrived on maintaining the pathology from the stolen children process, and continued the dependency of Aborigines on the goodwill of a government that does not understand and refuses to apologize.[3]

A vigorous focus on racial reconciliation in the United States followed several years of uncertainty and ambiguity within the Democratic leadership on the direction of national policies on race. President Clinton ordered each cabinet department to prepare a report on what works and what does not work in implementing affirmative action plans. "Mend it, don't end it," he intoned. The slogan struck a political balance akin to his policy on gays in the military: "Don't ask, don't tell." While intending to convey to the gay community that strict enforcement of punitive sanctions against homosexual acts within the armed forces would not be used to discriminate, the statement was simultaneously meant to sooth the religious right. They need not fear sending their sons away from home to serve their country, only to be sodomized.[4]

Similarly, the "Mend it, don't end it" policy was designed to convey to African Americans and affirmative action supporters that good programs would not be eliminated, while still signaling to the general population that the problem of unfair quotas and practices discriminatory to whites would be fixed. Just as the "Don't ask, don't tell" policy ran into constitutional difficulties, in an administrative twist, the "Mend it, don't end it" reports were never produced or were never publicly released. It was as if the policy analysts instructed to determine which affirmative action programs were working and which ones were not mistakenly thought their instructions were: "Don't ask, don't tell!"

There were other problems with the US racial reconciliation process. After announcing the initiative in 1997, the President failed to convene the group for months, and once it did meet, it was unable to articulate its agenda. Months went by with little visible output that emerged. Furthermore, as a top-down initiative—the President's initiative—the advisory board was a carefully picked mix of "respectable" whites, blacks, Asians, and Latinos.

No American Indians or Alaskan or Hawaiian natives were to be found on the seven-member commission.

Republican House Speaker Newt Gingrich and other leaders on the right argued publicly that the President's race reconciliation council was too one-sided and that the hearings finally held around the country were themselves a mockery of the reconciliation process because they failed to include diverse perspectives about the race problem in America.[5] One of the main fault lines of the US racial reconciliation process was the persistent opposition from the Republican leadership to the commission's composition. However, according to news reports, Newt Gingrich was contacted about membership of the group but his office never responded.

It is intriguing that there then emerged a call for racial healing in America from the right. It was as if it was intended to show that those on the right were not racists—even though they opposed affirmative action, welfare, minority scholarships, and the like. The new right called for acknowledgment and apology for slavery and the wrongs against blacks. Some even recommended compensation, putting claims of blacks forever behind us.

In this light, the American context of racial equality was one where racial reconciliation briefly was seen as a means toward ending black claims to special treatment. Cloaked in religious terms, racial healing and reconciliation served a useful purpose in undermining demands for whites to share their privilege.

ANTI-RACISM[6]

The United Nations World Conference against Racism, Racial Discrimination, Xenophobia, and Related Intolerance (UN-WCAR), through a multiyear, multi-national process, helped synthesize a large body of knowledge regarding definitions of race, racism, racial discrimination, and racial inequality (United Nations 2002). It brought together anti-racism organizations from across the globe in Durban, South Africa in August 2001and provided legitimacy to specific country anti-racism proposals that otherwise might not have been embraced. Convening these diverse anti-racism organizations revealed the wide differences in opinion about the problem anti-racism initiatives hope to solve. Indeed, as an analysis of upper-Midwest anti-racism initiatives revealed, there was a chilling ambivalence at times as to whether the problem was race at all.

The Durban WCAR provided perhaps the first formal international acknowledgment that current racism and racial discrimination have their roots in prior slavery. This acknowledgment has been resolutely avoided by the United States but nonetheless received formal support from most European participants:

> We acknowledge that slavery and the slave trade, including the transatlantic slave trade, were appalling tragedies in the history of humanity not only because of their abhorrent barbarism but also in terms of their magnitude, organized nature and especially their negation of the essence of the victims, and further acknowledge that slavery and the slave trade are a crime against humanity and should always have been so, especially the transatlantic slave trade, and are among the major sources and manifestations of racism, racial discrimination, xenophobia and related intolerance, and that Africans and people of African descent, Asians and people of Asian descent and indigenous peoples were victims of these acts and continue to be victims of their consequences. (United Nations 2002 [Section 13, p. 6])

The language of this statement owes as much to the significant lobbying by African American, Afro-Caribbean, Afro-Brazilian, and peoples of African descent elsewhere in the world as it does to the vigorous acknowledgment of indigenous groups and Asian human-rights groups of the role of colonialism, apartheid, and genocide in producing racial and ethnic economic inequality. Thus, the WCAR acknowledged not just African slavery, but other structures around the world that have had similar deleterious impacts on social and economic development of oppressed peoples. An important outcome of the WCAR was the galvanization of international support for reparations. Never before had there been such a massive global gathering with such unity on the idea of reparations. Although there is no explicit call for reparations in the final declaration signed by government bodies, the nongovernmental organizations (NGOs) succeeded in bringing the issue to the attention of the international community.

The main accomplishment of the Durban convention, however, was the effort to redefine anti-racism. Thousands of organizations were represented at the regional summits preceding Durban, and a reported 15,000 delegates from around the world attended the Durban NGO conference. One unintended consequence of this significant gathering, which included organizations representing Roma in Eastern Europe, Dalits in India, Maori in New Zealand, and Koori and Torres Strait Islanders in Australia, was the redefinition of anti-racism. At one point during the conference, there was even a call to rid the convention of race altogether by eliminating the term *race* in all documentation.

The Joint Center for Economic and Political Research's anti-racism initiative, the Network of Alliances Bridging Race and Ethnicity (NABRE), drew on research by Maggie Potapchuk (2002) and Ilana Shapiro (2002) to provide classifications of domestic anti-racism organizations. The dominant classifications include the anti-discrimination/civil rights advocacy approaches that are most closely aligned with conventional economic understandings of racial discrimination. If there are racial gaps in homeownership or lending, then the approach to remedying those gaps is enforcement of Title VIII of the Civil Rights Act of 1968 (Fair Housing Act), which prohibits discrimination in housing, or of the Equal Credit Opportunity Act, which prohibits discrimination in credit.

Other approaches included managing diversity, which focuses on institutions that are not well organized to integrate diverse populations, and democracy-building or community-building, which frame the problem in the context of neighborhoods or groups that are segregated or disenfranchised. Added to the list were conventional conflict-resolution/intergroup relations approaches familiar to social psychologists. The prejudice-reduction approach is familiar to anyone who has attended the well-known People's Institute training.

In short, an umbrella was created that permitted a wide range of organizations pursuing a diverse set of remedies to redefine and reconceptualize anti-racism. These widely divergent approaches to fighting racism were rooted in substantially different views of the nature and causes of racism; but, the organizations that embraced these divergent approaches all attested to being anti-racist.

As a part of a longer-term project examining racism in Minnesota, researchers sought out organizations that might be termed *solution-makers*. A file merging information from Guidestar IRS 1998–1999 data with information from the Minnesota Council of Non-profits produced a sample of 3,677 matches of schools, churches, foundations, and other nonprofit organizations. In September 2000, postcards were sent asking organizations if they considered anti-racism to be a major component of their work. There were 619 respondents. There were no statistical differences between the respondents and non-respondents in age of organization, income, or assets. Non-respondents were less likely to receive support from governmental units or from the general public and were more likely to receive the bulk of their funding from gross investment or unrelated business income.

Of the 619 respondents, 236 indicated that they were anti-racism organizations. No statistically significant difference was found in age, income, assets, or category of nonprofit (churches, schools, etc.) between those organizations that said they were anti-racism organizations and those that did not. Instead, the main factors differentiating the anti-racism organizations from other respondents were receipt of government or public funding and location in the metropolitan areas of Minnesota.

In the non-metro area, organizations were younger, had higher income relative to assets, and received their funding from government or public funds. Meanwhile, in the metro sample, the best predictor of anti-racism mission was having high assets, with no statistically significant impacts of age of organization, type of organization, or income.

Further analysis included interviews with anti-racism organization leaders. A total of forty-nine participants in ten focus groups were interviewed. The sample was 71 percent white and 63 percent female. The interviews were conducted prior to the Durban round. There was a general expression of feeling isolated from other anti-racism organizations in the state and in the national or international sphere. A dominant theme was the lack of a definition of racism. The majority of organizations interviewed did not adopt a formal definition of racism. Many of the respondents felt that racism was not about race, but about exclusion and bias, which can take many forms. Indeed, there was a consensus that the use of term *race* is often discomfiting.

The disagreement about remedies for racism rests in part on differences in perspectives about the nature of the problem that anti-racism is to solve. There are wide differences in beliefs about the subjects of analysis. The Durban round brought the human-rights plights of indigenous groups, Asians, migrants, children, and African Americans all under the same rubric. The Dalits in India and the Roma in Eastern Europe vied with African slave descendants in the Americas to bring their concerns to center stage.

Surprisingly, many anti-racism programs and initiatives, particularly in Minnesota, have been run by and for whites. Combating racism requires that one have a measureable and concrete conceptualization of racism. But, as the Durban round exposed, there are widely varying understandings of what racism is and how to remedy racism. As a result, anti-racism programs—often with noble goals and ambitious agendas—struggle to define what it is that they are attempting to remedy. The most glaring aspect of anti-racism initiatives is the tendency to gravitate toward "elimination of race" as part of the agenda. An extreme version of anti-racism is one that promotes the elimination of a race box in college admissions or in employment applications; advocates for the elimination of race in discourse about racial inequalities; and aspires for a world that is race-free.

SUMMARY

In this chapter, we have argued that the choice of remedy to racial inequality depends on the problem the remedy is attempting to resolve. When the problem is discrimination—whether current, passive, or general societal—the remedy might be designed to rectify disparities. But, some parts of observed disparities arguably are the result of things other than discrimination, immediately calling into question remedies such as anti-discrimination or affirmative action. If the problem is not really discrimination, how can one justify an anti-discrimination remedy or an affirmative action and race-conscious remedy designed to redress discrimination?

Race-neutral efforts can partially allay the concerns of critics who contend that the problem is not discrimination at all. But, then again, race-neutral remedies might not remove the underlying racial disparities.

When the problem to be remedied is blocked access to opportunities, remedies like equal opportunity remain the obvious choice for policy makers. Equal opportunity remedies are safe in the sense that they arouse far less opposition from groups that are not disadvantaged. Such remedies have the distinction of always being race neutral. Unfortunately, equal opportunity does not always assure that racial disparities will disappear or even diminish.

When the problem to be remedied is past wrongs or atrocities, remedies like reparations or racial reconciliation commend themselves. Anti-racism programs suffer, unfortunately, from widely differing conceptualizations of what racism is. Is it a sickness? Is it a normal and functional component of market economies? Would getting rid of racism require dismantling the overclass? Or, can we take the easy route of just saying no to race?

Reparations—a vital component of any comprehensive racial reconciliation program—are controversial both because they cost a lot and because they are seen as politically unfeasible. The administrative details of who would receive the reparations, how much, in what type of financial package, and at what cost to taxpayers are details that literally have never been fully resolved. The surprising support for reparations from the political and ideological right suggests that other forms of redress for historic wrongs would vanish once the reparations are paid.

Thus, all of the alternatives to race-neutral remedies suffer from the same sort of objections that arise when discussing the effectiveness of race-neutrality. The lesson from this chapter, then, is that the policy maker and analyst must be willing to focus separately on different types of remedies for different types of underlying racial inequalities. For inequalities that present themselves as racial discrimination, race-conscious interventions narrowly targeted to the groups affected work best. They may arouse objections as being unfair or unconstitutional. Yet, if narrowly tailored to remedy specific forms of discrimination and targeted toward groups experiencing the discrimination, the race-conscious remedies will do what they are intended to do.

For racial inequalities that present themselves as historic wrongs, racism, hate crimes, or atrocities, racial reconciliation requires multiple stages to be effective in remedying those wrongs. One must disentangle the portions of the atrocities like slavery that can never truly be remedied or reconciled and the parts that emerge after generations of foregone opportunities and advancement. Reparations might be able to recover some small component of the monetary damages but true racial reconciliation requires a massive government effort similar to that undertaken in Australia and South Africa. And, such an effort demands an apology, acknowledgment, and a guarantee of non-recurrence. Reparations are only a small part of true racial reconciliation.

The most politically feasible and easiest to implement race-neutral remedies fall into the category of remedying barriers to access to opportunities. Equal opportunity remedies are a mainstay of the American psyche. Unfortunately, since historically there has not been equality of opportunity for certain racial and ethnic groups, provision of equal opportunity now for disadvantaged groups assures that those groups will remain behind. Race-neutrality in this sense becomes a form of keeping racial disparities alive for generations.

NOTES

1. This section draws upon Samuel L. Myers Jr., "If Not Reconciliation, Then What?" *Review of Social Economy* 58(3), 361–380, 2000. http://dx.doi.org/10.1080/00346760050132373.

2. September 9, 1998, Office of the Press Secretary, "Remarks by the President to the advisory board on race," and January 12, 1998, Office of the Press Secretary, "Remarks by the President in the race initiative outreach meeting."

3. In May 1997, Prime Minister John Howard refused to accept the Australian high court judgment on Aboriginal claims to leasehold land and to officially apologize for past government policies that removed 100,000 Aboriginal children from their families. Commonwealth of Australia, *Bringing them home: Report of the National Inquiry into the Separation of the aboriginal and Torres Strait Islander Children from their Families* 1997, 249.

4. October 1998, White House Office of Communication, Clinton-Gore Administration: A Record of Progress for Gay and Lesbian Americans; July 19, 1998, White House, Office of Press Secretary, Remarks by the President at National Defense University.

5. Gingrich and Connerly, "Face the Failure of Racial Preferences," 1997. Newt Gingrich was speaker of the US House of Representatives. Ward Connerly chaired the American Civil Rights Institute and was a University of California regent.

6. This section draws upon Myers, Lange, and Corrie, "The Political Economy of Antiracism Initiatives in the Post-Durban Round," *AEA Papers and Proceedings* 93(2), 330–333, May 2003.

Epilogue

This book was conceived ten years ago as a result of collaborative research on race neutrality in public procurement and contracting. Our original intention was to make the case for maximizing race-neutral remedies to observed racial disparities in contract awards among business enterprises. We reasoned that race-neutral remedies would be preferable in the post-Obama era when (a) explicit and unlawful forms of discrimination appeared to have diminished and (b) constitutional challenges to affirmative action and related race-conscious remedies made such remedies less feasible.

Never in our wildest dreams did we anticipate when we began writing this book that in just a short span of eighteen months the political and cultural landscape would revert to the very type of open racism and explicit forms of discrimination that race-conscious programs initially were designed to combat. We never thought that we would see a dismantlement of diversity arguments and a massive retrenchment in support for equal opportunity. While we anticipated the continued opposition to race-conscious, preferential treatment initiatives in college admissions, public employment, and procurement and contracting, we never expected that basic civility in racial discourse would disintegrate in America.

Let's consider the case study of Dylann Roof. One of the most horrific hate crimes in modern US history occurred on June 17, 2015, and took place at Emanuel African Methodist Episcopal Church in Charleston, South Carolina, when Dylann S. Roof systematically murdered nine African American Bible-study class members. Unemployed and a high-school dropout, Dylann confessed to the shootings and justified his acts as part of an effort to ignite a national race war. All indicators were that this unemployed young white male was living on the margins of society, frequently using and abusing drugs, and angry at the advantages that African Americans and other nonwhites appeared to have gained at his expense and the expense of other whites like him. The narrative of the angry white male would resonate, but for the fact that Dylann Roof was mentally ill.

The *New York Times* reported on "how an awkward adolescent had progressed from reclusive consumer of internet hate to ruthless and remorseless jihadist" stating that unsealed psychiatric reports revealed a young man tormented by mental illness:

> The documents provide, for the first time, a multidimensional portrait of a withdrawn but strikingly intelligent misfit whose tastes ran to Dostoyevsky, classical music and NPR but who said his "dream job" would be working at an airport convenience store. He exhibited disturbingly introverted behavior from an early age—playing alone, never starting conversations—but received little treatment for what defense experts later concluded was autism and severe social anxiety, with precursor symptoms of psychosis. (Sack, 2017)

Roof had repeatedly been arrested in prior months for other crimes and normally would have been prohibited from purchasing a lethal weapon. However, apparently, clerical errors resulted in his prior arrests not being registered at the time of his application for a firearm. The Charleston, SC, massacre resulted in national outrage about gun availability, mental illness, and auxiliary factors that seemed to explain away or diminish the explanation of heightened white male unemployment that might contribute to violent acts of racism.

At least in 2015, one could feel comfort in knowing that Dylann Roof's form of racism was a form of mental illness.

Since 2017, we are not so sure.

We have witnessed escalating incidents of overt racist behavior not only among unemployed loners, also but among the top-elected officials in the nation. We have witnessed alarming acceptance of what can only be called openly hostile and explicitly offensive racial (and sexual) harassment and abuse in the workplace, in public spaces, and even in the hallowed halls of the White House and Congress.

None of the remedies discussed in this book are likely to address the new forms of explicit racism arising in American life. The question, then, is no longer one of whether race-neutral remedies to racial inequality can replace race-conscious ones to appease the various critics of conventional affirmative action efforts. The question now becomes one of how and whether race-neutral remedies can address the widening cultural divide in America that has made overt racism popular and acceptable once again.

We are dumbfounded by the recent turn of events in the United States where race-baiting, normalization of racially demeaning behaviors and the escalation of anti-immigrant, anti-Muslim, anti-equality themes send warning signals to advocates for racial equality. It is not clear to us whether abandoning race-conscious remedies—flawed as they may be—in favor of race-neutral remedies will be sufficient to reverse the unimaginable and unthinkable racist shift observed among top governmental officials and their hundreds of thousands of loyal followers. Our only hope is that the 2017 experience in America is merely an aberration and that soon the nation will return to the work of remedying racial economic inequalities.

Bibliography

Abravanel, M. D. (2002). Public Knowledge of Fair Housing Laws: Does it Protect Against Housing Discrimination? *Housing Policy Debate* 13(3), 469–504.

ACLU vs. LAPD in racial profiling suit. (2000, February 11). *Nando Times*.

Adams, J. et al. (1996). *Minnesota's Housing: Shaping Community in the 1990s*. Minneapolis, MN: Humphrey Institute, Center for Urban and Regional Affairs, p. 102.

Ahlburg, D. et al. (1995). *Are Good Jobs Disappearing? What the 1990 Census Says About Minnesota*. Minneapolis, MN: Humphrey Institute, Center for Urban and Regional Affairs.

Aigner, D. J., and Cain, G. G. (1977). Statistical Theories of Discrimination in Labor Markets. *Industrial and Labor Relations Review* 30(2), 175–187.

Akerlof, G. A. (1970). The Market for "Lemons": Quality Uncertainty and the Market Mechanism. *The Quarterly Journal of Economics* 84(3), 488–500.

Alesina, A. F., and La Ferrara, E. (2005). Ethnic Diversity and Economic Performance. *Journal of Economic Literature* 43(3), 762–800.

———. (2000). Participation in Heterogeneous Communities. *The Quarterly Journal of Economics* 115(3), 847–904.

Alesina, A., Baqir, R., and Easterly, W. (1999). Public Goods and Ethnic Divisions. *Quarterly Journal of Economics* 114(4), 1243–1284.

Alexis, Marcus. (1973). A Theory of Labor Market Discrimination with Interdependent Utilities. *The American Economic Review* 63(2) (May), 296–302.

Alvarez, M., and Brehm, J. (1997). Are Americans Ambivalent Towards Racial Policies? *American Journal of Political Science* 41(2), 345–374.

Ancona, D. G., and Caldwell, D. F. (1992). Demography and Design: Predictors of New Product Team Performance. *Organization Science* 3(3), 321–341.

Anderson, B. E. (1997). Affirmative action policy under executive order 1146: A retrospective view. In S. L. Myers, Jr. (ed.) *Civil rights and race relations in the post Regan-Bush Era* (pp. 47–60). Westport: Praeger Publishers.

Andorra, B. (1998, December 1). *Affirmative Action in Employment: Background and Current Debate*. Washington, D.C.: Congressional Research Service.

Antunes, G., and Hunt, A. L. (1973). The Deterrent Impact of Criminal Sanctions: Some Implications for Criminal Justice Policy. *Journal of Urban Law* 51(2), 145–161.

Ards, S. D., and Myers, Jr., S. L. (2001a). The Color of Money: Bad Credit, Wealth and Race. *American Behavioral Scientist* 45(2), 223–239.

———. (2001b). *Credit and Knowledge: The African American Experience.* Presented at the Southern Economic Association meetings in Crystal City, November 11, 2000, and the Eastern Economic Association meetings in New York, February 25, 2001.

———. (2001). *The Political Economy of Affirmative Action Retrenchment.* Revised. Hubert Humphrey Institute of Public Affairs, University of Minnesota, Minneapolis, Minnesota. Unpublished.

———. (1997). *The Political Economy of Affirmative Action Retrenchment.* A paper prepared for the National Economic Association panel on the Political Economy of Affirmative Action Retrenchment, Allied Social Science Association Meetings, New Orleans, Louisiana. Unpublished.

Ards, S., Chung, C., Hagerty, B., Malkis, A., and Myers, Jr., S. L. (2003, May). Decomposing Black-White Differences in Child Maltreatment. *Child Maltreatment* 8(2), 112–121.

Ards, S. D., Chung, C., and Myers, Jr., S. L. (2001). Letter to the Editor: Sample Selection Bias and Racial Differences in Child Abuse Reporting: Once Again. *Child Abuse and Neglect: The International Journal* 25(1), 7–12.

———. (1999). Letter to the Editor. *Child Abuse and Neglect: The International Journal* 23(12), 1211–1215.

———. (1998). The Effects of Sample Selection Bias on Racial Differences in Child Abuse Reporting. *Child Abuse and Neglect: The International Journal* 22(2), 103–115.

Aronson, J., Quinn, D. M., and Spencer, S. J. (1988). Stereotype threat and the academic underperformance of minorities and women. In J. K. Swim and C. Stangor (eds.) *Prejudice: The target's perspective* (pp. 83–103). San Diego, CA: Academic Press.

Arrow, K. J. (1973). The theory of discrimination. In O. Ashenfelter and A. Rees (eds.) *Discrimination in labor markets* (pp. 3–33). Princeton: Princeton University.

Arrow, K. J., and Hahn, F. H. (1971). *General Competitive Analysis.* New York: North- Holland Pub. Co.

Assembly seeks ban on racial profiling. (2001, May 25). *Times Union*, Albany, NY.

Bane, M.-J. (2001). Presidential Address—Expertise, Advocacy and Deliberation: Lessons from Welfare Reform. *Journal of Policy Analysis and Management* 20(2), 191–197.

Bankston, W., and Cramer, J. (1974). Toward a Macrosociological Interpretation of General Deterrence. *Criminology* 12(November), 251–280.

Barrilleaux, C. J., and Miller, M. E. (1988). The Political Economy of State Medicaid Policy. *American Political Science Review* 82(4), 1089–1107.

Bates, R. H. (2000). Ethnicity and Development in Africa: A Reappraisal. *American Economic Review* 90(2), 131–134.

Bates, T. (2009). Utilizing Affirmative Action in Public Sector Procurement as a Local Economic Development Strategy. *Economic Development Quarterly* 23(3), 180–192.

———. (1984). Urban Economic Transformation and Minority Business Opportunities. *Review of Black Political Economy* 13(3), 21–36.

———. (1981). Effectiveness of the Small Business Administration in Financing Minority Business. *Review of Black Political Economy* 11(3), 321–336.

Baumol, W. J. (1986). *Superfairness: Applications and Theory.* Cambridge, MA: The MIT Press.

Bean, F. D., and Leach, M. A. (2005). Critical Disjuncture? The Culmination of Post-World War II Socio-Demographic and Economic Trends in the United States. *Journal of Population Research* 22(1), 63–78.

Becker, G. (1971). *The Economics of Discrimination* (2nd ed.). Chicago, IL: The University of Chicago Press.

———. (1968). Crime and Punishment: An Economic Approach. *Journal of Political Economy* 76(2), 169–217.

Becker, G. (1957). *The Economics of Discrimination.* Chicago: University of Chicago Press.

Bejan, A., Jones, E. C., and Charles, J. D. (2010). The Evolution of Speed on Athletics: Why the Fastest Runners are Black and Swimmers White. *International Journal of Design and Nature and Ecodynamics* 3(5), 1–13.

Berkovec, J. A., Canner, G. B., Gabriel, S. A., and Hannan, T. (1994). Race, Redlining, and Residential Mortgage Loan Performance. *Journal of Real Estate Finance, and Economics* 9(3) (November), 263–294.

Bernstein, N., and Newman, A. (2001, November 8). Before child's death, a history of abuse and efforts to help. *The New York Times,* Section 1, Page 1, Column 2, Metropolitan Desk.

Berry, W. D., Ringquist, E. J., Fording, R. C., and Hanson, R. L. (1998). Measuring Citizen and Government Ideology in the American States, 1960–93. *American Journal of Political Science* 42(1), 327–348.

Bertrand, M., and Mullainathan, S. (2004). Are Emily and Greg More Employable than Lakisha and Jamal? A Field Experiment on Labor Market Discrimination. *American Economic Review* 94(4), 991–1013.

Best Graduate Schools: Public Affairs (Master's) (Ranked in 2001). (2001a, November). *U.S. News and World Report.* Retrieved November 26, 2001, from http://www.usnews.com/usnews/edu/beyond/gradrank/gbpubadm.html.

Betsey, C., Lindsey-Taliaferro, D., and Amdet. (2001). *Freddie Mac's Consumer Credit Survey: Family Influences on Credit Outcomes.* Presented at the Southern Economic Association meetings in Crystal City, November 11, 2000, and the Eastern Economic Association meetings in New York, February 25, 2001.

Bhagwati, J. N. (1982). Directly Unproductive, Profit-Seeking (DUP) Activities. *Journal of Political Economy* 90(5), 988–1002.

Black, D. E. (1983). Effectiveness of the Mandatory Minority Business Set-Aside Contracting Goals: A Regression Analysis. *Evaluation Review* 7(3), 321–336.

Blanchflower, D. G., Levine, P. B., and Zimmerman, D. J. (2003). Discrimination in the Small-Business Credit Market. *Review of Economics and Statistics* 85(4), 930–943.

Blinder, A. S. (1973). Wage Discrimination: Reduced Form and Structural Estimates. *Journal of Human Resources* 8(4), 436–455.

Board of Governors of the Federal Reserve System. (1997). *Survey of Consumer Finances, 1995*. [Electronic data tape]. Washington, D.C.: Board of Governors of the Federal Reserve System.

———. (1996). *Report on the Audit of the Board's Consumer Compliance Examination Process A9508*. April. Washington, D.C.: Office of Inspector General.

———. (1995). *Consumer Compliance Handbook*. Washington, D.C.: Board of Governors of the Federal Reserve System.

Bond, M. T., Seiler, V. L., and Seiler, M. J. (2003). The Effects of Multicultural Diversity in Real Estate Brokerage. *Journal of Real Estate Research* 25(4), 529–542.

Boston, T. D. (1999). *Affirmative Action and Black Entrepreneurship*. New York, NY: Routledge.

Bowers, W., and Salem, R. G. (1972). Severity of Formal Sanctions as a Repressive Response to Deviant Behavior. *Law and Society Review* 7, 427.

Boyd, L. A. (1997). Discrimination in Mortgage Lending: The Impact on Minority Defaults in the Stafford Loan Program. *The Quarterly Review of Economics and Finance* 37(1), 23–27.

Bozeman, B. (2007). Chapter eight: Public values. In Bozeman (ed.), *Public values and public interest: Counterbalancing economic individualism* (pp. 132–158). Washington, D.C.: Georgetown University Press.

Braithwaite, J. (1985). *To Punish or Persuade: Enforcement of Coal Mine Safety*. Albany, NY: State University of New York Press.

Braithwaite, J., and Makkai, T. (1991). Testing an Expected Utility Model of Corporate Deterrence. *Law and Society Review* 25(1), 7–13.

Brandl, J. (1998). *Money and Good Intentions Are Not Enough*. Washington, D.C.: Brookings Institution.

Brandl, John E. (1988). Presidential Address: On Politics and Policy Analysis as the Design and Assessment of Institutions. *Journal of Policy Analysis and Management* 7(2), 419–424.

Brewer, G. D., and deLeon, P. (1983). *The Foundations of Policy Analysis*. Homewood, IL: Dorsey Press.

Brief of Amici Curiae Steelcase, Inc., 3M, Bank One Corporation, Abbott Laboratories, E. I. Du Pont De Nemours and Co., Inc., The Dow Chemical Company, Eastman Kodak Company, Eli Lilly and Company, General Mills, Inc., Intel Corporation, Johnson and Johnson, Kellogg Company, KPMG International, Lucent Technologies, Inc., Microsoft Corporation, PPG Industries, Inc., The Procter and Gamble Company, Sara Lee Corporation, Texaco Inc., and TRW Inc. Gratz et al. v Bollinger; Grutter et al. v Bollinger. (2000). (No. 97–75928, No. 97–75231). October 16.

Brief of Amici Curiae The Civil Rights Project at Harvard University Gratz et al. v. Bollinger et al., Patterson et al. (Nos. 01–1333, 01–1416, 01–1418). (2001). May.

Browne, L. E., and Tootell, G. M. (1995). Mortgage Lending in Boston: A Response to the Critics. *New England Economic Review* (September/October), 53–78.

Bustillo, M. (2000, April 28). Davis backs bill banning profiling. *Los Angeles Times*, Part A. Part 1, Page 3, Metro Desk.

Bureau of National Affairs. (1995). *EEOC Compliance Manual.* Washington, D.C.: Bureau of National Affairs.

California governor signs bill on racial profiling. (2000, September 27). *FindLaw Legal News.*

Canner, G., Smith, D., and Passmore, W. (1994). Residential Lending to Low-Income and Minority Families: Evidence from the 1992 HMDA Data. *Federal Reserve Bulletin* 80, 79–108.

Carr, J. H., and Mebbolugbe, I. F. (1993). The Federal Reserve Bank of Boston Study on Mortgage Lending Revisited. *Journal of Housing Research* 4(2), 277–313.

Carter, D. A., Simkins, B. J., and Simpson, W. G. (2003). Corporate Governance, Board Diversity, and Firm Value. *Financial Review* 38(1), 33–53.

Cavalluzzo, K. S., and Cavalluzzo, L. C. (1998). Market Structure and Discrimination: The Case of Small Business. *Journal of Money, Credit, and Banking* 30(4), 771–792.

Centers for Disease Control and Prevention. (2011). *Unintentional Drowning: Fact Sheet.* Retrieved June 8, 2011, from Centers for Disease Control and Prevention http://www.cdc.gov/HomeandRecreationalSafety/Water-Safety/waterinjuries-factsheet.html.

Chambers, D. (2010). Does A Rising Tide Raise All Ships? The Impact of Growth on Inequality. *Applied Economics Letters* 17(6), 581–586.

Chang, M. J., Astin, A. W., and Kim, D. (2004). Cross-Racial Interaction Among Undergraduates: Some Consequences, Causes, and Patterns Research. *Higher Education* 45(5), 529–553.

Cherry, R. (2001). *Who Gets the Good Jobs? Combating Race and Gender Disparities.* New Brunswick, NJ: Rutgers University Press.

City of Richmond v. J. A. Croson Co., 488 U.S. 469 (1989).

Cloud, C., and Galster, G. (1993). What Do We Know About Racial Discrimination in Mortgage Markets? *The Review of Black Political Economy* 22, 101–120.

Coates, T. (2014, June). The case for reparations. *The Atlantic.* Retrieved from http://www.theatlantic.com/magazine/archive/2014/06/the-case-for-reparations/361631/.

Cohn, D. (1999, October 5). Credit study attacked; Freddie mac data called incomplete. *The Washington Post*, p. B1.

Colamery, S. N. (1998). *Affirmative Action: Catalyst or Albatross?* Commack, NY: Nova Science Publishers, Inc.

Collier, P. (2000). Ethnicity, Politics and Economic Performance. *Economics and Politics* 12(3), 225–245.

Commonwealth of Australia. (1997). Bringing them Home: Report of the National Inquiry into the Separation of the aboriginal and Torres Strait Islander Children from their Families, 249.

Corkery, M. (2012, January 26). Public pensions increase private-equity investments. *The Wall Street Journal*, https://www.wsj.com/articles/SB10001424052970203806504577181272061850732

Couch, K. A., and Fairlie, R. (2008). Last Hired, First Fired? Black-White Unemployment and the Business Cycle. IZA Discussion Paper No. 3713.

Coulton, C. J., Korbin, J. E., and Su, M. (1999). Neighborhoods and Child Maltreatment: A Multilevel Study. *Child Abuse and Neglect* 23(11), 101940.

Criminal justice: Minnesota's arrest, incarceration numbers are nation's highest in racial disproportion. (1995, October 18). *Star Tribune*, Minneapolis, p. 14A.

Crowly, S. (2006). Where is home? Housing for low income people after the 2005 hurricane. In C. Hartman and G. D. Squires (eds.) *There is no such thing as a natural disaster: Race, class, and Hurricane Katrina* (pp. 121–166). New York, NY: Routledge.

Darity, Jr., W. A. (2008). Forty Acres and a Mule in the 21st Century. *Social Science Quarterly* 89(3), 656–664.

Darity, Jr., W. A. (2005). *Affirmative Action in Comparative Perspective: Strategies to Combat Ethnic and Racial Exclusion Internationally.* Sanford Institute of Public Policy, Duke University, Durham, NC. Unpublished paper.

Darity, Jr., W. A. (2005). Stratification Economics: The Role of Intergroup Inequality. *Journal of Economics and Finance* 29(2), 144–153.

Darity, Jr., W. A. (1997). Reparations. In S. L. Myers, Jr. (ed.) *Race relations and civil rights in the post-Reagan Bush era* (pp. 231–242). Westport, CT: Praeger.

Darity, Jr., W. A. (1995). The Undesirable, America's Underclass in the Managerial Age: Beyond the Myrdal Theory of Racial Inequality. *Daedelus: Journal of the American Academy of Arts and Sciences* 124(1), 145–165.

Darity, Jr., W. A. (1989). What's left of the economic theory of discrimination? Chapter 12. In Steven Shulman and William A. Darity, Jr. (eds.) *The question of discrimination: Racial inequality in the U.S. labor market* (pp. 335–373). Middletown, CT: Wesleyan University Press.

Darity, Jr., W. A., Guilkey, D., and Winfrey, W. (1995). Ethnicity, Race, and Earnings. *Economic Letters* 47(3–4), 401–408.

Darity, Jr., Hamilton, D., and Dietrich, J. (2001). *Passing on Blackness: Latinos, Race and Labor Market Outcomes.* Working paper. University of North Carolina, Chapel Hill.

Darity, Jr., W. A., Lahiri, B., and Frank, D. V. (2010). Reparations for African-Americans as a Transfer Problem: A Cautionary. *Review of Development Economics* 14(2), 248–261.

Darity, Jr., W. A., Mason, P., and Stewart, J. (2006). The Economics of Identity: The Origin and Persistence of Racial Identity Norms. *Journal of Economic Behavior and Organization* 60, 85–305.

Darity, Jr., W. A., and Myers, Jr., S. L. (2000). Languishing in inequality: Racial disparities in wealth and earnings in the new millennium. In J. Jackson (ed.) *New directions: African Americans in a diversifying nation* (pp. 86–118). Washington, D.C.: National Policy Association Report #297.

Darity, Jr., W. A., and Myers, Jr., S. L. (1995). Family structure and the marginalization of black men: Policy implications. Chapter 9. In M. B. Tucker and C. Mitchell-Kernan (eds.) *The decline in marriage among African Americans: Causes, consequences and policy implications* (pp. 263–308). New York, NY: Russell Sage Foundation.

Darity, Jr., W. A., Stewart, J. B., and Mason, P. L. (2000). *The Economics of Identity: The Origin and Persistence of Racial Norms*. Working paper.

Darity, Jr., W. A., and Williams, R. M. (1985). Peddlers Forever?: Culture, Competition, and Discrimination. *American Economic Review, Papers and Proceedings* 75(2), 256–261.

Davila, R. L., Ha, I., and Myers, Jr., S. L. (2012). Affirmative Action Retrenchment in Public Procurement and Contracting. *Applied Economics Letters* 19(18), 1857–1860.

Day, T., and Liebowitz, S. J. (1996). *Mortgages, Minorities, and HMDA*. Paper presented at the Federal Reserve Bank of Chicago, April.

del Río, C., Gradin, C., and Cantó, O. (2011). The Measurement of Gender Wage Discrimination: The Distributional Approach Revisited. *The Journal of Economic Inequality* 9(1), 57–86.

Dery, D. (1984). *Problem Definition in Policy Analysis*. Lawrence, KS: University Press of Kansas.

Doleac, J., and Stein, L. (2010). *The Visible Hand: Race and Online Market Outcomes, Discussion Paper 09-015*. Stanford, CA: Stanford Institute for Economic Policy Research.

Donohue, J., and Heckman, J. (1991). Continuous vs. Episodic Change: The Impact of Affirmative Action and Civil Rights Policy on the Economic Status of Blacks. *Journal of Economic Literature* 29(4), 1603–1643.

Doxsey, P. (2001, August 25). Dutchess strives to avoid racial profiling by police. *Daily Freeman*.

Drake, B., and Rank, M. (2009). The Racial Divide among American Children in Poverty: Reassessing the Importance of Neighborhood. *Children and Youth Services Review* 31(12), 1264–1221.

Dunn, W. N. (1994). *Public Policy Analysis: An Introduction* (2nd ed.). Upper Saddle River, NJ: Prentice Hall.

Dunstan, R. (n.d.). (2013). *History of Gambling*. Retrieved January 17, 2013, from California State Library. http://www.library.ca.gov/crb/97/03/Chapt2.html.

Dye, T. R. (1984). Party and Policy in the States. *Journal of Politics* 46(4), 1097–1116.

Easterly, W., and Levine, R. (1997). Africa's Growth Tragedy: Policies and Ethnic Divisions. *Quarterly Journal of Economics* 112(4), 1203–1250.

Echaustegui, M. E., Fix, M., Loprest, P., Von der Lippe, S. C., and Wissoker, D. (1997). *Do Minority-Owned Business get a Fair Share of Government Contracts?* Washington, D.C.: The Urban Institute.

Eddings, K. (2001, June 29). Racial profiling bill becomes law in Westchester. *The Journal News*.

Ehrlich, I. (1972). The Deterrent Effect of Criminal Law Enforcement. *Journal of Legal Studies* 1(2), 259–276.

Electronic Code of Federal Regulations (e-CFR) current as of May 24, 2006; Title 49: Transportation PART 26.

Erickson, K. (1966). *Wayward Puritans; A Study in the Sociology of Deviance*. New York: John Wiley and Sons.

Erikson, R. S. (1971). The Relationship between Party Control and Civil Rights Legislation in the American States. *Western Political Quarterly* 24(1), 178–182.

Evelyn, Jamilah, and Hamilton, Kendra (2000, May 25). Department, Program, Institute or Other. *Black Issues in Higher Education* 17(7), 27.

Fairlie, R. W., and Meyer, B. D. (2000). Trends in Self-Employment among White and Black Men during the Twentieth Century. *Journal of Human Resources* 35(4), 643–669.

Fairlie, R. W., and Robb, A. M. (2008). *Race and Entrepreneurial Success: Black-, Asian-, and White-Owned Businesses in the United States.* Cambridge, MA: MIT Press.

Feagin, J. R., and Imani, N. (1994). Racial Barriers to African American Entrepreneurship: An Explanatory Story. *Social Problems* 41(4), 562–584.

Ferraro, P. J., and Cummings, R. G. (2007). Cultural Diversity, Discrimination, and Economic Outcomes: An Experimental Analysis. *Economic Inquiry* 45(2), 217–232.

Fisher, J. D., and Houseworth, C. A. (2012). The Reverse Wage Gap among Educated White and Black Women. *Journal of Economic Inequality* 10(4), 449–470.

Flood, S., King, M., Ruggles, S., and Warren, R. J. (2017). *Integrated Public Use Microdata Series, Current Population Survey: Version 5.0.* [dataset]. Minneapolis: University of Minnesota. https://doi.org/10.18128/D030.V5.0.

Fox, J. (1993). 1994 affirmative action briefing. *Newsletter in Law Firm of Fenwick and West*.

Franklin, J. H., and Moss, Jr. A. A. (2000). *From Slavery to Freedom: A History of African Americans*. New York: Alfred A. Knopf.

Freddie Mac. (1999). *Freddie Mac News Release* [On-line]. September 2, 1999. (Originally accessed www.freddiemac.com/corporate/reports/cceipoll.htm, later removed. A copy can be found at http://www.bad2goodcredit.com/CreditSurvey.htm).

Freedman, L. S. (2002). *The Microeconomics of Public Policy Analysis*. Princeton, NJ: Princeton University Press.

Freeman, D. G. (2003). Trickling Down the Rising Tide: New Estimates of the Link between Poverty and the Macroeconomy. *Southern Economic Journal* 70(2), 359–373.

Freeman, R. B. (2001). The Rising Tide Lifts. . .? *NBER Working Paper Series, w8155*. National Bureau of Economic Research, Inc.

Friedman, L. S. (2002). *The Microeconomics of Public Policy Analysis*. Princeton, NJ: Princeton University Press.

Friedman, L. S. (1984). *Microeconomic Policy Analysis*. New York, NY: McGraw-Hill.

Fryer, R., and Loury, G. C. (2005). Affirmative Action in Winner-take-all Markets. *Journal of Economic Inequality* 3(3) (December), 263–280.

Gao, Y. (2014). *The Deterrent Effects of Reverse Discrimination Claims on Federal Rule Compliance at Law and Society Association Annual Meetings*, Minneapolis, MN, May 30.

Garand, J. C. (1985). Partisan Change and Shifting Expenditure Priorities in the American States: 1945–1978. *American Politics Quarterly* 13(4), 355–391.

Garland, A. F., EllisMacleod, E., Landverk, J., Granger, W., and Johnson, I. (1998). Minority Population in the Child Welfare System: The Visibility Hypothesis Reexamined. *American Journal of Orthopsychiatry* 68(1), 142–146.

Gawronski, B. (2002). What does the Implicit Association Test Measure? A Test of the Convergent and Discriminant Validity of Prejudice-Related IATs. *Experimental Psychology* 49(3), 171–180.

Geva-May, I. (1997). *An Operational Approach to Policy Analysis: The Craft: Prescription for Better Analysis.* Boston, MA: Kluwer Academic.

Gibbs, J. (1975). *Crime, Punishment and Deterrence.* New York, NY: Elsevier.

Gingrich, N., and Connerly, W. (1997, June 15). Face the failure of racial preferences. *New York Times.*

Glennon, D., and Stengle, M. (1994). *An Evaluation of the Federal Reserve Bank of Boston's Study of Racial Discrimination in Mortgage Lending.* Economic and Policy Analysis working paper no. 94–2. Office of the Comptroller of the Currency, Washington, D.C.

Goering, J., and Wienk, R. (1996). *Mortgage Lending, Racial Discrimination, and Federal Policy.* Washington, D.C.: Urban Institute Press.

Graham, H. D. (1990). *The Civil Rights Era: Origins and Development of National Policy 1960–1972.* New York, NY: Oxford University Press.

Grasmick, H. G., and Green, D. E. (1980). Legal Punishment, Social Disapproval, and Internalization as Inhibitors of Illegal Behavior. *Journal of Criminal Law and Criminology* 71, 825–835.

Grasmick, H. G., and Bursik, R. J. (1990). Conscience, Significant Others, and Rational Choice, Extending the Deterrence Model. *Law and Society Review* 24(3), 837–861.

Greenwald, A. G., McGhee, D. E., and Schwartz, J. L. K (1998). Measuring Individual Differences in Implicit Cognition: The Implicit Association Test. *Journal of Personality and Social Psychology* 74(6) (June), 1464–1480.

Gupta, N. D., Oaxaca R., and Smith, N. (2006). Analysing Trends in US and Danish Gender Wage Gaps in the 1980s and 1990s. *Applied Economics Letters* 13(10), 643–647.

Gurin, P. (1999). *The Compelling Need for Diversity in Education.* Expert report prepared for the lawsuits Gratz and Hamacher v Bollinger, Duderstadt, the University of Michigan, and the University of Michigan College of LSandA, U.S. District Court, Eastern District of Michigan, Civil Action No. 97–75231; and Grutter v Bollinger, Lehman, Shields, the University of Michigan and the University of Michigan Law School, U.S. District Court, Eastern District of Michigan, Civil Action No. 97–75928.

Habyarimana, J., Humphreys, M., Posner, D. N., and Weinstein, J. M. (2007). Why Does Ethnic Diversity Undermine Public Goods Provision? *American Political Science Review* 101(4), 709–725.

Hajnal, Z. L., Gerber, E. R., and Louch, H. (2002). Minorities and Direct Legislation: Evidence from California Ballot Proposition Elections. *Journal of Politics* 64(1), 154–177.

Halligan, P. (1991). Minority Business Enterprises and Ad Hoc Hypotheses: Guidelines for Studies by Local Governments. *Urban Lawyer* 23(2), 249–279.

Harrel, C. M. (1999). *Barriers to Minority Participation in Special Operations (MR-1042)*. RAND Corporation. http://www.rand.org/pubs/research_briefs/RB7526/index1.html.

Hartman, C., and Squires, G. D. (2006). *There is no Such Thing as a Natural Disaster: Race, Class, and Hurricane Katrina*. New York, NY: Routledge.

Hastings, D. W., Zahran S., and Cable, S. (2006). Drowning in Inequalities: Swimming and Social Justice. *Journal of Black Studies* 36(6), 894–917.

Hawley, C. B., and Fujii, E. T. (1991). Discrimination in Consumer Credit Markets. *Eastern Economic Journal* 17(1), 21–30.

Hawkesworth, M. E. (1988). *Theoretical Issues in Policy Analysis*. Albany: State University of New York Press.

Heckman, J. (1998). Detecting Discrimination. *Journal of Economic Perspectives* 12, 101–116.

Heckman, J. (1990). The Central Role of the South in Accounting for the Economic Progress of Black Americans. *American Economic Review* 80(2), 242–246.

Higgin, M., and Mihalopoulos, D. (2000, January 23). Lawsuits bring profiling into open. *Chicago Tribune*, p. 6.

Higginbotham, F. M. (2005). *Race Law: Cases, Commentary, and Questions*. Durham, NC: Carolina Academic Press.

Hines, Jr., J. R., Hoyes, H. W., and Krueger, A. B. (2001). *Another Look at Whether a Rising Tide Lifts All Boats. NBER Working Paper Series, w8412*. National Bureau of Economic Research, Inc.

Hogwood, B. W., and Gunn, L. A. (1984). *Policy Analysis for the Real World*. Oxford, UK: Oxford University Press.

Hong, L., and Page, S. E. (2004). Groups of Diverse Problem Solvers Can Outperform Groups of High-Ability Problem Solvers. *Proceedings of the National Academy of Sciences* 101(46), 16385–16389.

Horne, D. K. (1994). Evaluating the Role of Race in Mortgage Lending. *FDIC Banking Review* (Spring/Summer), 1–15.

———. (1997). Mortgage Lending, Race, and Model Specification. *Journal of Financial Services Research* 11(1–2) (April), 43–68.

Huck, P. (2001). Home Mortgage Lending by Applicant Race: Do HMDA Figures Provide a Distorted Picture? *Housing Policy Debate* 12(4), 719–736.

Hungerford, T. L. (2011). How Income Mobility Affects Income Inequality: US Evidence in the 1980s and the 1990s. *Journal of Income Distribution* 20(1), 117–126.

Hutter, B. (1997). *Compliance: Regulation and Environment*. Oxford, UK: Oxford University Press.

Interagency Policy Statement on Discrimination in Lending. (1994). *Federal Register* 59(73) (April), 15.

It doesn't take long for an out-of-towner to spot Minnesota nice. (1993, September 29). *Star Tribune*, Minneapolis, p. 19A.

It's time for all to take an oath. (1994, January 5). *Star Tribune*, Minneapolis, p. 15A.

Jenkins, S., and Diamond, B. E. (1985). Ethnicity and Foster Care: Census Data as Predictors of Placement Variables. *American Journal of Orthopsychiatry* 55(2), 26776.

Jenkins-Smith, H. C. (1990). *Democratic Politics and Policy Analysis.* Pacific Grove, CA: Brooks/Cole Publishing Company.

Jones, R. L. (2001, July 26). Mayor backs bill to make police report race in frisks. *New York Times*, Section B., Page 2, Column, 1, Metropolitan Desk.

Kahn, A. E. (1988). *The Economics of Regulation.* Cambridge, MA: The MIT Press.

Kahneman, D., and Tversky, A. (1979). Prospect Theory: An Analysis of Decision under Risk. *Econometrica* 47(2), 263–291.

Kellough, J. E. (2006). *Understanding Affirmative Action: Politics, Discrimination, and the Search for Justice.* Washington, D.C.: Georgetown University Press.

Kemmelmeier, M. (2003). Individualism and Attitudes toward Affirmative Action: Evidence from Priming Experiments. *Basic and Applied Social Psychology* 25(2), 111–119.

Kennedy, R. (1999, September 13). Suspect policy: Racial profiling usually isn't racist; it can help stop crime; and it should be abolished. *The New Republic.*

Kinder, D. R., and Sanders, L. M. (1996). *Divided by Color: Racial Politics and Democratic Ideas.* Chicago, IL: University of Chicago Press.

King, M., Ruggles, S., Alexander, J. T., Flood, S., Genadek, K., Schroeder M. B., Trampe, B., and Vick, R. (2010). Integrated Public Use Microdata Series, Current Population Survey: Version 3.0. [Machine-readable database]. Minneapolis, MN: University of Minnesota.

Klarman, M. J. (2007). *Brown v. Board of Education and the Civil Rights Movement.* New York, NY: Oxford University Press.

Ladd, H. F. (1998). Evidence on Discrimination in Mortgage Lending. *Journal of Economic Perspectives* 12(2), 41–62.

Lamb, C. (2005). *Housing Segregation in Suburban America since 1960: Presidential and Judicial Politics.* Cambridge, UK: Cambridge University Press.

Lamberth, John. (1996). Report of John Lamberth, Ph.D. In the Courts, ACLU Freedom Network. http://www.aclu.org/court/Lamberth.html.

La Noue, G. R. (2008). Follow the Money: Who Benefits from the Federal Aviation Administration's DBE Program? *American Review of Public Administration* 38(4), 480–500.

———. (1994). *Minority Business Programs and Disparity Studies (Local Officials Guide).* Washington, D.C.: League of Cities.

———. (1993). Social Science and Minority Set-Asides. *The Public Interest* 110 (Winter), 49–62.

———. (1992). Split Visions: Minority Business Set-Asides. Affirmative Action Revisited. *Annals of the American Academy of Political and Social Science* 523, 104–116.

Langbein, L., and Kerwin, C. M. (1985). Implementation, Negotiation and Compliance in Environmental and Safety Regulation. *Journal of Politics* 47(3), 854–880.

Lazear, E. P. (1999). Culture and Language. *Journal of Political Economy* 107(6), S95–126.

Leiter, W. M., and Leiter, S. (2002). *Affirmative Action in Antidiscrimination Law and Policy: An Overview and Synthesis*. Albany, NY: State University of New York Press.

Lempert, R. O. (1982). Organizing for Deterrence: Lessons from a Study of Child Support. *Law and Society Review* 16(4), 513–566.

Leonard, J. S., and Levine, D. I. (2006). The Effect of Diversity on Turnover: A Large Case Study. *Industrial and Labor Relations Re*view 59(4), 547–572.

Liebowitz, S. (1993, September 1). A study that deserves no credit. *Wall Street Journal*, p. A14.

List, J. A. (2004). The Nature and Extent of Discrimination in the Marketplace: Evidence from the field. *Quarterly Journal of Economics* 119(1), 49–89.

Listokin, D., and Casey, S. (1980). *Mortgage Lending and Race: Conceptual and Analytical Perspectives of the Urban Financing Problem*. New Brunswick, NJ: Rutgers University, Center for Urban Policy Research.

Lopez, R. (2015, September 18). Black leaders say state has done too little on racial income disparity. *Star Tribune*, Minneapolis.

Loury, G. C. (1998). Discrimination in the Post-Civil Rights Era: Beyond Market Interactions. *Journal of Economic Perspectives* 12, 117–126.

Mason, P. L. (2001). Annual Income and Identity Formation among Persons of Mexican Descent. *American Economic Association Papers and Proceedings* 91(2), 178–183.

———. (1999). Male Interracial Wage Differentials: Competing Explanations. *Cambridge Journal of Economics* 23(3), 261–299.

———. (1997). Race, Culture, and Skill: Interracial Wage Differences among African Americans, Latinos and Whites. *Review of Black Political Economy* 25(3), 5–39.

———. (1996). Some heterodox models of inequality in the market for labor power. In T. D. Boston (ed.) *A different vision: Vol 2– Race and Public Policy* (pp. 350–379). New York: Routledge.

———. (1995). Competing Explanations of Male Interracial Wage Differentials: Missing Variables Models Versus Job Competition. *Cambridge Journal of Economics* 23(3), 261–299.

Mason, P. L. (1995). Race, Competition and Differential Wages. *Cambridge Journal of Economics* 19(4), 545–568.

May, P. J. (2005). Regulation and Compliance Motivations: Examining Different Approaches. *Public Administration Review* 65(1), 31–44.

McKinney, R. I. (1997). *Mordecai, the Man and His Message: The Story of Mordecai Wyatt Johnson*. Washington, D.C.: Howard University Press.

Meier, K. J., Haider-Markel, D. P., Stanislawski, A. J., and Mcfarlane, D. R. (1996). The Impact of State-Level Restrictions on Abortion. *Demography* 33(3), 307–312.

Mincer, J. (1974). *Schooling, Experience and Earnings*. New York: National Bureau of Economic Research.

Minnesota Department of Human Services. (2001). *Social Service Information System Data File Extract*. Prepared under agreement with the University of Minnesota.

Minnesotans munch to the beat of a different drumstick. (1995, August 19). *Star Tribune,* Minneapolis, p. 1E.

Montalvo, J. G., and Reynal-Querol, M. (2005). Ethnic Diversity and Economic Development. *Journal of Development Economics* 76(2), 293–323.

Morton, T. (1999). Letter to the Editor. *Child Abuse and Neglect: The International Journal* 23(12), 1209.

Mukamel, D. B., Murthy, A. S., and Weimer, D. L. (2000). Racial Differences in Access to High-Quality Cardiac Surgeons. *American Journal of Public Health* 90(11), 1774–1777.

Munnell, A. H., Tootell, G. M. B., Browne, L. E., and McEneaney, J. (1996). Mortgage Lending in Boston: Interpreting HMDA Data. *The American Economic Review* 86(1), 25–53.

Munnell, A. H., Browne L. E., McEneaney, J., and Tootell, G. M. B. (1992). *Mortgage Lending in Boston: Interpreting HMDA Data* (Working Paper Series No. 92–7). Federal Reserve Bank of Boston.

Myers, Jr., S. L. (2011). The economics of diversity. In N. J. Norman and J. H. Syara (eds.) *Justice for all: Promoting social equity in public administration* (pp. 100–118). Armonk, NY: M.E. Sharpe.

———. (2011). The economics of diversity: The efficiency vs. equity trade off. In S. Chen (ed.) *Diversity management: Theoretical prespectives and practical approaches* (pp. 47–62). New York, NY: Nova Science Publishers, Inc.

———. (2011b). *Does a Rising Tide Lift all Ships? Comparisons between China and the USA.* A paper prepared for presentation at the workshop on "Economy and Society Development in China and the World." Hosted by the Institute of Ethnology and Anthropology, Chinese Academy of Social Sciences, Beijing October 13 and 14.

———. (2010). Rebuttal to Supplemental Report of Plaintiffs' Expert. Civil Action No. 04–2425, GEOD CORPORATION, et al. Plaintiffs v.NEW JERSEY TRANSIT CORPORATION, et al. Defendants, March, 2010.

———. (2008). Rebuttal Report of Defendants' Expert. 2007–10–23, Civil Action No. 04–2425, GEOD CORPORATION, et al. Plaintiffs v.NEW JERSEY TRANSIT CORPORATION, et al. Defendants, April 5, 2008.

———. (2007). Final Report: The Deterrent Effects of Media Accounts and HUD Enforcement on Racial Disparities in Loan Denial Rate. Submitted to the United States Department of Housing and Urban Development, August 15, 2007, Revised October 11, 2007.

———. (2007). Initial Report of Defendants' Expert, 2007–10–23. Civil Action No. 04–2425, GEOD CORPORATION, et al. Plaintiffs v. NEW JERSEY TRANSIT CORPORATION, et al. Defendants, November 13, 2007.

———. (2002). Presidential Address – Analysis of Race as Policy Analysis. *Journal of Policy Analysis and Management* 21(2) (Spring), 169–190.

———. (2002). Analysis of Racial Profiling as Policy Analysis. Curriculum and Case Notes. *Journal of Policy Analysis and Management* 21(2) (Spring), 287–300.

————. (2002). Government-Sponsored Enterprise Secondary Market Decisions: Effects on Racial Disparities in Home Mortgage Loan Rejection Rates. *Cityscape: A Journal of Policy Development and Research* 6(2), 85–113.

————. (2000). If Not Reconciliation, Then What? *Review of Social Economy* 58(3), 361–380. http://dx.doi.org/10.1080/00346760050132373.

————., ed. (1997). *Civil Rights and Race Relations in the Post Reagan Bush Era.* Westport: Greenwood Publishers.

————. (1993). 'The Rich Get Richer And. . .' The Problem of Race and Inequality in the 1990s. *Law and Inequality: A Journal of Theory and Practice* XI (2) (June).

————. (1993). Measuring and detecting discrimination in the post-civil rights era. Chapter 9. In J. H. Stanfield, II and R. M. Dennis (eds.) *Race and ethnicity in research methods*, Sage Focus Editions, Vol. 157 (pp. 172–197). Newbury Park, CA: Sage Publications.

————. (1992, December). *Widening Racial Economic Disparities: A Problem of 'Minnesota Nice'.* Technical Report. Humphrey Institute, University of Minnesota.

————. (1985). Statistical Test of Discrimination in Punishment. *Journal of Quantitative Criminology* 1(2), 191–218.

Myers, Jr., S. L., Ards, S. D., Mazas, J. L., and Ha, I. (2015, June). Bad Credit and Intergroup Differences in Loan Denial Rates. *The Review of Black Political Economy* 42(1–2), 19–34.

Myers, Jr., S. L., and Chan, T. (1996). Who Benefits from Minority-Business Set-Asides? The Case of New Jersey. *Journal of Policy Analysis and Management* 15, 202–225.

————. (1995). Racial Discrimination in Housing Markets: Accounting for Credit Risk. *Social Science Quarterly* 76(3), 543–561.

Myers, Jr., S. L., and Chung, C. (1996). Racial Differences in Home Ownership and Home Equity among Pre-Retirement-Aged Households. *The Gerontologist* 36(3), 350–360.

Myers, Jr., S. L., Chung, C., and Darity, Jr., W. A. (1998). Racial Earnings Disparities and Family Structure. *Southern Economic Journal* 65(1), 20–41.

Myers, Jr., S. L., Chung, C., and Saunders, L. (2001). Racial Differences in Transportation Access to Employment in Chicago and Los Angeles, 1980 and 1990. *American Economic Review, Papers and Proceedings* 91(2), 169–174.

Myers, Jr., S. L., Cuesta, A., and Lai, Y. (2017). Competitive Swimming and Racial Disparities in Drowning. *Review of Black Political Economy* 44, 77–97. https://doi.org/10.1007/s12114–017–9248-y.

Myers, Jr., S. L., and Darity, W. (1995). *The Widening Gap: A Summary and Synthesis of the Debate on Increasing Inequality.* Prepared for the National Commission for Employment Policy, April.

Myers, Jr., S. L., and Husbands Fealing, K. (2012). Changes in the Representation of Women and Minorities in Biomedical Careers. *Academic Medicine* 87(11), 1525–1529.

Myers, Jr., S. L., and Ha, I. (2009). Estimation of Race Neutral Goals in Public Procurement and Contracting. *Applied Economics Letters* 16(3), 251–256.

Myers, Jr., S. L., and Lai, Y. (2017). *The Labor Market for Lifeguards and Racial vs. Ethnic Disparities in Drowning Rates.* A paper prepared for presentation at the Western Economic Association and American Society of Hispanic Economist Meetings, San Diego, California, June 26.

Myers, Jr., S. L., Lange, L., and Corrie, B. (2003). The Political Economy of Antiracism Initiatives in the Post-Durban Round. *AEA Papers and Proceedings* 93(2) (May), 330–333.

Myers, Jr., S. L., and Saunders, L. (1996). The Effect of Commute Time on Racial Earnings' Inequality. *Applied Economics* 28, 1339–1343.

Myers, Jr., S. L., and Sabol, W. J. (1988). *Crime and the Black Community: Issues in the Understanding of Race and Crime in America.* Monograph commissioned by the Political Participation Subcommittee of the Committee on the Status of Black Americans, National Research Council, January.

Myers, Jr., S. L., and Xu, M. (2015, December). *Relative Incomes of Blacks in Minnesota. Minnesota Economic Trends.* St. Paul, MN: Minnesota Department of Employment and Economic Development.

———. (2015, November 10). *Are Blacks Better off in Mississippi than in Minnesota? Research Brief, Revised and Are Blacks Better Off in Mississippi than in Minnesota? Research Brief, Revised and Update.* Roy Wilkins Center, University of Minnesota.

Myrdal, G. (1996). *An American Dilemma: The Negro Problem and Modern Democracy (Black and African American Studies).* Piscataway, NJ: Transaction Publishers.

Nagel, S. S. (1984). *Contemporary Public Policy Analysis.* Tuscaloosa, AL: University of Alabama Press.

Nardinelli, C., and Simon, C. (1990). Customer Racial Discrimination in the Market for Memorabilia: The Case of Baseball. *The Quarterly Journal of Economics* 105(3), 575–595.

National Bureau of Economic Research. (2013). *US Business Cycle Expansions and Contractions.* Retrieved June 26, 2013, from http://www.nber.org/cycles/cycles-main.html.

National Center for Health Statistics. (1988). *Vital Statistics of the United States, 1988, Vol. III, Marriage and Divorce.* (DHHS Publication No. (PHS) 961103). Washington, D.C.: Public Health Service. Retrieved from http://www.cdc.gov/nchs/data/vsus/mgdv88_3acc.pdf.

National Collegiate Athletic Association. (2006, April). *1999-00 – 2005-06 NCAA Student-Athlete Race and Ethnicity Report.* Indianapolis: The National Collegiate Athletic Association.

National Cooperative Highway Research Program (NCHRP). (2010). *Report 644: Guidelines for Conducting a Disparity and Availability Study for the Federal DBE Program.* Transportation Research Board of the National Academies.

National Science Foundation, Committee on Equal Opportunity in Science and Engineering. (2003, April). *2005–2006 Biennial Report to Congress.* Arlington, VA.

———. (2004, December). *The 1994–2003 Decennial and 2004 Biennial Report to Congress.* CEOSE 04–01.

National Universities—Doctoral: Top 50. (2001b, October). *U.S. News and World Report*. http://www.usnews.com/usnews/edu/college/rankings/natudoc/tier1/ tlnatudoc.htm.

Nelson, Barbara J. (1999). Diversity and Public Problem Solving Ideas and Practice in Policy Education. *Journal of Policy Analysis and Management* 18(1), 134–155.

Nelson, Richard. (1977). *The Moon and the Ghetto: An Essay on Public Policy Analysis*. New York: Norton.

Nice, D. C. (1982). Party Ideology and Policy Outcomes in the American States. *Social Science Quarterly* 63(3), 556–565.

Noble, D. (1986). *Forces of Production: A Social History of Industrial Automation*. New York, NY: Oxford University Press.

Nunley, J. M., Owens, M. F., and Howard, R. S. (2010). *The Effects of Competition and Information on Racial Discrimination: Evidence from a Field Experiment*. Working Papers 201007. Middle Tennessee State University, Department of Economics and Finance, Murfreesboro, TN.

Oaxaca, R. L. (1973). Male-Female Wage Differentials in Urban Labor Markets. *International Economic Review* 14(3), 693–709.

Olney, M. L. (1998). When Your Word Is Not Enough: Race, Collateral, and Household Credit. *Journal of Economic History* 58(2) (June), 408–431.

Ottaway, S., Hayden, D., and Oakes, M. (2001). Implicit Attitudes and Racism: Effects of Word Familiarity and Frequency on the Implicit Association Test. *Social Cognition* 19(2), 97–144.

Partridge, M. D., and Rickman, D. S. (2008). Does A Rising Tide Lift All Metropolitan Boats? Assessing Poverty Dynamics by Metropolitan Size and County Type. *Growth and Change* 39(2), 283–312.

Patton, C. V., and Sawicki, D. S. (1986). *Basic Methods of Policy Analysis and Planning*. Englewood Cliffs, NJ: Prentice-Hall.

Pelled, L. H., Xin, K. R., and Eisenhardt, K. M. (1999). Exploring the Black Box: An Analysis of Work Group Diversity, Conflict, and Performance. *Administrative Science Quarterly* 44(1), 1–28.

Pope, D. G., and Sydnor, J. R. (2011). What's in a Picture? Evidence of Discrimination from Prosper.com. *Journal of Human Resources* 46(1), 53–92.

Potapchuk, M. (2002). *Holding up the Mirror: Working Independently for Just and Inclusive Communities*. Washington, D.C.: Network of Alliances Bridging Race and Ethnicity (NABRE)/Joint Center for Political and Economic Studies.

Powell, W. W., and Steinberg, R., eds. (2006). *The Nonprofit Sector: A Research Handbook* (2nd ed.). New Haven, CT: Yale University Press.

Putnam, R. D. (2007). *E Pluribus Unum*: Diversity and Community in the Twenty-First Century the 2006 Johan Skytte Prize Lecture. *Scandinavian Political Studies* 30(2) (June), 137–174.

Rachlis, M. B., and Yezer, A. M. (1993). Serious Flaws in Statistical Tests for Discrimination in Mortgage Markets. *Journal of Housing Research* 4(2), 315–336.

Racial profiling proposal approved. (2001, October 12). *Poughkeepsie Journal*, p. B2.

Raiffa, H. (1968). *Decision Analysis: Introductory Lectures on Choices under Uncertainty*. Reading, MA: Addison-Wesley.

Ravina, E. (2008). *Love and Loans: The Effect of Beauty and Personal Characteristics in Credit Markets.* Unpublished.

Reinan, J., and Webster, M. (2015, September 17). Black household income plunges in one year in Minnesota. *StarTribune*, Minneapolis.

Rice, M. F. (2005). *Diversity and Public Administration: Theory, Issues, and Perspectives.* New York, NY: M.E. Sharpe.

———. (1993). State and Local Government Set-Aside Programs, Disparity Studies and Minority Business Development in the Post-Croson Era. *Journal of Urban Affairs* 15(6), 529–554.

———. (1992). Justifying State and Local Government Set-Aside Programs through Disparity Studies in the Post-Croson Era. *Public Administration Review* 52(5), 482–491.

———. (1991). Government Set-Asides, Minority Business Enterprises, and the Supreme Court. *Public Administration Review* 51(2), 114–122.

Ricketts, E. L. R., and Sawhill, I. V. (1988). Defining and Measuring the Underclass. *Journal of Policy Analysis and Management* 7(2), 316–325.

Rodgers, III., W. M., and Armentrout, K. S. (1996). *How Much Can Job Training Aid in Narrowing Racial/Ethnic Wage Gaps: New Evidence from the National Longitudinal Survey of Youth.* Working paper. University of Wisconsin, Madison.

Rodgers, III., W. M., and Spriggs, W. E. (2002, April). *The Effect on Black-White Wage Differences in the Quantity and Quality of Education: Comment.* Industrial Labor and Relations Review.

Rodgers, III., W. M., and Spriggs, W. E. (1996). What Does the AFQT Really Measure: Race, Wages, Schooling and the AFQT Scores. *Review of Black Political Economy* 24(4), 13–46.

Ross, S. L., and Tootell, G. M. B. (1998). *Redlining, the Community Reinvestment Act and Private Mortgage Insurance.* University of Connecticut, Storrs. Unpublished manuscript.

Ross, S. L., and Yinger, J. (2003). *The Color of Credit: Mortgage Discrimination, Research Methodology, and Fair-Lending Enforcement.* Cambridge, MA: The MIT Press.

Sabol, W. J., and Couture, H. (2008). *Prison Inmates at Midyear 2007.* Bureau of Justice Statistics. http://bjs.ojp.usdoj.gov/index.cfm?ty=pbdetailandiid=840. Accessed July 16, 2010.

Sack, Kevin. (2017, May 31). Court files raise question: Was Dylann roof competent to defend himself? *The New York Times.* https://www.nytimes.com/2017/05/31/us/church-shooting-roof-charleston-hate-crime-.html?_r=0.

Samuelson, P. A. (1947). *Foundations of Economic Analysis.* Cambridge, MA: Harvard University Press.

Scholz, J. T., and Gray, W. B. (1997). Can Government Facilitate Cooperation? An Informational Model of OSHA Enforcement. *American Journal of Political Science* 41(3), 693–717.

School system will try 'cycle' of improvement; Minneapolis experiment defines goals, strategies. (1994, August 8). *Star Tribune*, Minneapolis, p. 1B.

Schuman, H., Steeh, C., Bobo, L., and Krysan, M. (1998). *Racial Attitudes in America: Trends and Interpretations.* Cambridge, MA: Harvard University Press.

Sedlak, A., Bruce, C., and Schultz, D. J (2001). Letter to the Editor. *Child Abuse and Neglect: The International Journal* 25(1), 1–5.

Sedlak, A. J., Broadhurst, D., Shapiro, G., Kalton, G., Goksel, H., Burke, J., and Brown, J. (1997). *Third National Incidence Study of Child Abuse and Neglect: Analysis Report.* Washington, D.C.: National Center on Child Abuse and Neglect, DHHS.

Shapiro, I. (2002). *Training for Racial Equity and Inclusion: A Guide to Selected Programs.* New York, NY: Aspen Institute.

Silverman, M. (1976). Toward a Theory of Criminal Deterrence. *American Sociological Review* 41(June), 442–461.

Simon, H. (1991). Bounded Rationality and Organizational Learning. *Organization Science* 2(1), 125–134.

Siskin, B. R., and Cupingood, L. A. (1996). Use of statistical models to provide statistical evidence of discrimination in the treatment of mortgage loan applicants: A study of one lending institution. In J. Goering and R. Wienk (eds.) *Mortgage lending, racial discrimination, and federal policy* (pp. 451–468). Washington, D.C.: Urban Institute Press.

Slack, J. D. (1997). From Affirmative Action to Full Spectrum Diversity in the American Workplace: Shifting the Organizational Paradigm. *Review of Public Personnel Administration* 17(4), 75–87.

Snyder, T. D., Dillow, S. A., and Hoffman, C. M. (2008). *Digest of Education Statistics 2007 (NCES 2008–022).* Washington, D.C.: National Center for Education Statistics, Institute of Education Sciences, U.S. Department of Education. http://nces.ed.gov/programs/digest/d07/. Accessed July 16, 2010.

Spriggs, W. E., and Williams, R. M. (1996). A Logit Decomposition Analysis of Occupational Segregation: Results for the 1970s and 1980s. *Review of Economics and Statistics* 78(2), 348–354.

Steeh, C., and Krysan, M. (1996). The Polls—Trends: Affirmative Action and the Public, 1970–1995. *Public Opinion Quarterly* 60(1), 128–158.

Steele, C. M. (1997). A Threat in the Air: How Stereotypes Shape Intellectual Identity and Performance. *American Psychologist* 52(6), 613–629.

Steele, C. M., and Aronson J. (1995). Stereotype Threat and the Intellectual Test Performance of African Americans. *Journal of Personality and Social Psychology* 69(5) (November), 797–811.

Stengel, M., and Glennon, D. (1999). Evaluating Statistical Models of Mortgage Lending Discrimination: A Bank-Specific Analysis. *Real Estate Economics* 27(2) (Summer), 299–334.

Stiglitz, J. E., and Weiss, A. (1981). Credit Rationing in Markets with Imperfect Information. *American Economic Review* 71(3), 393–410.

Still, T. (1999, June 4). ACLU sues California highway patrol over racial profiling. *The Recorder/Cal Law.*

Terenzini, P. T., Cabrera, A. R., Colbeck, C. L., Bjorklund, S. A., and Parente, J. M. (2001). Racial and Ethnic Diversity in the Classroom: Does it Promote Student Learning? *The Journal of Higher Education* 72(5), 509–531.

Thurow, L. W. (1969). *Poverty and Discrimination*. Washington, D.C.: The Brookings Institution.

Tittle, C., and Logan, C. (1973). Sanctions and Deviance: Evidence and Remaining Questions. *Law and Society Review* 7, 371–392.

Tootell, G. M. B. (1996). Turning a critical eye on the critics. In J. Goering and R. Wienk (eds.) *Mortgage lending, racial discrimination, and federal policy* (pp. 143–182). Washington, D.C.: Urban Institute Press.

Tyson, A. S. (2006, June 20). Pulling no punches in push for navy SEALs pentagon looking to increase ranks without easing the tough training. *Washington Post*. http://www.washingtonpost.com/wpdyn/content/article/2006/06/19/AR2006061901388_pf.html.

United Nations. (2002). World Conference against Racism, Racial Discrimination, Xenophobia and Related Intolerance declaration and programme of action, A/CONF.189/12. 25 January. Retrieved from http://www. unhchr.ch/pdf/Durban.pdf.

U.S. Bureau of Labor Statistics. (2013). *Labor Force Statistics from the Current Population Survey: Unemployment Rate - Men*. Retrieved June 26, 2013, from http://data.bls.gov/timeseries/LNS14000001Q?include_graphs=falseandoutput_type=columnandyears_option=all_years.

———. (2013). *Labor Force Statistics from the Current Population Survey: Unemployment Rate - Women*. Retrieved June 26, 2013, from http://data.bls.gov/timeseries/LNS14000002Q?include_graphs=falseandoutput_type=columnandyears_option=all_years.

U.S. Census Bureau, Population Division. (2008, May 1). *Annual Estimates of the Population by Sex, Race, and Hispanic Origin for the United States: April 1, 2000 to July 1, 2007* (NC-EST2007–03).

———. (2008, May 1). *In Annual estimates of the Black or African American alone population by sex and age for the United States: April 1, 2000 to July 1, 2007* (NC-EST2007–04-BA). http://www.census.gov/popest/national/asrh/NC-EST2007-asrh.html. Accessed July 16, 2010.

———. (2008, May 1). *Annual Estimates of the Population by Sex and Selected Age Groups for the United States: April 1, 2000 to July 1, 2007* (NC-EST2007–02). http://www.census.gov/popest/national/asrh/NC-EST2007/NC-EST2007–02.xls. Accessed July 16, 2010.

———. (1998). *Statistical Abstract of the United States*. Section 14, Income, Expenditures, and Wealth, Table No. 733, Average Annual Expenditures of all Consumer Units, by Race, Hispanic Origin, and Age of Householder, 1995. Washington, D.C.: U.S. Department of Commerce, Economics and Statistics Administration.

———. (1997). *American Housing Survey for the United States: 1997*. Current Housing Reports, Series H150/97, Table 3–15, Mortgage Characteristics- Owner Occupied Units. Washington, D.C.: U.S. Department of Commerce, Economics and Statistics Administration.

U. S. Commission on Civil Rights. (1994). *The Fair Housing Amendments Act of 1988: The Enforcement Report*. Washington, DC: US Commission on Civil Rights.

U.S. Congress, Senate. (1993). *Problems in Community Development Banking, Mortgage Lending Discrimination, Reserve Redlining, and Home Equity Lending,*

Hearings. Committee on Banking, Housing, and Urban Affairs, 103rd Congress, 1st session, February 3–24.

U.S. Court of Appeals, Ninth Circuit. (2005). *Western States Paving Co., Inc. v. Washington State DOT*.

U.S. Department of Health and Human Services, Administration for Children and Families, Administration on Children, Youth and Families, Children's Bureau. (2017). Child Maltreatment. https://www.acf.hhs.gov/cb/resource/child-maltreatment-2015 and https://www.acf.hhs.gov/cb/resource/child-maltreatment-1996.

———. (2008a, April). *The AFCARS Report: Preliminary FY 2006 Estimates as of January 2008*. http://www.acf.hhs.gov/programs/cb/stats_research/afcars/tar/report14.htm. Accessed July 16, 2010.

———. (2008b). *Child Maltreatment 2006*. Washington, D.C.: U.S. Government Printing Office. http://www.acf.hhs.gov/programs/cb/pubs/cm06/index.htm. Accessed July 16, 2010.

U. S. Department of Health and Human Services. (2002). *Child Maltreatment 2000: Reports from the States to the National Child Abuse and Neglect Data System*. Washington, D.C.: National Center on Child Abuse and Neglect, DHHS. http://www.acf.dhhs.gov/programs/cb/publications/ncands00.html.

U. S. Department of Health and Human Services. (1998). *Child Maltreatment 1996: Reports from the States to the National Child Abuse and Neglect Data System*. Washington, D.C.: National Center on Child Abuse and Neglect, DHHS. http://www.acf.dhhs.gov/programs/cb/publications/ncands96.html.

U.S. Department of Justice. (1977). *The Attorney General's Report to Congress Pursuant to the Equal Credit Opportunity Act Amendments of 1976*.

———. Proposed Reforms to Affirmative Action in Federal Procurement, p. 26,050.

U.S. General Accountability Office. (1996). *Fair Lending: Federal Oversight and Enforcement Improved but Some Challenges Remain*. GAO/GGD 96–145.

U.S. General Accounting Office. (2000a). *Better Targeting of Airline Passengers for Personal Searches Could Produce Better Results*. GAO/GGD-00–38.

U.S. General Accounting Office. (2000b). *Racial Profiling: Limited Data Available on Motorist Stops*. GAO/GGD-00–41.

Varian, H. R. (1993). *Intermediate Microeconomics a Modern Approach*. New York, NY: W. W. Norton and Company.

Walker, N. (1965). *Crime and Punishment in Britain?: An Analysis of the Penal System in Theory, Law, and Practice*. Edinburgh, UK: Edinburgh University Press.

Walter, J. (1995). The Fair Lending Laws and Their Enforcement. *Economic Quarterly* 81(4), 61–69.

Waters, M. (1999, October 9). Free for all [Opinion]. *The Washington Post*, p. A21.

Weimer, D. L., and Vining, A. R. (1989). *Policy Analysis: Concepts and Practice*. Englewood Cliffs, NJ: Prentice-Hall.

Weitzman, M. L. (1992). On Diversity. *Quarterly Journal of Economics* 107(2), 363–405.

White House Office of the Press Secretary. (1998). *Remarks by the President in the Race Initiative Outreach Meeting*. January 12.

———. (1998). Clinton-Gore Administration: A Record of Progress for Gay and Lesbian Americans; Remarks by the President at National Defense University, July 19, 1998. White House, Office of Press Secretary, October.

————. (1998). Office of the Press Secretary, Remarks by the President to the Advisory Board on Race. September 9.

Whitford, A. B. (2005). The Pursuit of Political Control by Multiple Principals. *Journal of Politics* 67(1), 29–49.

Williams, R. W. (1992). Racial inequality and racial conflict: Recent developments in radical theroy. In W. Darity (ed.) *Labor economics: Problems in analyzing labor markets* (pp. 209–236). Boston, MA: Kluwer Academic Publishers.

Williams, R. W., and Kennison, R. E. (1996). The Way we Were?: Discrimination, Competition, and Inter-Industry Wage Differentials in 1970. *Review of Radical Political Economics* 28(2), 1–32.

Wilson, K. A. C. (2000, August 26). Law Firm Says it will Sue Seattle over Racial Profiling. *Seattle Post-Intelligencer Reporter.* http://seattlep-i.nwsource.com/local/prof26.shtml.

Wiltse, J. (2007). *Contested Waters: A Social History of Swimming Pools in America.* Chapel Hill: The University of North Carolina Press.

Winters, R. (1976). Party Control and Policy Change. *American Journal of Political Science* 20(4), 597–636.

Winter, S. C., and May, P. J. (2001). Motivation for Compliance with Environmental Regulations. *Journal of Policy Analysis and Management* 20(4), 675–698.

Wong, E. (2013, January 13). On scale of 0 to 500, Beijing's air quality tops 'crazy bad' at 755. *The New York Times.*

Wray, L. R., and Pigcon, M.-A. (2000). Can A Rising Tide Raise All Boats? Evidence from the Clinton-Era Expansion. *Journal of Economic Issues* 34(4), 811–845.

Yezer, A. M., Phillips, R. F., and Trost, R. P. (1994). Bias in Estimates of Discrimination and Default in Mortgage Lending: The Effects of Simultaneity and Self-Selection. *Journal of Real Estate Finance and Economics* 9(3) (November), 197–217.

Yinger, J. (1998). Evidence on Discrimination in Consumer Markets. *The Journal of Economic Perspectives* 12(2), 23–40.

————. (1996). Discrimination in mortgage lending: A literature review. In J. Goering and R. Wienk (eds.) *Mortgage lending, racial discrimination, and federal policy* (pp. 29–74). Washington, D.C.: Urban Institute Press.

————. (1995). *Closed Doors, Opportunities Lost: The Continuing Costs of Housing Discrimination.* New York, NY: Russell Sage Foundation.

————. (1986). Measuring Racial Discrimination with Fair Housing Audits: Caught in the Act. *The American Economic Review* 76(5), 881–893.

Zandi, M. (1993). Boston Fed's Study Was Deeply Flawed. *American Banker* (August 19), 13.

Zimring, F. E., and Hawkins, G. J. (1973). *Deterrence: The Legal Threat to Crime Control (Studies in Crime and Justice).* Chicago, IL: University of Chicago Press.

Zycher, B., and Wolfe, T. A. (1994). Mortgage Lending, Discrimination, and Taxation by Regulation. *Regulation* 17(2) (Spring), 61–73.

Index

Page references for figures are italicized.

About the Authors

Samuel L. Myers, Jr. is the Director and Professor at Roy Wilkins Center for Human Relations and Social Justice at the Hubert H. Humphrey School of Public Affairs, University of Minnesota. He is an often cited Massachusetts Institute of Technology-trained economist who has published more than a hundred studies on applied microeconomic and policy issues in leading economics and interdisciplinary journals and in books and monographs. He is a pioneer in the use of applied econometric techniques to examine racial disparities in crime, to detect illegal discrimination in home mortgage lending and consumer credit markets, to assess the impacts of welfare on family stability, to evaluate the effectiveness of government transfers in reducing poverty, and to detect disparities and discrimination in government contracting. He is an expert on conducting disparity studies for state and local governments and analyzes race-neutral public procurement and contracting policies. He has served as an expert witness in the ground-breaking federal cases of *GEOD vs. New Jersey Transit* and *Geyer vs. MnDOT*. In 2009, he was a Senior Fulbright Fellow at the Chinese Academy of Social Sciences, where he conducted research on disability policies in the United States versus China.

Inhyuck "Steve" Ha (PhD, University of Minnesota-Twin Cities) is a Professor of Economics at Western Carolina University in Cullowhee, North Carolina. His areas of interest are economics of discrimination, spatial econometrics, community economic development, and economic impact analysis. He has extensive experience conducting statistical analysis and understanding the complexities of real-world data. His current research projects include studying the effects of affirmative action policies on public procurement and contracting, and labor market discrimination. He has over twenty years of experience working on issues of racial discrimination and numerous DBE goal-setting and disparity studies. Prior to his current position, Dr. Ha worked in the Humphrey School of Public Affairs at the University of Minnesota and in the Haas Center for Business Research and Economic Development at the University of West Florida as Forecasting Program Director.